Chas Hodges

CHAS & DAVE

All About Us

JOHN BLAKE

Published by John Blake Publishing,
80–1 Wimpole Street,
Marylebone
London W1G 9RE

www.facebook.com/johnblakebooks
twitter.com/jblakebooks

First published in hardback in 2008
This edition published in paperback in 2013

Paperback ISBN: 978-1-78219-232-9
Ebook ISBN: 978-1-85782-826-9

British Library Cataloguing-in-Publication Data:

A catalogue record for this book is available from the British Library.

Design by www.envydesign.co.uk

Printed and bound in Great Britain by Clays Ltd, Elcograf S.p.A.

5 7 9 10 8 6

MIX
Paper from
responsible sources
FSC
www.fsc.org   FSC® C018072

Every reasonable effort has been made to trace copyright-holders of material
reproduced in this book, but if any have been inadvertently overlooked the
publishers would be glad to hear from them.

John Blake Publishing is an imprint of Bonnier Books UK
www.bonnierbooks.co.uk

To Harry Albert Bob Garner

Special thanks to Daniel Bunyard

Foreword

We've just done a show and we're back at the hotel having a drink and a chat. We sit around for a while and I start to feel pretty knackered.

Chas says to me, 'I think I'll go up and do a bit more on the book.'

I think to myself, 'How can he get his brainbox working at this time of night?' (It's three in the morning). Maybe he wants to write something down before he forgets it. This is just one little instance I can recall when Chas was putting all this together and I for one am really glad he did.

There's tales in these pages even I hadn't heard before. It's all here, my mate's account from when he was a nipper in Edmonton, right up until the time he got tangled up with me.

Then the whole story up to now.

Have a butcher's. I think you're going to like it!

Dave Peacock

Contents

Introduction

Why are you reading this introduction? I never do! If I've bought a book about somebody I like I wanna get straight into the story to find out what sort of things he got up to and what makes him tick.

But perhaps you ain't bought it yet and you're reading this bit in the shop in hopes it'll give you an idea of what it's all about and if it's worth spending your money on? I'll tell ya one thing. It's got a few swearwords in it. But you see, that's the way I talk. I use 'em like perfect punctuation. You don't notice them. But you would if they weren't there. The same as if you had no full stops or commas, the words would be there but the flow and rhythm would be lost. Now I might slip up on me full stops and commas here and there, but I do know where to put a swearword.

So what's it about then? Well, for starters, it's about my life up until I got together with Dave. The school days. The early Rock 'n' Roll days. The fifties. London street life. The serious bits. The funny bits. The days spent on the road with mad but likeable blokes like Gene Vincent and Jerry Lee Lewis. The laughing and learning. The Soul Scene in the sixties with Cliff Bennett & The Rebel Rousers. Touring with The Beatles. The daft but exciting American tours in the seventies with Heads Hands & Feet. The skint and the rich times. The hit records and the flops. The wonderful and the wallies. In short, the bits you look back on as all part of growing up. And then there's meeting Dave…And that's where a whole new set of stories start!

I hope you do enjoy this book 'cos one day, when I am grown up, I might write another one.

Well I did actually.

The second half of this book was written a quarter of a century later after the first. Have I grown up? Don't know. But I enjoyed writing it and I hope you enjoy reading it. The main course, the Chas & Dave story, rambles from the 'Gertcha!' days to the Glastonbury days and everything in between. With Rock 'n' Rollers, royalty, and punks to politicians, all agreeing in principle that Rockney Rules. All in favour say, 'Gertcha!'

PART ONE

CHAS BEFORE DAVE

Chapter 1

First Memories

I'm Chas, the one who plays the piano in Chas & Dave. I was born in the North Middlesex Hospital, Edmonton on 28 December 1943. Albert and Daisy Hodges were the 'proud' parents. (So my Mum tells me, and I believe everything my Mum says.) Brother Dave was nearly three years old. Mum wanted me to be called Nicholas but Charles was the traditional family name on my Dad's side. So I became Charles Nicholas. 'Chas' was also the familiar nickname for Charles around Hackney, where my Dad came from, so 'Chas' it was.

My earliest memories were when I was about three. Music among the most vivid of 'em. My Dad was a lorry driver and worked for an Italian named Romano. Romano owned a farmhouse in Ashford, Kent, that was to let and Dad decided that we should move down there. Edmonton was alright, where we were living with my Mum's Mum and Dad, but he wanted something better for us. We moved to Kent in the summer of 1947. It was good down there: I loved it. Considering I was only young and we were only there for about six months, I have a lot of vivid memories about that time. The journey down in my Dad's old green van. Me asking Dad if it was putting your hands on the steering wheel that made it move along. Dad taking his hands off the steering wheel while we were going along to prove that it wasn't. I was impressed. The arrival at the farm. Being met by Ginger, the farm hand, who never lifted a finger, let alone a hand! Dad at the top of an apple tree slinging apples down to my Uncle Bert. Waking in the morning to see the hunt go by. I thought it was a magnificent sight. Stella our Alsatian. Peggy and Spike the greyhounds. Collecting new laid eggs and being chased by one of the cockerels. Was I frightened! He was nearly as big as me! I injured my finger slamming the door of the run and I remember Mum making me sit quiet with my finger in a glass of TCP. Dad wringing the cockerel's neck in case he pecked us kids' eyes out. Me getting chased again by the cockerel! (We had two cockerels. A wild one and a tame one. Dad had wrung the wrong one's neck!) Garlic in my Wellingtons. (An idea of Mum's to keep the colds away. Found out later this is what the Romans used to do.) The pond in the woods that had witches (another idea of Mum's to stop us kids going near it). New discoveries like oak apples, mole hills, cowpats and straw. Brother Dave chucking some 12-bore cartridges behind the Rayburn stove and Mum going mad even though Dave kept insisting that it didn't matter 'cos they were dead ones. Dad coming home with a rabbit for dinner. Spitting out the lead shot. The smell of Dad's van in the garage. Car fumes even now bring back happy memories! Me and my brother and Stella the Alsatian playing in the haystack. 'Housewives' Choice' on the radio. Songs like 'Cruising down the River' – a popular song I liked. I told my brother, 'That's my song!' 'No it's not, it's the lady on the radio's.' Little git. Early memory songs, 'Feniculee Fenicula'. 'The Thieving Magpie'. I'd watch magpies from my bedroom window with that tune going through my head.

One day we had company. My Mum announced them to me and my brother as being 'off the stage'. I remember standing in this sunny room as the couple went into their act. The lady played the piano and the man sang. The song was 'Blue Room'. They were on the posh side but they were quite good at what they did. (I had 'em sussed although I was only three.)

It was a good memory. It was music. Grown-ups always looked happy when they were singing. Especially when someone was playing the piano. Why didn't they do this all the time?

I have fond memories of that place. I loved it. It was where my Dad lived. When I think of him walking about, or drinking a cup of tea, or working on his old van, it was all down in Kent, I didn't remember him before that. I was too young. My Mum doesn't have the same affection for the place. But it was different for Mum. To her it was where my Dad died. The day before my fourth birthday my Dad died of wounds from a 12-bore shotgun. I remember it happening but I was too young to take it in. Not see him again?

Dead? No! All dead people died before I was born.

It was his own hand that fired the gun. Nobody knew why.

We left the farm before the New Year and came back to Edmonton to live with my Nan, Grandad, and Great-grandfather.

Chapter 2

11, Harton Road

Us kids, like kids do, adapted quickly once more to North London life. Mum earned money to keep us by playing piano in the pubs and clubs. Nan and Grandad helped bring us up while Great-grandfather Shaw, who was nearly ninety years old then, sort of acted the part of comic relief. He was a good old boy, five foot four inches tall and full of life.

He lived in the boxroom which had a smell of old stale pipes which I quite liked. He was music mad. He played clarinet in his younger days and would go out busking with my Mum on harmonium. I never heard him play clarinet, although he was supposed to have been quite good. I only heard him play the whistle which he played day and night, whatever the hour. I'd get private recitals in his room. He'd show me the scales, or play his latest piece that had just come through the door from Keith Prowse. Grandfather would be off, stopping every now and again to repeat a passage he felt needed improvement.

I loved every minute. When it was time for a break, he'd light up his old pipe and go into a story. Most times it would be about music. A brass band he'd seen years ago. He'd describe all the sounds and what they played. I could hear that band as clearly as if I'd been there. Then he'd ask me what I was up to, what new toys had I got? 'New toy car? Let's have a look.' I'd go and get it. Grandfather would inspect it with wonder. Try it out with glee! Sometimes I'd say, 'You can borrow it for a while if you want, Grandfather.' 'Thanks boy. Thanks very much. I'll take care of it.' He didn't get on with his son-in-law too well, though (Mum's Dad).

There was a thing in my house that was as important as the teapot or the gas stove or other household necessities.

It was the piss-pail.

He had one in his room. Nan and Grandad had one and me and my brother had one. We never had china piss-pots – didn't hold enough. We had galvanised piss-pails. Great-grandfather and Grandad would argue never-ending over who'd got whose piss-pail.

'You've got my piss-pail.'

'No I ain't, you silly old bastard!'

'Daisy!' Grandfather would shout to his daughter (Daisy was my Nan's name, too). 'Tell him he's got my piss-pail!' And so it would go on.

We kids had a white enamel piss-pail. It had a lid with holes on it. You could use it without taking the lid off, although I never owned up. My brother used to suss it when the lid felt warm, and I'd get a clump. I couldn't see the sense in takin' the lid off, as it all went in anyway.

The nearest school to me was Eldon Road School. I started there shortly after I was four years old. My brother Dave, nearly three years older than me, was already at the school, and

I couldn't wait to get there too. I begged my Mum to get me there as soon as possible. It must have been the glamour of it, big brother and all that, goin' off to school with all the lads. The morning I started I did just that. Went to school with all the lads. Now big brother, who was supposed to be lookin' after me, decided before we got close to Eldon Road that I was a bit of a nuisance and I was left to fend for myself. I'd got this Victoria plum my Mum had given me to take to school, and I decided to sit down against this wall outside the school gates to eat it. Some ol' gels (who were jawing on their front door steps) every now and then looked over at me.

'They've gone in, yer know,' they'd say, and then get back to their jawing. I never took no notice and carried on eating me plum.

To me the novelty had gone. I'd been to school with the boys but I didn't want to go in, and that was that. Sitting up against the wall eating my Victoria plum and thinking about goin' to school was heaven. Goin' to school was great, but now I'd been. Now I wanted to go home, and I did. Those questions about 'Do you like goin' to school?' made sense. I did. I liked comin' home from school too. But goin' *in* to school was a different matter. Do you want to *go* to school? – that was all I was asked.

My Mum decided I wasn't ready to attend school and I was kept home 'til I was five. Try again. I wasn't mad on it though I got to like it. When I started going to Eldon (and going in as well) I thought it was alright. Some teachers I didn't like, some I liked. My first teacher was an old Victorian trained lady named Miss Dames.

One day she was teaching us a poem about a 'Teeny Tiny Key' – 'I know a little cupboard with a teeny, tiny key, and in there are cakes for me, me, me.' I can't remember the rest. We all had to recite this poem together. As the class was reciting I remember feeling a pain in my stomach, something I'd probably ate, and I shit myself. It crept round my trousers all sort of warm. It wasn't lumpy and none dropped out, so I thought I'd be able to keep it a secret 'till I got home. It was four o'clock and the bell went at five past four. Now whether I had a funny look on my face or just chance I don't know, but Miss Dames said:

'Now before we all go home, children, Charles Hodges will come out and recite the poem to you all on his own.' I went out all caked in shit, but it clung there, not showing itself as I went into 'I know a little cupboard with a teeny, tiny key.' I did it all through, word perfect. The bell went and I was off home. I run indoors and all I could say was, 'I couldn't help it, I couldn't help it!'

'What couldn't you help?' said Mum. 'What's the matter? Tell me, tell me!' The 'couldn't help it' bit came about 'cos I'd gone home from school once laughing about a school mate who'd been in the same predicament. 'Ahh, he probably couldn't help it,' Mum had said, and I had latched onto that.

So after a bit she found out (it didn't take long!) that I'd shit myself. My Nan promptly took my trousers and pants off and put me outside on the toilet. What's she done that for? I thought. I've already done it! I sat there on the bog-hole. I decided I'd never laugh at my mates again. It could well have been apples. Too many of 'em, I was mad on apples.

One day Mum and Nan decided to take me and my brother to Southend for the day. Grandad said, 'Take this bag of apples with yer, give some to the kids and give the rest away when you get down to Southend.'

It wasn't a bag, it was a sackful! We had to catch the train at Lower Edmonton station, but the train was late. Me and my brother played up and down the station and I nicked an apple every time I got near the sack. Finally the train came along (the sack half empty by now) and off we went.

As we neared Southend, a thunderstorm started and, on top of that, so did one in my belly. Mum told my brother to take me to the toilet. He did, reluctantly. Boy, did I have the shits! My belly was aching like hell. I really thought I was gonna die. My brother Dave reported back to me Mum and then forgot what toilet he'd put me in. I could hear him shouting 'Chas!' underneath the toilet doors miles away. I was answering feebly. He found me in the end. When I recovered we spent the rest of the day under a shelter away from the storm. But that wasn't all. I got me fingers shut in the train door on the way home! I've still got the scars to prove it. Some yobs, running down the platform, slammed our carriage door shut and my fingers were in the hinges. Nan sorted them out though, and gave their earholes a walloping to go home with.

Now you'd think from that first experience I'd hate the place. But I grew to love it. A trip to Southend was second only to Christmas Day. My favourite pastime down Southend was crabbing, in the boating pool. A bit of string with a piece of cockle or mussel tied to the other end, drop it in the pool, wait for a tug, and slowly pull it up. Sure enough there'd be a crab. Years later when I took my own kids down Southend I tried the same thing in the same pool (the one near the pier). I got the same results. Kids watching at first thought I was mad. Crabs in the boating pool? But they were away after bits of string and cockles and mussels before you knew it! Try it yourself, when you're next down Southend. (Note, 2008. It ain't there no more)

Harton Road was a typical London street of terraced houses. Small front garden with evergreens. Downstairs was the front room (most people didn't use theirs and kept it as 'best' but we had to use ours), the kitchen (with the old black leaded stove), scullery, or 'washus' as it was called, back yard about thirty foot long by twenty foot wide, outside toilet and old dug-up Anderson shelter at the end, which became Grandad's shed. There were three rooms upstairs and eleven stairs. I know, I counted 'em 'cos my ambition at the time was to jump all eleven stairs in one go.

I worked my way up, first one, then two etc, until the day came to attempt the lot. I'd done ten stairs, one more to go. My Nan would shout, 'You'll jump your legs in.' I never knew what she was talking about but I presumed she meant I'd end up a midget. I remember poising myself at the very top, waiting for the right moment (like a footballer does when he's taking a penalty) to do what I had to do. It came. I took a flyin' leap, eyes fixed on the landing strip (the passage floor). I would have done it too if it hadn't been for the floor of the upstairs landing. I had to jump that bit higher to make the eleven stairs. Whack! My head hit the landing floor that jutted out above me, and I landed in a crumpled heap at the foot of the stairs. I never attempted it again. I stuck at ten.

The characters down our road were unique. Next door to us lived a gypsy family, who had mad kids. They had bows and arrows with real dart-heads screwed onto the arrows. They let their little sisters out of upstairs windows, cowboy-style, with ropes tied round their middles and all that. If you went in for a cup o' tea, you'd get it in a jam jar. Which, I gotta be honest, seemed a good idea. Why buy cups when you get jam jars for nothing? Though jam jars were handy too, when the roundabout man came round. For a jam jar you could get a ride on the roundabout. It was a small round wooden thing with sticks sticking out that the big kids grabbed hold of and pushed. The roundabout whizzed round full of little kids. We'd all get off feeling sick. But it was an occasion. This red, white, blue and green wooden roundabout thing turning up at the end of the street. Well, you had to have a go!

Mrs Barlow lived the other side. I played John Bunyan in the school play once and she lent me her long drawers. I played the part with, I thought, the dignity which it deserved. I couldn't make out why everyone was laughin'.

A woman who lived down the road really was mad. She was always on about spacemen and Mars and that. My Great-grandfather didn't know about this 'cos he was as deaf as a post. I remember one conversation I overheard that went, 'Where you goin' for your holidays?' Woman: 'I'm goin' to Mars.' Grandfather: 'I don't like them seaside places.'

Not everybody was mad in Harton Road though. Well, if you class being mad on music as bein' mad then perhaps a lot of 'em were. Music played a big part in our household. Mum played the piano which she taught herself, with the aid of Nan who had a great ear for music. 'Get your vamps right,' she'd say. She wasn't interested in the twiddly bits up the top, like most self-taught pianists played, with anything for the left hand. With her, the chords had to be right. She had the right idea. Mum learnt the hard way by just sloggin' at it 'till it was right. She had no teacher who knew how to play, only Nan who knew when it was wrong. Mum ended up with a unique style that was admired by many, me included. I could never figure out her chord shapes or exactly what she was doin' but it sounded great.

Nan did play a bit of mouth organ though. She was a great critic too. Later on when I began to make records she always had something constructive to say and would come out with good ideas. Grandad (Mum's Dad) was the only unmusical one. He'd just sit back with his pint and enjoy the racket. He did sing now and again though. I learnt 'Not me' from Grandad, which we put on our first 'Jamboree Bag' album.

Grandad took over when Dad died. He was great, he loved an outing. Southend for the day, fishin' off the pier or just fishin' in the Lea down at Broxbourne. Grandad enjoyed it as much as us kids.

Mum often said to me at the time, 'Why don't you take up the piano? You've got a good ear.' But I didn't want to know. I loved music but I also loved fishing and football, and playing in the street. It wasn't until the guitar became popular that I wanted to play. But that was later. There was too much goin' on at the time for me to actually sit down and learn to play an instrument. My every spare moment was spent in the open air. If I wasn't over the Lea fishing or just messing about, I was out in the street playin' games like 'runouts', 'end to the football', or 'Jimmy Knacker'.

Around 1953 when I was nearly ten I remember there were two gangs down our street. There was Lenny Macey's gang with Nobby Brook as his right-hand man. In our book they were the trouble-makers. The other gang was led by my brother Dave with me as his right-hand man (at least I thought so!). We were the peacemakers, but ready to fight for peace! Lenny Macey, a couple of years older than my brother, was talked about as being the best fighter in the street. When he spoke, everybody jumped, but not us. 'My brother could beat him any day,' I'd pipe up. 'Oh Yer?' would say his gang. 'Yer', I'd say. And so on.

One day, me, my brother and our gang were out in the street playin' a game like 'Kingy' or something. Anyway, Lenny Macey and his mob decided they'd join in, uninvited. Brother Dave and Lenny Macey got into an argument that developed into a fight that we all knew was inevitable sooner or later. Not only us kids but the grown-ups knew about the rivalry. One by one they came out of their front doors to watch the fight. They weren't about to stop it. They knew it had to happen. Soon almost the whole of the street were out watching. Nobody cheered or booed or nothing. They were there to witness a fair fight. Which it was. It seemed to go on for hours though it probably lasted more like about half an hour. They fought from one end of the street to the other. Finally Lenny Macey held up his hands. He was beaten. Brother Dave was champ!

From that day on I'd have no talk about Lenny Macey being the best fighter in the Street. I had proof and so did the rest. Nobby Brook, though, never let up. Now my brother had sorted out Lenny Macey, I decided it was my duty to sort out Nobby Brook. As I have said, I was ten and Nobby Brook was about thirteen, although we were roughly the same size. But Nobby Brook had a temper and when he lost it he really lost it!

I can't remember how it started, but shortly after my brother's fight with Lenny Macey, me and Nobby Brook got into a scuffle in the street. He was stronger than me so I wasn't gonna let the fight go on for hours. I knew I'd get beat. We were in a clinch in the middle of the road and I was going under. I reached out in desperation more than anything and my hand fell upon half a house-brick. Wallop! I hit him right on top of the head with it. He went mad and I mean mad! I was up and running and he was close behind me screamin' with rage! I had half the length of the road to run to reach my front door. I glanced behind to see Nobby Brook grab a school railing that we'd been playing javelin throwing with. He meant business so I hoped and prayed that the 'string' was in the door. This string came through a hole in the front door and was attached to the lock. A quick pull and the front door was open. It was! I grabbed the string, was in like a shot and slammed the door just in time. The school railing that was meant for me ended up embedded in the front door! Thank gawd the string was in.

There was always something going on in that street. If it wasn't a fight, (dog fights too), it was a party. Anybody who played an instrument down the street was well respected and sought after on such occasions. Mum was the best piano player down the street. If you got 'Daisy' to play piano at your party you knew it was gonna be a good one. In fact she was the best piano player for miles around. Everyone knew Daisy in and around Edmonton. The street was proud of her.

Music played a big part in that road. Johnny Wright (who taught me a few chords later on) played banjo. He still comes to see us now and is a good friend. There was Bob Weston over the road who played guitar, and his brother Tony. Before I started playin' people down the street would say to me, 'What do you play?' I didn't play anything! They were amazed. They knew about me Mum, Nan and Great-grandfather. 'You ought to, then,' they'd say. Perhaps the combination of my family's and the street's encouragement got me goin'. Who knows? It must have helped.

Coronation Day was a great occasion. Everybody did their bit only too willingly. A real excuse for a party! Let's go! A stage was built outside Huffys, the local shop. A piano was got from somewhere, beer arrived like magic and away they went. Every night for a week the whole street had a great time. I enjoyed every minute of it. The grown-ups looked happy and we kids stayed up late.

'You love music,' Mum would say. 'Why don't you learn to play something?' But life was too full up for me to take time out to sit down and learn to play an instrument. My hours and weeks and months were crowded. If I wasn't fishing down Picketts Lock I'd be train spotting or goin' up the Spurs with my brother, or playing football wishin' I was as good as my brother. He played for Edmonton. Too much was goin' on.

About that time, Great-grandfather married his sixth wife, who left him a week later. Him and his mate 'Scally' (they were both in their nineties) met two birds and decided they would get married. They did, and both moved up to Grimsby. A week later, Great-grandfather arrived back at 11, Harton Road with a bag of dirty washing.

'She's thrown me out, Daisy' he said to Nan. Great-grandfather was back in the fold. 'She wouldn't wash my dirty pants,' he said, and that was that. Scally came home shortly after. He'd got thrown out too. I remember Grandfather and Scally discussing their wives in Grandfather's room. Both of them were stone deaf. Entertaining!

In the meantime Mum married her second husband, Larry.

I wasn't mad on him, he didn't fit in. He didn't last either, and buggered off leaving Mum pregnant. 'The only good thing he ever done,' said Mum. She wanted a daughter and she had one. My half-sister Jean.

My Mum's next husband was Irish John. She met him while playing at the Exhibition pub in Edmonton. I was eleven.

Chapter 3

Irish John

The upset of Mum's last marriage had mellowed with time and contentment reigned. Life at home was good. Me, Mum, brother and sister lived upstairs. Great-grandfather in the box room, and Nan and Grandad lived downstairs. We all got on well together (after a fashion) and I was looking forward to starting my new school.

I'd scraped through the Eleven Plus and was going to Higher Grade, Edmonton. Halcyon days! But them Halcyon days were about to change, especially Sundays. Once Mum married Irish John, what used to be 'sitting round the ol' coal fire of a Sunday with a cup of tea, the pleasant wintery sun shining through the window and just the sound of the old clock ticking on the mantelpiece' soon became 'a room full of Irishmen drinking whiskey, farting, and playing poker'.

Actually John wasn't a bad bloke really. He was as silly as arseholes when he was pissed, which was a good part of the time. I think my Mum didn't really mind him getting pissed though, 'cos he would make her laugh. One day Mum was getting ready to go up the green, shopping.

'Oi'll get your fluten shopping for ye,' says John, 'Oi'm going up the fluten green anyway.'

We never saw him 'til next day. John's recollection of what happened was somewhat sketchy, to say the least, but between bits pieced together from acquaintances and policemen, the story went something like this.

John got the shopping. Then decides he'll go in the 'Ex' for a quick one before going home. John's 'quick one' ends up being a bit longer than originally planned. Before he knows what's happened, its two o'clock in the morning!

On the way home (he vaguely remembers this bit), he's realised he's left the shopping in the pub. It's foggy and he's pissed. It's a long way back to the pub, but he's been gone for over half a day and he ain't even coming home with the shopping. Dais' is gonna be none too pleased. But then he sees something (as though it were heaven sent!) that not only solves his problem, but will put him in Daisy's good books for evermore.

Through the mist he sees a lorry. The back is open and inside he sees something white. It looks like something that women like to buy for their kitchens. A fridge or a washing machine. He's dived in, nicked it and took it home on his shoulder for Dais'. He arrives home, puts it down on the door step to find his key, and then decides to have a look at what he's nicked. It turns out to be a washing machine. They had one in the digs where he used to stay. But didn't the big hole in the top use to have a lid on it? Where's the lid? He'd only forgotten the lid. Dais' will want a lid on it. He remembered seeing a round white bit in the back of that lorry. He must go back for the lid. He did. But so as not to spoil the surprise in case Daisy came out, he took the washing machine with him. An hour later he arrives back at the scene of the crime. The lorry was still there. The back was still open. The lid was still there.

John went in after it. Now as it happened, the fog had begun to clear, and it turned out the lorry was parked outside Edmonton Police Station.

John emerged from the lorry with the lid, hoisted up the washing machine and off he went. But he was spotted. John just heard 'Oi!' and ran with the washing machine and lid down the road. The coppers gave chase. John runs in and out of turnings trying to sidetrack 'em but the boots behind him were getting closer. As a last resort, he slung the washing machine over his head into their path. Some of the boots stopped but a couple dodged out the way and finally caught up with him.

The first we heard was a 'phone call we got at four o' clock in the morning saying it was the police and they'd got Mr John Rice in their custody.

The headline in the local paper was: MAN THROWS MANGLE AT POLICEMAN.

He got off light. He was fined £68, which his brother Packy paid. Mum never sent him shopping no more.

Chapter 4

Schooldays and Rock 'n' Roll

Looking back, I had two sorts of mates at school. Almost complete opposites. Perhaps this reflects the different directions I was torn between. One of my mates, Johnny Hitchens, was a smashing fellow and I thought the world of him. We went up the Spurs together, we went fishing together, but he always did his homework and I didn't. I was always late for school but he wasn't. I admired him for this but instead of modelling myself on him, I accepted the fact that we were different in these respects and went my own way. He still comes to see us at the Millfield Theatre Edmonton. He's a retired teacher now. I bet he was a good one. Better than the ones we had at Eldon Road.

Apart from Miss McSweeny, who I fell deeply in love with when I was nine. She was Burmese, smelt lovely and had lovely brown sandy coloured hands. I still see her regularly today. Joan don't mind. We all went to her 90th birthday this year (2008). She hasn't changed.

My other sort of mates were the ones that were just a little bit more daring than I was. I admired them too. I enjoyed their company. It was exciting. For instance, one of my mates, Tony Webster, was another fishing companion. We used to go camping together over at Cheshunt. One day I hit on the idea (to get our camp fire going better) that we go along the railway lines collecting bits of coal that had fallen from the trains. We spent a good couple of hours doing this and came back with half a sack of coal. We had a good camp fire that night and decided we'd go back and collect some more coal the next day. But here comes the difference between him and me. I didn't mind wandering along the lines picking up stray bits of coal, but it wasn't quick enough for him. He's spotted a coal yard and he's over the fence.

'There's fuckin' loads of it over here!' I've heard, and then he's back with two sacks full. In my mind collecting coal from the trackside wasn't stealing so it was acceptable, but in Tony's mind we were collecting coal and the quicker you got it the better, no matter how. I sort of felt it wasn't quite right, but I liked his initiative.

Our camp fire for the rest of the week outshone everybody else's. It was the talk of the camp site. So much so the camp site bailiff came down to see us.

'Where did you get that coal from?' he said. We told him we got it from along the railway lines.

'Well you'd better bring it up to my house 'cos you're not supposed to have it.'

I felt we'd been found out and it was the only thing to do, but not Tony.

'Bollocks!' he said to me after the Bailiff had gone. 'He only wants it for his own fire!'

'You're right,' I thought, and although I had a nagging feeling that it belonged more to the coal yard than to us, it was still more ours than his. (There's a moral in this somewhere, but I can't figure it out at the minute.)

As I began my new school at Higher Grade, the Rock 'n' Roll era was beginning and I was about to be hooked.

Although, at first, I didn't like it. All the kids were going mad on this bloke called Bill Haley. I couldn't see it. He was okay but he was not as good as Tennessee Ernie or Kay Starr or the boogie-woogie piano players I'd heard. But I hadn't heard Little Richard, or Jerry Lee then. Little did I know what I was in for!

I became a bit of an 'erbert at that school. Nobody got the cane more than me, nobody had longer hair than me. I suppose I was a bit cheeky sometimes, but even though I say it myself I was never nasty and I think most of the teachers liked me. I didn't mind the cane if I knew I was guilty, but I wouldn't accept it if I wasn't.

The Headmaster was a bastard. If you got sent to him you knew you were gonna be caned on the arse and that wasn't pleasant. It wasn't so much the pain. The worst part was the sick feeling you felt a few minutes after. You really felt you'd eaten something bad. Outside his study was a painting of a boy with a rabbit. That was all you had to look at as you was waiting to see the head who you knew was going to cane you. I've seen that picture since and the same feeling came over me. I wanted to go and have a shit. The poor sod who painted it never meant it to give off that feeling, I'm sure! The Headmaster loved caning kids. I'd look through my legs at the old bastard as he bent the cane about before he laid into you. He'd hardly listen to what you had to say for yourself. He didn't want to in case there might be a reason for letting you off. I was a 'bounder' and a 'thug' and had to be 'dealt with accordingly'.

I wasn't sure what 'bounder' meant although it didn't sound too bad, but I objected to being called a thug for kickin' a football through the school window. We used to make up stories of him and the Headmistress having a 'do' at playtime. With her whackin' him on the arse for a change.

The crafty fag smokin' sessions round the back of the bike sheds was an enlightening experience. We'd talk about who you was going to 'tit up' on the field and who you would like to 'tit up'. We had a PT teacher with nice tits. Miss Bebb. She taught us English.

She'd come into class with her PT shorts on. If you played up, you were made to come and sit next to her. So I played up. I remember once havin' to sit at her desk while she sat in front of the class with her foot up on a stool. I could see right up the leg-hole of her shorts to full crutch-piece. No knickers. This was my punishment for being a naughty boy. Looking back I thought, 'Oh no! She don't realise what she's showing!' But now I think she knew alright! Nice memory.

My feelings towards girls began to change. They started to become not just nuisances who played silly games and messed up yours. I began to 'see' something in girls that was worth exploring. My first girlfriend at school was Gillian Marchi. She was the girl behind me in class who piped up when I was told off for having long hair.

'Oh, it's lovely!'

It got me to notice her and then I fancied her. The fact that her big brother was captain of Spurs made her even more attractive. I was a regular up the Spurs at the time. Everybody in the football world pronounced his name as Tony 'Mark-Eye'. I was better informed. It was Tony 'Markee'. 'No, it's not.' 'Oh yes it is, 'cos I go out with his sister.' Anything I said about football from then on was taken as gospel.

At school I was okay at football but wanted to be better. I had a lot to live up to. My brother Dave played for Edmonton.

I played in goal for the school and I thought I guarded goal well, but I never got picked to play for Edmonton. I thought I was as good, if not better than any goalie I'd witnessed at the time, but those that picked the Edmonton team didn't.

I'll tell you something now that will make me sound like a rotten little git.

When I was about seven I buried all my brother Dave's football medals in the front garden.

I didn't have anything against him but I must have been so fed up with relations coming round admiring 'em and then saying 'Why ain't you got any?' That I thought, 'Right! Now he ain't gonna have any. So that's evened that up.'

I couldn't have been all bad though 'cos I owned up and dug 'em all up.

Later on I did excel in one athletic sport. High jump. Before the days of the Fosbury Flop, I broke the school record doing the Western Roll. To me, if you've got to jump over a fence then you can't expect there to be three soft mattresses the other side. You've got to land on your feet. Makes sense. Fosbury Flop? Bollocks. But there you are. When I broke the school high jump record I landed on my feet. Sensible jumping I'd say.

The finalists were me & Geoffrey Geeves. It couldn't be decided in school hours so the showdown high jump was set up in the playground, after school.

Among the crowd, Maureen Clarke was watching.

I knew she had her eye set on classmate Alan Watkins, but she had a pretty face and I made that final leap for her. Interesting ain't it? She was watching but she never knew. I won the contest and never saw her after or since. She inspired me to win it though.

But jumping, playing football, goin' up the Spurs, fishing, even girls (for a while) were about to take second place.

Chapter 5

I Become a
Rock 'n' Roller

It was Little Richard who turned me onto Rock 'n' Roll. I was listening to Radio Luxembourg one night around 1956 and he came on. I was gone! This was the most exciting music I'd heard in my entire life! I went to school next day raving about him but nobody had heard of him. 'Just wait 'til you do. He sings a song called 'Rip-it-up'. He makes Bill Haley sound like Perry Como!' I wouldn't shut up about him. Not long after, me and my mates went to see 'The Girl Can't Help It'. Little Richard sang 'Ready Teddy' in the film. This was real Rock 'n' Roll. My mates had to own up.

And I decided I wanted to be in there playing it.

I was about to find out that taking up music wasn't as easy as taking up fishing or football. But once took up, it was gonna be impossible to put down.

I tried the piano, but couldn't make head nor tail of it. Then all the time other Rock 'n' Rollers were coming along and the feeling of wanting to do what they were doing became an obsession. It was where I was heading. I had no choice. Fats Domino, Jerry Lee, Larry Williams, Eddie Cochran, Gene Vincent and (although he wasn't Rock 'n' Roll but most definitely as exciting in his own way) Lonnie Donegan.

With him came Skiffle groups. Washboards, tea-chest basses and guitars. Guitar! 'Now I think I'd get on alright with that,' I remember saying to my Mum who really did want there to be a musician in the family. 'Mum, I'd like to learn to play the guitar.' Mum promised she'd get hold of one for me if I promised to learn to play it. I did and she did.

It was an old Spanish guitar she got off my Uncle Alf. It was the same guitar she remembered having round the house when she was a kid. I went over to Uncle Alf's in Hackney to get it. I can still remember the smell of that guitar now. Uncle Alf had done it up. Filled all the cracks up with filler and given it a fresh coat of varnish. I arrived home proud. All I had to do now was to learn to play it and I was away. It looks pretty easy watchin' 'em play on the telly, I thought. I could strum alright so I was halfway there. It shouldn't take long.

'How long does it take to play a guitar?' It's a question I've often been asked. When they find the answer to 'How long is a piece of string?' perhaps I can answer it. If one bloke knows two chords and his mate knows none, his mate thinks the two-chorder can play the guitar. But he don't think so when he meets someone who knows four chords, and so on. In music you never stop learnin'. The advice I always give is to play every day even if it is only five minutes every day. Now that don't sound long but you can bet your boots that once you've actually taken the step of pickin' up the guitar you won't put it down for at least an hour. Time flies when you are playing. Learn a new bit every day. Never think of the tenth step after the first, think of the second step. You'll reach the tenth step sooner than you know it (as long as you don't bang your head on the landing floor!).

I thought it was goin' to be easy but I pretty soon owned up that although my strummin' hand was reasonable, the noise that was comin' out was rough. It needs tuning up, I decided. But how do I do that? My Mum got close. She tuned it to a piano chord and I began to play it by stickin' one finger across all frets at different intervals to change to different chords. This didn't sound bad but I had a feeling it wasn't right. The guitar players I saw on the telly made different shapes with their fingers on the fretboard. I had to find out why.

Skiffle groups were beginning to spring up all over the place and there was one down our street. Bob Weston over the road had one. There was talk about how good he was on the guitar. 'There's the man to tune your guitar,' Mum said. 'Catch him on his way home from work and ask him to tune it.'

I waited at my front door one evening and waylaid him. He tuned it and impressed me with the few chords he casually strummed.

I came runnin' in. I had found the key. Eureka! But when I ran my fingers over the strings it didn't sound as good as my Mum's tuning. (The proper guitar tuning is not tuned to a 'chord', so it doesn't sound very musical when played 'open', I found out later.) I was more confused than ever. I got hold of a chord book next, and things began to look a little clearer. Then after study and right 'shapes' were played, it began to sound like a guitar.

But Mum really started me off. She figured out how to play the chords of 'Bring a Little Water Sylvie'. Then she left off for me to carry on. I struggled with these chords. But I now knew how. And it was just a matter of time and practice.

My next-door neighbour but one, Johnny Wright, played the

banjo and he taught me a few chords. I began practising like mad and I began to get quite good on the guitar. Now, as it happened, Mum noticed an advert in the sweet shop window round the corner that said 'Guitarist/Banjo player wanted for the Horseshoe Skiffle Group'. That was Bob Weston's Skiffle group, over the road. 'Go and have a go,' Mum said. I didn't think I was quite good enough yet, but she kept on and I did.

I not only passed the audition, but I knew I had really impressed 'em with my guitar and banjo playing. (I had bought an old banjo for a shilling at a jumble sale.) I was in the group! Mum was right. I must be better than I thought I was. The first paying gig I ever did ('playing jobs' you called them in those days) was a hall over the top of the Britannia pub, Edmonton. Everyone remembers their first gig. We got paid as well! I felt a bit guilty about it. It wasn't that we didn't play well. We played alright, but in my experience you got paid money for doing something you didn't like doin', not for something you loved doin', and would have done anyway. It didn't make sense. Nevertheless I got used to it.

The band got better and we did more and more gigs in and around North London. The personnel changed as the band progressed. An electric guitar was added and I wanted to put Rock 'n' Roll songs into the act. Little Richard's 'Rip-it-up' was the first and it didn't sound bad. Skiffle had been a big help to me, but I was ready to move on.

I was now a Rock'n'Roller.

Chapter 6

Jerry Lee for Me

Skiffle had played its part, and an important part. It got me started. Throughout pop history a relatively simple type of music every now and then becomes popular. It is good because it makes kids think, 'Perhaps I can do that,' and they do, and in a short time some of them are sounding as good as the records. The serious ones move on from there, but that start is important.

Skiffle was like that. It progressed to Rock 'n' Roll and Blues (in England) and players like Eric Clapton and Albert Lee, whose roots lie in Skiffle, began to be popular. But not many kids, in their wildest dreams, thought they could pick up a guitar and learn something quick that sounded like them. They were too far advanced. Something simpler was needed to give the kids the feeling again of 'I can do that!' Then Bob Dylan came round and thousands of youngsters overnight bought guitars and were strummin' 'Blowin' in the Wind' in parks, on Tube trains, in the streets, everywhere, and most of 'em sounded as good as him, if not better. 'New Wave Skiffle!' The next time it happened was Punk. These were really important eras for getting new musicians off the ground. But back to the Horseshoe Skiffle Group.

We were now a Rock 'n' Roll group. We were called The Horseshoes and did songs like 'Ready Teddy', 'That'll Be the Day', 'Oh Boy!', 'Let's Have a Party' – the choice of material was limitless. Up 'till now I'd experienced all my Rock 'n' Roll idols on film or on record, I'd never seen any of 'em live. I'd missed the Buddy Holly concerts at the Regal, Edmonton. I don't know why I didn't go, I can't remember. All the kids at school went and were ravin' about him. Perhaps that's what made me determined not to miss the next concert at the Regal. It was to be Jerry Lee Lewis.

That performance was a milestone in my life. The line-up was piano, bass and drums (coincidence: that is me and Dave's line-up now! Or is it coincidence?). They had an electric bass, the first I'd ever seen, the loudest drummer I'd ever heard, and Jerry Lee playin' piano like it was a new instrument. I had a piano indoors, but it never sounded like that! I still loved Little Richard, but this man played music that was even closer to my heart. His piano playing, although I hadn't heard anything like it before, made sense. This was the way I'd like to play piano if I ever became a pianist.

I liked the songs he sang and the way he sang 'em. I decided then and there I'd catch as many of his English tour gigs as possible before he went home. Two days later he was deported. All because he married some thirteen-year-old girl! I couldn't believe it! The Home Office decided he would be a bad influence on us youngsters. 'Are they mad? Don't they realise that me and the rest just like him for his music? They're protecting us?' From what? I was beside myself with rage. What he did in his private life didn't concern me in the least. Of course I was right but the letter I wrote to the Home Office didn't make any difference. They kicked him out and that was that. If someone had told me then that one day I'd record an album with him, sing a duet and do gigs with him, and he'd record a song I helped write, what would I have said? 'You're mad!' But he did!

That Jerry Lee concert was in May 1958 and at that time I was coming up to school-leaving age. I'd had fun at school despite the ups and downs. I learnt to play guitar while I was at school and my first attempt at Skiffle was also at school. Me and Brian Juniper used to have a few sessions round his house. (It was through Brian that I met Dave Peacock much later. Brian was in the same junior school as Dave and formed a group with Dave when he left school.) My headmaster now and again threw a few compliments my way. I couldn't handle that. It was out of character. He'd come into the class and give a lecture on the evils of hanging around street corners late at night. 'Why not take a leaf out of Hodges' book and learn to play a musical instrument?' I almost thought, 'He's not so bad after all.' The music teacher never gave me any encouragement, though. All Rock 'n' Roll was rubbish in his book. I marked him down as a know-nuffink dumb-cluck.

But my being in favour with the Headmaster was short-lived. It was Christmas 1958 and the School Party.

It was the year canned beer was introduced and it was a bit of a novelty. Me and my mates decided to have a go and bought some Long Life beer to drink in the school bog. We had a line of cans set up along the top of the toilet doors. Me and my mate Don Philips were just drainin' the last dregs out of our cans ready to go back and join the party. I said (feelin' really big), 'I bet ol' Dunnie (the Head) would do his bollocks if he walked in now!'

I sensed a presence as I said it. I lowered my eyeballs as I was guzzling, and they fell upon a pair of horribly familiar baggy trousers. In 'em stood the Headmaster. Without a word he took the empty beer cans from us and once more it was 'lookin' through the legs time'.

The next morning we were both hauled up in front of the school and were asked to leave at the Christmas holidays. I was actually fourteen when I left (or was politely expelled) but I was fifteen just after Christmas, so legally able to start work, which I did.

Chapter 7

First Real Job

The first job I got was at Turners, the jeweller's shop on Edmonton Green, as a watch and clockmaker's apprentice. My Mum knew the guv'nor, who used to go in the Exhibition pub where she played piano. My brother worked there when he left school a couple of years earlier, but he didn't get on with the job and moved on.

The idea of messing about with old clocks, takin' 'em apart and puttin' 'em back together appealed to me. I asked Mum if she could get me a job there. I went up to be interviewed and I started in January 1959. 1 liked that job. At the time I had never dreamed of earnin' a livin' playin' music. I never knew anyone who was a professional musician, I had a job and as far as 'proper' jobs go, it wasn't bad. It was a little old nineteenth-century shop. I was on my own most of the time. I became quite good at mendin' old clocks quite quickly, though I wasn't mad on watch mending. All you did with watches was find out what was wrong and send away for a new part. But clocks; some of the old ones you'd get in, you'd have to use your initiative, and make new parts to get them going. The feelin' of bringin' them old clocks back to life was nice.

I worked hard when I was there but I was constantly late for work. I couldn't get up in the mornings, and I still can't. I hated mornings and still do. I'm a different person in the morning and always have been, regardless of what time I go to bed. I'm not proud of the fact, I'm just being honest about myself. It's nothing to do with hangovers or anything like that. I was the same when I was at school. I am not very good tempered in the mornings and don't want to speak to anybody. I get annoyed at stupid things that I'm ashamed of later in the day. When me and my brother had to get up together to go to school, we wouldn't speak. But the sound of him crunching his toast used to make me want to punch him. Now ain't that terrible?

I become a different person after midday and when I think of my instinctive feelings earlier that morning I am ashamed. I mean, 'Stop crunchin' that fuckin' toast!' WALLOP! What a little bastard! Thank Christ it wears off. I make a point of avoiding mornings at all costs, though sometimes I can't. I feel I'm being victimised when I'm woke up in the morning to go and do something. I do it – but grudgingly. And them bright and breezy morning people! I feel they're bein' like they are just to annoy me. It can't be natural. It can't be natural to be laughin' and jokin' while it's still mornin'. They're doin' it just 'cos they know it annoys me! Once again in the afternoon I'm thoroughly ashamed of myself. I'm thinkin', I really had the hump with him this morning, laughin' and jokin' like that. I can tolerate him now and he's still laughin' and jokin'. But now it's afternoon.

The best thing I've learned to do in the morning is to keep my mouth shut and don't say nothing. As I said, I'm not proud of it and if the two of me ever met, the morning me and the afternoon or evening me, well, I don't think they'd get on too well together. The evening me would not tolerate such a short-tempered little git as the morning me, and the morning me would not tolerate such a cheerful genial chap as the evening me.

When I started that job at Turners, the guv'nor was off sick and his son Charley took over 'til he got better. Charley was a good bloke. He'd moan at me for being late but he knew I worked well when I did get in so it never got to the sack. But when the boss got back he couldn't accept my tardiness and I was soon given an ultimatum: 'Get in early or get out.' I couldn't see the sense. All the work got done on time even if I had to take work home to finish it. I didn't mind, I enjoyed it. But I didn't like mornings and I couldn't get up in them. I turned up late again to be greeted by the guv'nor with me cards. 'Oh fuck him,' I thought, 'if he can't see I'm a good worker then bollocks.' I was earning more money playing local gigs than I was working there anyway.

The Horseshoes by this time had drifted apart and I began playing with new musicians. I met up with Tony Ollard, a great guitar player. We began swapping ideas. We started playin' gigs at the King's Head, Edmonton – a good Rock 'n' Roll gig. The King's Head was a great meeting place (I also met my wife there!). There really were some good musicians in and around North London at that time and the King's Head was a good place to find 'em on a Friday night. For a while I was in no regular band. Whoever was available just got together and away we went. Invaluable experience. The musicians got to know each other, swapped ideas, talked about guitars and Rock 'n' Roll. I had found a crowd I could identify with. The bass guitar began to be talked about. Not many had seen one, let alone heard one, apart from on Rock 'n' Roll records. I had seen one. Jerry Lee's bass player had one. I fancied playin' bass. I fancied playin' double bass at one time, but it wasn't practical. It wouldn't fit in the luggage compartment on the bus like the old tea chest used to! On some Friday night gigs, four or five guitar players would turn up. We made a bit of a row sometimes. We were still young and our tunin' quite often was not spot on. One night I tuned my bass strings down a couple of tones and played sort of bass lines. Were the boys impressed! So was I. A new sound! I had discovered a frequency range uncluttered by anybody else's, and it sounded good. That was it, I was going to become an electric bass player. I saw an advert for a Hofner Bass Guitar that you could buy on the knock from Bell Accordions in Surbiton, Surrey. My Grandad signed as guarantor, the deposit was sent off and the bass guitar arrived.

I tried it out indoors in my little amp, playing along to records. It sounded absolutely fantastic! I couldn't wait to get together with the boys at the King's Head. Up Town Road I went early on Friday evening, amp in one hand, bass guitar in the other. I arrived, proud, at the gig.

As I was plugging in my amp, the rest of the boys were admiring my guitar. 'Blimey, ain't the strings thick. It's fantastic.' 'You wait 'til you hear it,' I said. I tuned it up sittin' close to me amp and away we went. Did that bass sound good? It sounded fuckin' terrible! 'Fart, Rasp, Rattle.' I couldn't believe it. In my front room it sounded great but my poor little amp couldn't cope with the rest of the band in that big hall. I never knew that a bass needed a bigger speaker and cabinets, etc.

'I don't think you realise what you let yourself in for, Chas,' said Billy Kuy the guitar player. 'You're gonna have to fork out for a bigger amp and you won't be able to carry it up and down Town Road like you can that one.' I didn't want to believe him but I knew he was right. It was an obstacle that had to be overcome. I was hooked on the bass guitar.

Now although I didn't have a bass amp, I suddenly found myself in demand by all the bands that played down the King's Head. Bands were willing to provide a bass amp if I would sit in with 'em. No one else in Edmonton had a bass guitar. It made their band sound professional and I weren't complaining. I was earning money playing with all these bands. Playing the bass gave me the chance to work with nearly all the musicians around North London and eventually a band was formed which I was pleased to become a part of: Billy Gray and The Stormers. Me on bass, Reg Hawkins rhythm guitar, Billy Kuy lead guitar, Billy (Gray) Halsey singer, and Bobby Neate on drums. This was the band for me and I thought it was time I got a bass amp of my own. Bobby Neate had an open-backed van. He had to carry his drums but there was enough room for a proper bass amp. He agreed to lug it about if I got one. So I set to work.

Billy Kuy told me that the bass player with Dave Sampson and the Hunters, Johnny Rogers, had a bass amp for sale. He'd bought it from Jet Harris, the Shadows' bass player. I'd seen Cliff and the Shadows when Jet Harris was using the amp. I thought it was fantastic. Johnny Rogers wanted £20 for the lot. I was round there like a shot and got it.

Now this bass amp was built like a little house and was about as heavy as one. It was about four foot high, three foot wide and three foot deep. A solid wooden box (two inch thick wood) within a box and the cavity was filled with sand. You can imagine the weight. It was made by Wallace in Soho Street. I think it was the first British bass amp ever made. Bobby Neate, who had promised to lug it about, looked a bit dismayed when he found out what he'd agreed to. But he didn't back out and it came with us on the road. It had a sound and a half! (Some years later I gave that cabinet to some geezer I'd just met named Dave Peacock. He sawed a fuckin' great hole in it, all the sand fell out and it ended up in his back garden. It's probably still there now!)

Billy Gray and The Stormers began to get a name as the best band round North London. Through someone or other we heard that there were auditions going for Butlins Holiday Camps. We brushed up the act and went for the audition at the Majestic in Finsbury Park. There were some good bands there from all over London. We had competition. But a few days later we got a letter through saying that we had passed. We were to go to Filey Holiday Camp in Yorkshire for the 1960 summer season at £20 each a week. An absolute fortune for a sixteen-year-old and all we had to do was play music! I couldn't wait to get there and it was to turn out even better than I had expected.

Chapter 8

Butlins with Billy Gray & The Stormers

It was heaven. Parties every night, go to bed when you like, get up when you like, a new girlfriend every week. You'd watch 'em file in to the dance on the night of arrival, smile at the one you fancied and you were away! I never knew it was as easy pulling birds. Why didn't I try this before? I wasn't used to all this!

I'd had a couple of girlfriends in the past. I was courting a girl who I packed up just before I went to Butlins. I shan't ever forget that. I was courting her for about three months. At the time I thought I was in love. We'd have rows and at the end she'd say 'Go on then, go if you want to.' And me like a fool didn't, and would talk her round. I remember thinking if ever I wanted to pack her up it would be easy, she wouldn't give a monkeys. One mornin' I woke up and I remember thinkin', I don't want to see her anymore. There was no feeling or nothing. The worm had turned. So, I didn't go round her house. It was easy. After a week I'd forgotten all about her. Then there came a knock on the door. I looked out of the window and it was her with her mate. I was getting ready to go up the King's Head at the time.

'Hello,' I said. 'What do you want?'

'I want my Ricky Nelson records!' she said.

'Oh alright, I'll chuck 'em out of the window to you.'

'No, bring 'em down. I want to talk to you. Anyway, I might miss 'em and they might break.'

I didn't want to talk to her. It was all finished as far as I was concerned. I didn't want to break her records though. I went downstairs. They were only 45s. I thought I'll probably be able to poke 'em through the letterbox. But they were just too big. I opened the door quick, stuck 'em in her hand and went to shut the door, but she was there pushing on the door from the other side with all her might to keep it open. I managed to shut the door, then: 'Whaaaaaaaa' she started cryin'. She just sort of switched it on. It frightened me.

'Shut up!' I shouted through the letter-box. 'Whaaaaa!' she said.

'Shut up and I'll come out!' I shouted again. I thought the whole street must be out. She stopped. I opened the door.

'I want you to come back to me. Whaaaaa!' 'Shut up!' I said. 'What's the matter?' shouted Nan from the front room. 'Nothing, Nan.' I went out to the doorstep and shut the door. 'I think we should finish with each other,' I said.

'Whaaaaaaa!'

Oh, bleedin' hell, the street'll think she's bein' murdered.

'Just let me come with you to the King's Head tonight.'

'No!'

'Whaaaaa!'

'Alright, just be quiet. I'll walk you to the bus stop but you can't come in to the King's Head. Let me get me coat and me bass.' I was in and out like a shot and off we went up the street.

All the time she kept askin' 'Why?' I didn't know why, I just knew I'd got fed up with her. On top of that the more she pleaded the more I didn't want to know. At the top of the road I suddenly decided to leave her there.

'I'm goin' and you're not comin' with me.'

'Whaaaaa!'

'Alright! Stop it, I'll walk on a bit further.'

Silence. 'What am I goin' to do?' I asked myself. 'This is goin' to go on forever.'

I finally made the decision as we were taking a short cut through the alley to the bus stop.

'I'm goin', I said, and I went.

'Waaaaaaaaaaaa!'

I couldn't have left her in a worse place. The echo between those two brick walls in that alley was deafening. This girl who once could twist me round her little finger, hollering like that! I was confused but I felt I was doing the right thing. Anyway, soon I'd be off to Butlins and having the time of my life. I lived for the moment and Butlins was the moment. But it was going to end only too quick.

At the end of the summer we came back home and I thought, 'Oh well, it's a shame that's over but we're bound to get loads of gigs, so it won't be so bad.' But two of the band got married and the interest waned. So did the gigs. I had to get a job.

Down the employment exchange I've gone with Billy Kuy. I was asked all the usual questions.

'What did you like at school?'

'Nothin'. Well, football and woodwork.'

'Right, I can't fix you up with a job at the Spurs, but there's a job goin' at a woodwork factory in Edmonton. Get down there.'

Off I've gone.

Now Billy Kuy had always worked in office jobs. He wore detachable collars and you never ever saw him without a tie. There were no office jobs going at the factory, but he was skint. He was no good at woodwork but the man at the employment exchange said they needed someone sweepin' up, so Bill came too. On the way I've thought, 'Oh well, makin' somethin' out of wood might not be so bad.' I remembered making a split-cane fishin' rod and a veneered cigarette box at school and I quite enjoyed it. We've turned up at the factory, Billy Kuy has been given a broom and off he's gone.

'Right, Mr. Hodges, come over here.' It was a deck chair makin' factory. Not very creative, but makin' the best of it I am thinkin' p'raps I can get into it. Drillin' the holes, shapin' the wood, fittin' the canvas, sanding down and polishing and being proud of the finished product. Yeah, it won't be so bad.

'Right, Mr. Hodges, here's what you do. See them sticks with holes in?'

'Yeh.'

'Well, put them round sticks in them round holes and bang a nail in to stop 'em comin' out.'

'Right. What do I do next?'

'That lot over there,' he said, pointing to a mountain of sticks with holes in and hole-shaped sticks.

'If you need any more nails, come and see me.'

I've never seen a bigger tin of nails! It was like a bad dream. There was I, left all alone with a pile of sticks that had to be banged together. A monkey would have been humiliated at the task. I made a start. In front of me was a dingy window that hadn't been cleaned for years. Through it I could see a blurred vision of the bright autumn sunshine. I'm thinkin', 'This time last week I was at Butlins Holiday Camp. Heaven and Hell! Yes, that's it, I'm in Hell. This is what it must be like.'

I've managed to get through to tea-break, then I saw Billy Kuy. That depressed me even more. The Jack the Lad of the band, number one bird puller, smooth talker, always wore a clean collar, man about town, looked a wreck. There he was, no collar, hair all over the place, red face, sweepin' up. He's come over to me with his broom.

'Chas, I've had enough, I am fuckin' off home!'

'Go, Bill,' I said. As much as he got on me nerves sometimes, with his smoothie ways and dapper habits back at Butlins, I didn't want to see him like this.

'Go, Bill,' I said. 'I'm gonna stick it out, I think.'

Bill's gone. Dinner-time's come and I'm fed up and depressed and everything. I've gone out to get me bike to go home for dinner. I can't find me bike. Some bastard's pinched me bike! Right, that's it, I've had enough. How can I work with a load of thievin' bastards! I'm not havin' it. That's the last time I'm comin' to work here.

On the way home I began to feel happier. Although me bike was pinched it gave me the excuse to leave. 'I mean, you can't expect me to work with a bunch of thieves,' I've told Mum when I got home. 'I mean, what are they gonna pinch next?'

'Well, you've got to earn some money somewhere, Chas,' said Mum. 'So you'd better start thinkin'.' My usually easy-going Mum was right and I knew it. I've gone back on Friday to get me cards and me morning's money and I'm just goin' out of the gate when someone said:

'Oi, you, come here. Did you come here on a yellow bike?'

'Yes,' I said, 'and one of your mob's nicked it!'

'Nicked it? We brought it in out of the rain. It's in the shed over there.'

I felt rotten the way I'd run 'em down. I called 'em all the bastards under the sun and all they'd done was bring it in for me 'cos it was gettin' wet in the rain. They weren't so bad after all. But the thought of going back to that job filled me with dread. I couldn't wait to get away from the place. But I was out of work and the band by now had split. What do I do next?

Chapter 9

The Outlaws

Just before The Stormers split we did a couple of test recordings and also backed a singer called Danny Rivers, (who we met at Butlins), on a couple of demos. Danny Rivers had a couple of brief spots on 'Oh Boy'. He sung 'Stuck on You' on one appearance, but had trouble reaching the high note in the middle. 'Tear' was the word. The line was, 'A team of wild horses couldn't tear (high note) us apart.' Jack Good got Dickie Pride to sing 'tear' behind the scene while Danny mimed the word. It worked. You'd never have spotted it if you didn't know.

Danny was managed by Peter Yaquinandi who was a bit of a character. One night not many days after the bike pinchin' episode fate took a hand. There was a knock on my door. It was Peter Yaquinandi, or 'Yak' as we called him. He was managing a singer called Mike Berry who had passed an audition with an independent recording engineer named Joe Meek. Joe was well impressed with Mike Berry but not too impressed with his band. Yak was on his way round to see the rest of our band. If he could get them back together, would I be willing to audition at Joe Meek's as a backing musician to Mike Berry? He played me some demo tapes and Mike was like Buddy Holly (not 'like' him but almost *him*!). Buddy Holly ranked highly among my Rock heroes along with Jerry Lee Lewis and Little Richard.

I was all for it. The rest of the boys agreed: Reg Hawkins on rhythm guitar, Billy Kuy on lead (ex-broom!) and Bobby Neate (who now called himself Bobby Graham) on drums. An audition with Joe Meek was arranged. We passed the audition and before we knew it we had a record out on the market. My first record! 'Will You Love Me Tomorrow' by Mike Berry and The Outlaws (Joe's new name for us). That one didn't do too good, but soon after, The Outlaws recorded 'Swingin' Low' which made the top fifty. We were on our way, but the chart thing was really an extra for me. The main thing was, I was back playing and enjoying myself. The deck chair factory? A bad dream I'd woken up from!

Joe Meek was alright. By that I mean that his heart was in the right place. He was a bit of a bum boy, as I found out later. At the time I met him, I'd heard these stories about blokes stickin' their winkles up other blokes' bums – but who could really believe that? I mean, I was told havin' a Jodrell sent ya blind and – and, well, I could go on for ever! I was sixteen years of age. Old enough to realise that schoolboys told these fairy tales to each other while havin' a crafty dog end round the back of the bike sheds. But I was in for a shock.

A mate of mine, Tony Ollard, played me a tape he'd got from somewhere, of some guitar playing. I'd never heard the like of it before. He told me he thought it was a bloke called Chet Atkins but he didn't know who the other bloke was. I thought it could be one bloke double-tracked. Later on I found out it was Chet Atkins but it wasn't double-tracked. The man just played like two guitar players! I begged Tony to lend me the tape and I'd get it copied and return it straight away. Who do I know who's got two tape recorders? Joe Meek! Next time we did a session I asked Joe if he'd do a copy of this tape for me.

'Bring it up tomorrow and I'll do it.' I was there. He's done the tape, I was well pleased, caught the last bus home and played that tape 'till the sun came up. Next day I'm ravin' about this tape to the boys.

'Never mind the tape', they said. 'What about Joe? Did he give you one?'

'Bollocks!' I've gone, 'he's alright, how old are you?' Christ, some people just don't grow up, do they?

Now Joe wrote most of the instrumentals for the band. I say 'wrote', his method was more like 'get an idea for a tune, find a record that was the right tempo and sing his tune to it'. The resulting demo (which I had to decipher) was a din; he sang out of tune too. I had to work out what I thought he was trying to get across. Most of it I figured out but I had to put my own bits in for the bits I couldn't decipher. Joe always seemed pleased with the result, so all was well. Anyway he'd invite me up to listen to his latest creation and I'd take the acetate home and try to make it playable by the band.

This happened on many occasions. Not a move was made, bum-boy-wise. Ol' Joe's alright!

One Saturday afternoon I've gone up there to listen to another Joe Meek 'composition', heard it, worked it out with difficulty and worked out how we're gonna do it. Got it! Great! Ready to go home.

'Do you want a cup of coffee 'fore you go, Chas?'

'Alright, Joe.' I can remember feeling a bit uneasy but 'He's alright', I told myself.

In his sitting room he had this sofa. No matter where you sat on it, you were sort of bounced towards the middle and ended up sittin' next to whoever else was on it. Even if you both sat down at the extreme ends of the sofa. Which we did.

So there we were. Me and Joe. 'I hope my mates are wrong,' I'm thinking as we sat together in the middle of the sofa. Now in them days wrestling was just becoming popular, and Joe had it on the telly. It was popular in the Sixties and was always on of a Saturday afternoon. As I'm trying to knock back the cup of coffee he made me which had too much sugar in it – funny how you remember silly details – Joe said to me:

'I love wrestling, do you?'

My whole life flashed before me. I thought, 'Oh no! It's the bums he likes! My mates were right.' Too late! The next minute, there was a hand groping round my bollocks and I froze. Petrified. It must have been only a fraction of a second that I sat there rigid but it was enough to make Joe think, 'He likes it,' 'cos his hand started scrunching quicker and he started bobbing up and down. My eyes started watering. I looked at Joe. His eyeballs were bulging but he looked ever so happy. I leapt out of that seat like my arse was alight. It very nearly could have been. I found my voice, but the best I could come up with was:

'I've got to be going now. I've got to go and meet my big brother.'

I had always mentioned my 'big' brother when I was threatened by anybody at school. It was the best I could think of. I was out of his flat like a shot. I kept running until I saw a bus that was heading in the general direction of home and I leapt on it. The conductor asked for me fare in a normal voice and I felt safe. I was back in the land of the un-bum boys.

Next day though, I thought, 'I believe now there are blokes that stick their winkles up other blokes' bums.' I was growing up. I rang Mike Berry and told him of the episode.

'The dirty bastard,' was all he kept saying between the gaps of my story.

'Yes,' I said in the end. 'Isn't he?'

I never spoke to Joe for days afterwards but as I started to weigh it up I thought, 'Well, it does go on; but at least I got away and didn't get raped.' I s'pose it's the same as some geezer fancyin' some bird. He weren't to know I liked birds and not geezers. He fancied me so he had to find out. But now he's found out he knows where he stands.

He rung up and apologised a few days later. 'That's OK, Joe,' I said, 'but let's have no more of it.' That was the end of that, but Charlie Hodges could now say when the subject of bum boys came up,

'Oh yes, it goes on alright. You don't believe it? Oh, come now. How naive can you get!'

Joe with all his eccentricities was well before his time in the recording field. DI-ing the bass, for instance, was a matter of course for Joe. DI-ing or 'Direct Injection (nothing to do with bum boys!) meant the bass player didn't use an amp. The bass was plugged more or less direct into the tape machine. No amp was used in the actual studio and this meant there were no stray notes or floatin' around to be picked up by other microphones. This technique meant a much cleaner and purer sound for the electric bass. All studios do it now. Joe always had five or six mikes on the drum kit instead of one or two which was usual for the time. He loved a sound that had 'presence'. He wanted the snare drum, hi-hat, bass drum, cymbals recorded close. It worked. They all do this now. Joe would have been in his element with a multi-track machine. He never got one as far as I know; they were still a novelty in England when Joe died not many years later.

Now The Outlaws were doing alright. We were out on the

road with Mike Berry and started doing a few sessions up at Joe Meek's. Joe was always recording somebody or the other. Most of 'em never came to anything but we did some sessions with an actor, John Leyton. 'Johnny Remember Me' was one of the songs we did, and suddenly I was on a Number One Hit. My friends and relations thought I was rich, but you got £7. 10s a session regardless of whether it was a hit or not. I earned far more off Joe's flops. I thought this fair enough, still do, but they'd go, 'What! He got all that money and all you got was £7. 10s?' They probably thought I'd copped a fortune, and was keeping it dark.

We did a few other recordings with John Leyton. Among 'em was the follow-up, 'Wild Wind', on which I played fretless bass. It had frets on it at the beginning of the session, but I got this idea halfway through that a bass guitar without frets might sound a bit like a double bass. I couldn't wait to try it so levered 'em out on the session. It didn't sound too bad. As far as I knew it was the first fretless bass guitar. (I've still got this bass. My original Hofner. I got it fixed up recently and used it on my new album this year. 2008. It sounds great. The last time I recorded with it was on 'Dontcha Think it's Time' in 1963. Forty-six years ago! Daft ain't it?)

We backed John Leyton for a week in Brighton later on. There was a bit in 'Wild Wind' he used to sing which I thought was comical. He sung the song in an American accent but when he got to the word 'trouble' he sort of went all Cockney. It was the best part of the whole song for me but I'm not sure he meant it to be a laugh. You see, he had to really holler that word to get it out as it was the highest note in the whole song. He had to really open his mouth wide. Now you can't sing 'trouble' in American style ('trerble') with your mouth wide open like a barrow boy's. It *has* to come out as 'trubball'. Good though.

The Outlaws

That original Outlaws band was a good line-up. Bill, Bob, Reg and me. Reg was a real rhythm guitarist. Not like most of them. In those days most of them were frustrated lead guitarists. He was my best mate in the band, and we still see a lot of each other today. Dave likes Reg, too. He's got a great sense of humour and is always good company. I first met Reg at Higher Grade School. He was a year older than me but him and his mate, and me and my mate, Rodney Clark, used to knock around together. It was unusual to mix with anyone in a different year to you but we all used to laugh at the same things. It was coincidence that we ended up in the same band together. We lost touch after we left school then met again a few years later up the King's Head (the birth place of The Outlaws).

I was with Reg when I learnt my first chords on the piano. Apart from having the same taste in humour we also had the same taste in music. He introduced me to the music of Jack Elliot and Derrol Adams. We both loved Big Bill Broonzy and Chet Atkins. We'd sit around for hours on end doing our best to copy 'em.

We were both Jerry Lee fans too. When we were at Butlins we found out there was a way of sneaking into the Viennese Ball Room after it was shut. It had a grand piano! We'd sit up all night singing and I began to get off some bits I thought sounded like Jerry Lee. How much like Jerry Lee it was I don't know but Reg liked it and that gave me encouragement.

Bobbie Graham was a great drummer. A bit of a jazzer when he joined us, I don't think he was too mad on Rock 'n' Roll, (it wasn't considered 'cool' then) and I don't think he was too mad on me at the time, trying to get him to play like Jerry Lee's drummer.

Perhaps I was too young to explain what I meant. I knew Bob

was a better drummer than Jerry Lee's but the feel wasn't right. (I don't even think the musical term 'feel' was used in those days, I just used to say, 'It don't sound right, Bob'.) He did eventually get into Rock 'n' Roll (p'raps I wore him down) and there was no one to touch him.

Billy Kuy? Now what can I say about ol' Bill? A bit short-tempered in his younger days (to say the least!) but you could have a laugh with him. He knew his instrument and was particularly good at chords. I remember saving Bill's life once.

Me and Bill had just finished a gig at The Angel, Edmonton. Irish John, my stepfather, told me there was a party going afterhours over the top of the 'Ex'. I asked Bill if he fancied going, his eyes lit up and off we went.

We had to walk through Edmonton Green on the way. Now Edmonton Green was renowned for pulling bits of stray after dark and Bill spotted a bit of stray. But the bit he spotted (Bill wasn't to know and probably wouldn't have cared anyway as he was three parts pissed) was the dodgiest bit of stray in Edmonton. Everyone knew her (except Bill).

Bill's homed in and started giving her the 'Billy Kuy chat'. 'Bill, you're mad,' I tell him. 'Come here.' Too late. He's back with her on his arm and a big 'Look what I got' smile on his face. He's invited her to the party.

Anyway we've arrived, seen Irish John, we're in. Straight up to the bar. Great. I'd forgotten about the bird, so had Bill. It was me and Bill, after-hours in a pub.

'What d'yer want to drink, Chas?'

'I'll have a pint, Bill.' I've gone off to the bog.

I've come back. No Bill. Now where's he gone? He's supposed to be getting the pints in.

I've looked round, and there he is. Rabbitin' away nineteen to the dozen to some great big Irishman. The look on Bill's face told me it wasn't no matey conversation. Bill was wild-eyed, and by the look on the Irishman's face he was none too friendly either.

I've gone to the rescue. As I've got near, I've recognised the Irishman, Big Mick, one of my stepfather's workmates. Bill's picked on a wrong 'un this time! I've moved in.

'Hallo Mick,' I've gone. 'How ya doin'?' He's looked round, wild an' all, but soon as he saw me he softened a little.

'Chassy boy! How yer fluten doin'?' Thank God he's recognised me. I've breathed (for Bill's sake) a sigh of relief.

'Not too bad, Mick. What d'ya want t'drink?'

'Oh, I'll have a wee Scotch with ya, Chassy boy.'

I've done it! I thought. But no.

'Oh no you fuckin' won't! We've got some business to finish!' says Bill. Mick's friendly look changed back to the wild one again.

'You little git! Oi'l morder ye!' he's said, leaping at Bill's throat.

'Hold up, hold up, hold up!' I've gone. 'Look, Mick! Talk to *me*! What's the matter?'

I've moved round the front so he can see my eyes. He's dropped Bill.

'He says I've been chatting up his girlfriend. Oi wasn't! I swear oi was only *talking* to the woman!'

I believed Mick, but I couldn't believe Bill. Getting all possessive over this 'ol bird! He'd forgotten all about her for the last hour. I've given him a look, as if to say, 'Are you mad? This bloke's three times the size of you! Bugger off quick while you're in one piece.'

'Look, Mick,' I've said, 'me and Bill's been out and had a few pints. We've had a good time and Bill's a bit pissed. Let's forget it, come on I'll buy you that Scotch.'

Mick would've gone for it, but oh no.

'*I'm* not pissed, Chas.' 'Oh, *shut up*, Bill!' 'And your Irish mate's a cunt!'

With that Mick's gone for Bill in a big way, and he meant it. He's lifted Bill up like a bit of rag and pushed him through the nearest door. Which happened to be the bog-hole. I've run in, and there was Mick with Bill on the floor, trying to grind his head in the piss trough with his boot. Bill's head was jerking from left to right, deftly dodging every stomp, but it would have been only a matter of time.

'Mick!' I've hollered, grabbing hold of him. Mick's turned round ready to take a swing, then saw it was me.

'Mick,' I said. 'Leave him alone. He's not worth the bother. Come and have a drink.'

Mick was torn between two emotions. Bill at last saw the light and was up and away. I dragged Mick to the bar and bought him that Scotch.

Bill did end up fighting someone that night. It was Freddy the Fly, a mate of ours. They had a punch-up all up and down Edmonton Market. I don't know why, but it was the way Bill liked to round his evenings off.

Around 1962 the original Outlaws folded up. Reg decided the business wasn't for him and settled down with a regular job. Bob joined Joe Brown and Bill buggered off somewhere or other. That left me and Mike Berry. If I remember right, the first new Outlaw was drummer Don Groom.

In fact I think he did a couple of gigs with Reg and Bill before they left. Mike got hold of Ray 'Biffo' Byhart to play rhythm guitar, so now we had drums, rhythm and bass. All we needed was a lead guitarist.

Mike heard about this lead guitarist who had been working with Screaming Lord Sutch. (Sutch had a reputation for finding good Rock 'n' Rollers). But the guitarist would only consider joining if we took his piano-playing mate on too. We didn't want a piano player, but we thought we'd get 'em down and if we liked the guitarist we'd talk him into joining us on his own.

They've both turned up, and I've never seen such a weird-looking couple of geezers. The guitar player was about four foot six tall with bleached blond hair and a face straight out of a Brueghel painting. The piano player was about six foot tall, as skinny as a rake and looked dopey. Neither one of 'em hardly said a word. 'Oh, well,' I've thought. 'Let's get it over and done with, think of something diplomatic to say as to why we don't want 'em, and think again.'

Now I want you to try to imagine how a young, enthusiastic and talented Rock 'n' Roller looked at things in those days. You see, we knew the *feel* of our music, but we weren't particularly *masters* of our instruments. We simply hadn't been playing long enough to become so and any player that was nimble or 'fast', as we called it, gained our immediate admiration. But usually the ones that were fast didn't have the feel and vice versa.

Anyway, I'm plugging in me bass, thinking about who can we ring tomorrow who might know of a lead guitarist, when I heard a sound that made me freeze. It really did. My life for two seconds was in suspended animation. I can remember how far the jack plug was from the hole and everything.

'DIDDLY DIDDLY DIDDLY DIDDLY DUM BEOODLY BLAT BAP WEEDLY WOP'

I've heard a guitar run that was not only fast, and I mean *fast*, but had a real Rock 'n' Roll *sound*. Now anything you experience in life that you don't believe is possible, don't register immediately. You know it happened but your brain tells you it's impossible, so it tries to blank it out. I've looked round at the guitarist, he's casually fiddling with the controls on his amp.

59

'Do that again,' I've said.

'What?' he said.

'What you just did.' So there he's gone again:

'DIDDLY DIDDLY DIDDLY DIDDLY DUM BOOBABABABLAT BLAT WEEDLY WOP'

'What, that?'

'Fuck me, yer! Let's do a song, what do you know?'

I'd forgotten the piano player.

'The piano player likes Jerry Lee,' said the guitarist, lookin' toward his mate who's sat there at the piano motionless lookin' like a shop window dummy that's been on a hunger strike.

Alright, how about 'I Could Never Be Ashamed of You' I've said, at the same time tryin' to think how I'm gonna get rid of the piano player and keep the guitarist. Bonk! We've gone into it.

The piano player from the back looks like he's not started. His body and head never moved. But, am I imagining it, or is the most incredible noise comin' out of that piano? It can't be. He's not movin', I've walked over to the piano. Only his hands were movin' but the sound they were makin' were Jerry Lee! My favourite Rock 'n' Roll pianist!

Now, like I said, you've got to realise that English Rock 'n' Roll musicians were new at the game. American Rock 'n' Rollers had the edge. You had to get *near* 'em before you ever thought of *overtakin*' 'em. Here were two musicians that were not only near 'em, they *topped* 'em. We've gotta have 'em! What a band we'll be!

But they never joined.

To this day I don't know why, but they didn't. Perhaps I was too enthusiastic, perhaps I should have been a bit more cool. I don't know. They stayed with Sutch. Perhaps they got the hump when we said we didn't want the piano player at first, and had just come down to taunt us.

The Outlaws

Anyway they didn't join. (The piano player, by the way, was to become a quite famous session man. Nick Hopkins. I did a few sessions with him later on. He played piano on John Lennon's 'Imagine'. The guitar player was Bernie Watson. He was supposed to have turned towards classical music, but nobody ever discovered his whereabouts, so nothing was proved.)

No, they didn't join us, but they suggested another ex-Sutch guitarist, Roger Mingaye or 'Scratch and Scrape Bailey'. No one's gonna top that Bernie Watson, I thought, but I was pleasantly surprised when Roger turned up. He wasn't as 'fast', but he had a great sound and a good Rock 'n' Roll feel.

He joined The Outlaws and once more we had a working band. Me on bass, Biffo rhythm, Scratch lead guitar, Don on drums and Mike vocals. One of the first tours we did was Scotland. We had 'Just a Matter of Time' out, which the new band was on.

Life on the road with a bunch of blokes you hardly know is always interesting, to say the least. You soon do get to know each other and have to learn to get along. It wasn't unusual for a clash of personalities to be sorted out with a punch-up. Scratch used to have digs at Biffo. Poor old Biffo. Scratch would really give Biffo stick, about how his guitar was always out of tune, and how all he liked was the 'Shads'.

We used to say to Biffo, 'Stick up for yourself. He won't let up 'til you do.' But Biffo was too easy – until one day. We were sittin' in a cafe. Scratch started on Biffo again. Right out of the blue (and we all sat back in amazement) Biffo said, 'Say one more word, Scratch, and I'll punch you straight on the fuckin' nose.' Well done, Biffo! Scratch was struck dumb. He made an attempt at a joke, lookin' towards us for support, got none and bottled out. Biffo got no more trouble from Scratch. Scratch became a nicer bloke after that and we all got on better. But Scratch was to get that punch on the nose, only not from Biffo.

We were on stage somewhere in the middle of Scotland, setting up for a sound check. Mike Berry was in a bad mood about something. Don't know what. But he came stormin' on to the stage, said something to Scratch, Scratch called him a cunt, and Wallop! Mike had turned round about three times with his fist stuck out, caught Scratch on the jaw and sent him flying off the stage to the middle of the dance floor. I was shocked to see poor old Scratch flyin' through the air. He wore glasses and was littler than Mike. I leapt at Mike and pushed him.

'What did you fuckin' do that for? He didn't deserve that,' I said.

Mike immediately felt guilty and we jumped down to see how Scratch was.

His glasses were all bent up, and all he kept sayin' was, 'I'll fuckin' get you, Berry.'

We straightened his glasses out as best we could while Mike was trying to apologise. But Scratch didn't want to know.

'I'll fuckin' get you, Berry,' was all he kept sayin'.

That night Scratch's face blew up like a football. The next day it was worse. We took him down the hospital. They x-rayed his jaw and found it was broken. They had to wire it up and he spent the rest of the tour like that, drinking soup. Mike had exhausted his apologies but every now and then Scratch would say through his wired-up teeth, which made it sound even more threatening, 'I'll fuckin' get you, Berry.'

He never did, but Mike feels guilty to this day. So you should, you big bully!

(Mike & Scratch met for the first time since then, in 2004, over forty years later, at a Screamin' Lord Sutch annual reunion memorial gig at the Ace Café. All was forgiven and they rocked well together on stage.)

Biffo was the first one to leave that band. Scratch suggested as a replacement a Canadian bloke he knew. Ken Lundgren. Ken was to become a big mate of mine and still is. Apart from bein' good on the guitar (and steel guitar) Ken was good at organising things. This was what we needed. Ken drove the van (on the wrong side of the road at first!), rang agents, fixed gigs and did just about everything, and drank like a fish. I liked a couple of pints but I wasn't in Ken's class. We'd be drivin' home from a gig in the ol' Thames van. Ken'd have a crate o' beer beside him to 'keep me awake'. I'd be behind him with a rolled-up road map ready to whack him on the back of the head when he started nodding off, which was often. Poor ol' Ken was the only one who had a licence to drive.

The Outlaws were now doing a lot of gigs on their own. We were becoming less available to back Mike Berry on his gigs so he formed his own backing band. With Ken as our new rhythm guitarist we recorded 'Sioux Serenade' and 'Ku-Pow'. We spent about six months on the road with this line-up. The next one to go was Scratch. He announced one day, right out of the blue, that he was going to emigrate to Australia, on his own.

A lead guitar player was needed, so we did the auditioning bit. No good. None of 'em was as good as I was on the guitar. Perhaps this was the answer. It might be easier to find a bass player and I go on lead guitar. I liked playin' either instrument so it didn't matter to me. I suggested it to Joe Meek (it was at Joe's place we'd been holding the auditions). Joe thought it was a great idea.

'I know a bass player who came up from Southampton with a group to audition,' Joe said. 'I think we could get him.'

'What's he like?'

'Well, he's tall, quite good lookin'.'

'No, for fuck's sake, what's he like on the *bass*?' Trust Joe.

'I'll get him down and see what you think of him.' He turned up. His name was Heinz Burt.

I wasn't impressed. He was a bit image-conscious, to say the least. Not a very desirable quality for a musician to have, in my book. I hoped he was goin' to be useless. It would have made it easier. As it happens he was passable. But he didn't fit in. He was too ambitious. Wanted to be a 'star'. No good for us. We didn't want to be stars if it meant pandering to the masses. We wanted to enjoy ourselves and play good music and fuck about and that. I decided to take the easy way out and rather than tell Joe I didn't like him, I told Joe I didn't think I was up to playing lead guitar and I wanted to go back on bass.

'Okay,' said Joe. 'We'll carry on auditioning for a lead guitarist. But I shall build a band round Heinz.'

By this time Don Groom had got fed up and went off to join Mike Berry's new group, The Innocents. We now needed a drummer as well as a lead guitarist. The advert went back in the *Melody Maker*, now saying, 'Drummer and Lead Guitarist wanted for Hit Recording Artists, The Outlaws'. Things were looking gloomy. But every cloud has a silver lining. I got a phone call from someone who had been up at Joe Meek's, who said he had just seen Alan Caddy and Clem Cattini (Johnny Kidd's guitarist and drummer) walk into Joe Meek's to audition for The Outlaws.' Great! I'd heard them play. Perfect! I've rang Joe.

'Is it true?'

'Yes,' said Joe. 'But they're no good for you so I'm forming a group with them round Heinz.

'But I know how they play. I *like* 'em.'

'Well, they're now in my new group I'm forming called The Tornados.'

Fanks, Joe!

We carried on auditioning. We found a drummer who suited us. Mick Underwood. All we needed was a lead guitarist. Me and Ken remembered seeing a guitar player (another one who was with Sutch) that we liked. Let's find out what he's up to. We found out his name was Ritchie Blackmore and we got him down. He wasn't particularly quick at pickin' up a tune but he had a style of his own, a good sound and a good Rock 'n' Roll feel. He was in.

Chapter 10

Jerry Lee Lewis Tour

The new Outlaws had fire. Me, Ken, Mick Underwood and Ritchie were a Rock 'n' Roll band to be reckoned with. Right. All we need is gigs to prove ourselves and we're away. Someone saw in one of the music papers that Gene Vincent was looking for a backing group. Ken got on the phone. Don Arden came down with Gene Vincent to have a look at us, liked us, and we got the job. The tour that was coming up was a tour with Jerry Lee. Fantastic! On the same bill as Jerry Lee! I'll get to meet the bloke. But the best was yet to come. Don Arden called us into his office a couple of days before the tour.

'Fellas, you've got a choice. Jerry Lee needs a backing group. You can back Gene Vincent or Jerry Lee.'

Got a choice? There was only one. Gene Vincent was one of my Rock 'n' Roll heroes, but Jerry Lee was God! It was too good to be true. Something had to happen to take the edge off it, and it did. Joe Meek called us into his office to announce that Heinz had now left the Tornados to become a star in his own right.

'Oh, great. Good luck to him.'

'He is going to be added to the Jerry Lee tour.'

Mistake, I thought, but it wasn't none of my business. I should have guessed what he was leading up to, though.

'He needs a backing group and I would like The Outlaws to back him.'

Hold up a minute. I had nothing personal against Heinz but in my book he just wasn't any good. Jerry Lee and Gene Vincent were. Also, his image was all wrong for the show, he was too flash and slimy.

The greasy, lary Jerry Lee and Gene Vincent followers were not gonna take kindly to the 'White Tornado'. He was a dumb cluck crumpet Rock 'n' Roller. His image was fashioned to the 'pin up a wanker on your bedroom wall' dozy tart brigade. The audience we were gonna get would be 90 per cent herberts and I didn't wanna be associated with him. No, sod that. Not under any circumstances can we back Heinz.

But they say everyone has his price, and on this occasion we were skint. On top of all that our gear was falling apart. Amps held together with gaffer tape, bass strings that had been boiled for the tenth time (a cheap way of puttin' a bit of life back in 'em), and the arses were hangin' out of our trousers.

'Look,' said Joe, sensing not a lot of enthusiasm, 'before you turn it down I would like you to meet someone.' In comes this geezer, a typical hard-nosed businessman. He was introduced to us and we waited to see what he had to say. It was like something out of a Rock 'n' Roll film. And it's the scene where you laugh and say, 'That don't happen in real life!'

'Boys, I'll come straight to the point. I am a millionaire and I am to become Heinz's manager. I would like you to back Heinz on this tour. If you accept, you will each be given an open cheque book, and providing everything you spend is to the benefit of the band, you may spend as much as you like. New amplifiers, guitars, basses, drums, clothes, new van, whatever. Just make sure I get a bill for everything. You will be on a retainer of £30 a week for your food, etc. In return I shall expect 50 per cent commission on your earnings when you become famous.'

Famous! He could have said 200 per cent of our earnings, it wouldn't have made any difference. We never had no plans to become famous. We just wanted to enjoy ourselves, play good music and fuck about and that. Good music! I pulled myself together to ask an important question, my compromise.

'If we back Heinz, does it affect us backin' Jerry Lee?' Even all this I would've turned down if he'd have said it did. 'No, I see no reason why you shouldn't back Jerry Lee too.'

Great!

The next minute there we were, hoppin' up and down Charing Cross Road like we'd just been let out of a nut house. We've gone mad! Gibson guitars! Epiphone bass! Twelve string guitar! Drumkit, strings, cases, Gibson amps, Fender amps! We bought the lot. Ken took time off to ring his local garage to order a new van. Every now and then it crossed my mind that the price we had to pay was having to back Heinz. But that won't be too bad. We were still backing Jerry Lee – and we had all this new gear! New amps, new guitars! It's gonna be great! I can cope.

Or could I?

The show opened in Birmingham Town Hall. We'd been filming in the morning, a film called 'Live It Up' in which Heinz was starring. We arrived in Birmingham just in time for a quick run-through with Jerry Lee. We did 'Great Balls of Fire' and a couple of others, and I could tell Jerry Lee was impressed with our band. I swelled with pride!

The show started. We were to open, then Heinz, then Gene Vincent, and Jerry Lee was to close. Off we went with a few Outlaws Rock 'n' Roll tunes. We went down great. It was Heinz's turn. We announced him to the backing of 'C'mon Everybody'. The crowd waited, and so did we. Then, from off stage (this was his idea for his entrance) Heinz started singin' 'Well come on everybody'. I say singin', it sounded more like an old blow-lamp that kept goin' out. The crowd showed no emotion but waited expectantly wondering what they were about to witness. Then a white head appeared around the corner by a body movin' sort of like Elvis having just shit himself.

He just about got to the centre of the stage, the crowd still quiet. Then one lone voice in the audience hollered, 'Fuck off you cunt!'

The place erupted. A hail of ice-cream cartons, beer cans and anything they could get their hands on flew towards the stage from all directions. I gotta admit I didn't help things. I sort of tried to pretend I wasn't with him. It wasn't very professional of me but I couldn't help it. You see, when I was in the role of the punter I was as bad as them and I'd holler and hoot if I didn't think the band was any good. Mind you, it was only the poser-type bands I did it to. The flash bands that had no talent. Now I was thinkin', 'If I was out there, would I look upon me as being part of a flash band?' I squirmed at the thought. I backed away from Heinz like he had the plague and joined in with the crowd. Like I said, it wasn't very professional of me and I wasn't proud of myself but I couldn't help it.

I must say he had guts. He didn't let up. He went through the whole of his act, layin' on the floor and all that, but it didn't work. He was simply booked on the wrong show. He was a 'dumb cluck tarts' act. On some other tour he might have been passable. But not this one. Gene Vincent and Jerry

Lee fans were hardly the most polite bunch, even to the best support bands.

Backing Jerry Lee on tour was fantastic. It was made up for backing Heinz. We finished off at the Star Club in Hamburg, Jerry Lee only, thank fuck.

Richie fell in love at the Star Club. Her name was Margret. I remember him saying, 'Who's that bird down the front who looks like Doris Day?' And our tour manager, Henry Henroid, saying, 'Blimey! He's well hooked, ain't he?' He was right.

Ritchie bought her an engagement ring and brought her back to England like a lot of musicians did who went to Hamburg. They all got hooked up with German birds. I think she was in the puddin' club, though I can't be certain (I don't wanna get sued), but I remember the day they married alright!

It wasn't long after we all got back from Hamburg. We all went to the wedding and had to rush away to a gig in Salisbury. It had been a sort of unusual affair. Not the kind of wedding atmosphere I had been brought up with. I'd seen a few weddings in my time too. What with Great-grandfather's and Mum's. Richie got married and perhaps he felt different, but we all felt we'd been to a court case. Something that was our duty to do. We done it, and that was it. Now we had to get to the gig.

We were second on the bill. This new band were topping the bill. They'd just got a record in the charts. A scruffy load of jumped-up Skifflers called The Rolling Stones. The place was packed. Mostly teenage girls who were there to see The Rolling Stones. We came on to do our set which normally went down a bomb, but they weren't there to see us.

Some of 'em gave us the time of day, but there was a bunch of girls down the front who, after every number started chanting, 'We want The Rolling Stones!' and all that.

One of the girls at the front, who was directly in line with

Ritchie, was drinking a bottle of Coke through a straw. She decided it was a good idea to suck up Coke through the straw and blow it over Ritchie's trousers. Every time she hit the target her mates fell about. She was having a great time. Little did she know that Margret was in the wings watching all this.

Now I could see what Ritchie meant when he likened Margret to Doris Day, but Margret was the German version of Doris Day. She was just a bit bigger all round, and I don't mean fat, she had muscles. I don't mean that unkindly. She told me once that a woman should take pride in the physical condition of her body. She should be fit and strong. Margret was. The girl who was blowing Coke over Ritchie's trousers (and her mates) were about to find out.

The girl was sucking down her straw for the fifth go at squirting Ritchie's trousers when Margret's run onto the stage, grabbed the girl and give her a punch that sent her sprawling among her mates. She stood there as the girl's mates got up from the floor. Then one of 'em made a grab for Margret. She caught hold of Margret's skirt. The rest joined in but all they succeeded in doing was pulling her skirt off. Margret, now stood there in her drawers, dived off the stage in among the lot of 'em.

And she laid into 'em!

A big circle was formed and the girls who weren't flattened just run for it. The band kept playing, by the way, and though I was motioning to Ritchie to get down there and help her, he just gave me a wide-eyed and dumbstruck look. I suppose he thought, 'I'll carry on doing what I do best. She don't look as though she needs any help from me or anybody.' She didn't, either. 'I spend ze morning pressing my Reechie's trousers,' she said later. 'I have no one spoilin' zem.' Quite right too.

That girl's eyes (and her mates'!) must water to this day

everytime they hear a Rolling Stones record. Those around her must think she is weeping through nostalgia. But those who know, know better.

Coming home from the Star club also meant Jerry Lee going home to America. The end of a heavenly tour. What now? Post Rock 'n' Roll depression again. Like coming home from Butlins.

But the next best thing was only just around the corner!

Don Arden said Gene Vincent loves your band and wants you on the road with him. That don't sound bad to me!

Chapter 11

Gene Vincent

Poor old Gene Vincent. I liked Gene. He was a bit mixed-up and used to annoy a few people he worked with, but once you got to know Gene you realised it was all front. He couldn't handle the 'being a star' bit. Then again, when he'd fallen from favour, he couldn't handle that, either. He liked a laugh, though, when he was in one of his better moods. Deep down I think he just wanted to be one of the boys.

The first time we backed Gene I was thrilled. Even more so when he came up to me after a few gigs and asked me personally if I'd go with him to Geneva. He couldn't take the whole band but would I go with him to show the resident Swiss band the chords and routine, etc.

'They absolutely love me over there,' he said. 'They actually roll out a red carpet when I arrive. I am treated like God! Of course, if you're with me you'll get the same treatment.'

Fantastic! I thought. Unbelievable! One of my Rock heroes wants me as right-hand man. I'm there like a shot.

'We've got to leave at 6am for the airport,' says Gene. 'It'll be best if you stay at my flat so's we're ready to go. What have you got to wear? Have you got a suit? Never mind, I'll sort you out one of mine.' I'd not long been courting at the time (I was going out with this girl called Joan). I dropped a note round her house after that night's gig, telling her that Gene Vincent's asked me to go to Geneva with him, so I couldn't see her that night. (She's still got this note, incidentally.) I went straight on round to Gene's house.

Me and Gene sat up all night. I was fascinated by his stories and also a bit wary every now and then when he went into things like, 'You know, I shot a man in Rochester?' And staring at me with his big bally eyeballs.

'Oh yer, Gene. Whatever happened to Cliff Gallup?' (The guitarist on Gene's hits.)

Cockin' a deaf'un, he'd get his collection of Nazi armbands and guns out. Then he'd put 'em all away and drag me into his bedroom to show me his newborn baby, and get a bollockin' from his missus. I thought this was out of order – the bollockin' I mean. I mean, you can't say to the famous Rock 'n' Roller, Gene Vincent, 'Why don't you stop makin' so much noise and bugger off to bed?' Can ya? 'Be-Bop-a-Lula' wasn't like this.

Anyway, I've finally got me nut down about 4am. An hour later, Gene's woke me up with a light ale and a suit on a hanger.

'I'd sooner have a cup of tea, Gene.'

'Try this suit on, Chas,' he goes. I'm taller than Gene but I've tried the jacket on. It wasn't too bad. Sleeves a bit too short, but passable. He's give me the trousers. They were a bit on the short side too, to say the least, but I buttoned up the jacket and worked 'em down a bit. Not bad at all. At least it's a suit. Red carpet! Geneva! Gene Vincent's personal arranger! I'm getting excited.

Gene Vincent

At 5 o'clock I'm ready to go. Guitar, clean shirts, passport. I'm ready. Gene's ready. Suitcase, crutches, half a bottle of Scotch. 'Bang', there's a knock on the door.

'Gene!' I've heard, in one of the loudest voices I'd ever heard.

'It's Don,' says Gene. He opens the door. Don Arden walks in. Gene's manager.

'Come on, Gene. Put the Scotch back in the cupboard, we've got half an hour to catch the plane.'

Gene waddles out to the car. I'm right behind him carryin' me gear. Ignoring me completely, Don Arden's said to Gene, 'Who's he?'

'Well Don,' says Gene, 'I thought, Geneva. Strange band. I thought, well p'raps they won't know the tunes, I just thought ...'

'I told you Gene. No musicians! Band's laid on. They know your act better than you do. Now come on, get in.' Gene's got in without so much as a 'See ya' to me. Don's got in and they're away. I'm left standin' there in the middle of some mews in the West End, guitar in one hand, suitcase in the other, lookin' like Norman Wisdom in Gene Vincent's poxy suit. The car disappeared round the corner.

Good ol' Gene! I got your number. Nevertheless we ended up backin' him on the road for something like the last half of 1963.

Lookin' back, I enjoyed it. He could be a pain sometimes, but deep down he was OK. He'd say things like, 'You know, Chas, "Be-Bop-a-Lula" sold three million records.' Looking at you with his great big bally eyeballs.

'Did it, Gene? I really loved that record.' I did too.

'You don't believe me?'

I did believe him. 'I'm telling you, Chas, I earned a fortune out of that song!'

I believed him! 'I believe you Gene, it was a great record.' I meant it.

'Chas, *I'm telling you that record sold three million copies*! How much do you think I earned out of that record, then? Peanuts? What would you expect to get from a three-million selling record?'

'Oh bollocks, Gene, I'm fucked if I know,' I've gone, wearying of the subject.

'Certainly not peanuts, Chas, I'm telling you!'

Am I goin' mad? How can anybody start an argument when you're agreeing with him? Gene Vincent could!

When he wanted he could put on a fantastic show, He had a unique talent. Trouble was, he had a frustrating habit of not using it when you really wanted him to. We went back to the Star Club, Hamburg, with Gene in November 1963. (Cliff Bennett was there at the time. That's when I got to know him.) The first night was absolutely packed solid. The place was heaving. Half an hour before we were due on the Germans were chanting 'Zheen Wincent! Zheen Wincent!'

The Outlaws have gone on, done a couple of numbers and we've announced Gene. The roof's lifted off as Gene's waddled on. I'm glowin'! Go on, Gene, give it to 'em! I can't wait.

Our cue to start was 'Be-Bop-a-Lula, She's My Baby'. Snare drum beat and all in. Gene's stood still in the middle of the stage, dodgy leg stuck out, clutching the mike, the crowd's gone quiet waitin' for it. We're excited, waiting for the 'Be-Bop-a-Lula' cue. But it don't come. Gene decides to have a little chat to 'em instead.

'Ah bin havin' some trouble with mah leg. Ah don't suppose ya all know but ah first broke it in a motor bike accident and then ah broke it again in a car crash when mah poor friend Eddie Cochran died. Ah've had a new plaster put on this week and ah've bin told by the doctors ah've got to exercise it. But *they* don't know! *They* don't know the *pain* ah'm in!'

Gene Vincent

The Deutschers are just standin' there silent. They just want to rock 'n' roll. But Gene's turned to us and said, 'I think for a change tonight, fellas, we'll kick off with a song I recorded a few years back, "Lavender Blue". Gimme a chord.'

Plang! 'Lavender Blue, dilly dilly...'

The crowd sort of looked let down. 'Gene,' I think to myself, 'I don't think they really wanted "Lavender Blue".'

But then we'd go to some little Corn Exchange gig where nobody hardly took any notice and Gene would pull it out of the bag. And he would put on a great show if anybody he knew had come to see him special. One of his best shows was when Johnny Kidd turned up one night. Gene had that way about him. *He* decided when to put on a good show.

Gene was with us on the road towards the end of our Flour Bag Throwin' era. We got the idea a few months earlier when we were on tour with The Saints who were now backin' Heinz. Our vans would follow each other from gig to gig. We both had vans that had sliding doors. We'd stop at cafes together, jump back in our vans together, overtake each other, slide back the doors and chuck things. I think it was Ritchie Blackmore who hit on the brilliant idea of buying bags of flour and throwin' 'em from the van at people we passed. I know Ritchie was the best shot. It's not easy to hit a movin' target when you're movin' even faster in the opposite direction, but Ritchie could, almost every time.

We'd make a small split in the bags. This made sure of the desired effect on impact. It was every bit as good as you imagined it would be. Clouds and clouds of flour! We picked our victims carefully. No old people or kids. The perfect victim was a cocky geezer who thought he was *it*, dressed up to go out for a night with the boys. The sort of bloke that would murder you if he got hold of you, but that added to the excitement.

Those boring long journeys (before there were many motorways) were now looked upon in a different light. The longer the journey, the more fun we were going to have. We'd have a whip-round before the set off, arm ourselves with a cardboard box full of flour bags and off we'd go. This particular day, Gene was with us in the van. We knew he liked a laugh and couldn't wait to show him the Flour Bag Throwin' bit. We were goin' to Swansea in the days before the M4. Normally that journey would be moaned about, but now we had flour bags we could chuck.

We had the whip-round and with a big box full of flour bags we set off. We threw them at herberts all up the A4. Through towns and villages we left a trail of flour. Gene loved it. Sometimes the aim wasn't too accurate and the bag would burst on the edge of the van door or something. The inside of the van was white, we were white and we were enjoying ourselves. As we neared Swansea, we spotted a perfect target. Some geezer had broken down at the side of the road. He had his bonnet up and his head in it. As we drove past, Wallop! We dropped a flour bag on his head. We fell about. He must have just got the engine runnin' 'cos the fan gave out a nice effect! The whole car was obliterated by clouds of flour. As we were lookin' through the back window of the van, havin' hysterics, we saw through the haze the man slam down his bonnet and jump in his car. He was off after us. In seconds he was on us. He drew up alongside and leaned out. His face was a picture. Pure white with a big bushy beard that was the same colour!

He aimed a fuckin' great brick at us. 'Doiyng!' It hit the side of the van and we put our foot down. Gene was lookin' worried! We did lefts and rights and detours and after about four or five miles we managed to lose him. We finally arrived at the gig on the outskirts of Swansea, still laughin'.

We were early and couldn't get in, so we sat there waitin' for someone to turn up.

Someone did. But it wasn't anybody to do with the gig.

It was the flour-bag victim!

He'd been determined to catch us and he had. He parked his motor and walked over to our van. He looked like a statue that had come to life.

'Oi, cunt!' he said to Gene who was sittin' in the passenger seat, 'You bin slingin' flour bags about?'

'No, Sir!' said Gene in his polite Southern manner.

'Don't fuckin' "No Sir" me!' he said. He stuck his head in the van window. There we all were. The inside of the van was white and so were we. He was wild, but p'raps seeing all us lot in there changed his mind about punching Gene.

'I happen to think it ain't very funny,' he said. 'You ain't heard the last of this.'

He was right too. He reported us to the police and we ended up gettin' nicked for it. We had to go to court somewhere along the A4. We had no insurance or tax at the time so we really got the book thrown at us. He got his own back alright.

We had to cut out the flour-bag throwin' from then on. It was a shame and we missed it, but we couldn't chance gettin' nicked again 'cos we still weren't insured. Y'see, no one would insure young musicians to drive, unless you paid a fortune, so we just left it.

By this time the 'Heinz management' deal was over. We abused it rotten, generally fucked about and enjoyed ourselves. Heinz's manager had enough of us and dropped us. We still kept the gear, though. The flour-bag era was over, but we did have a little fling with catapults and goosegogs (good old English hard, green and sour gooseberries.)

Once again, Gene was in the van. We'd stopped at a level

crossing. Some bird walked past the van with one of them Sixties PVC macs on. The old catapult was loaded. 'Wop!' A goosegog hit her right in the middle of the back. It couldn't have hurt her, 'cos it made too much noise. The baggy mac took the impact. It sounded like an old slack bass drum, but she was mad! She flew at poor Gene (he always had the best seat, the passenger seat), grabbed hold of him and started shakin' him. He looked round for help.

'Leave him alone,' someone said. 'He's got a bad leg.' She's let go and started laying into him verbally. The crossing gates opened and 'Zoom!' Off we went. Gene told that story to everyone. He loved it,

'Wup! it went,' he'd say. Then he'd go into the flour-bag stories.

Gene would tell us stories about when he was a kid in Virginia. He said they used to have a favourite trick of findin' a fresh bit of dog shit, placing it on someone's doorstep with some newspaper over the top, set light to the newspaper and knock at the door and run away. The first thing the bloke did on openin' the door was see the burnin' newspaper and stamp on it to put it out, look around to find out who done it, see no one and go back indoors to tread dog shit all up his passage.

Cliff Gallup, the guitar player on 'Be-Bop-a-Lula', 'Race With the Devil' etc, never went on the road with Gene. He was under the thumb, so Gene said, and cried when he left the band. Johnny Meeks, the guitar player who took his place, was Gene's big mate on the road.

Me and Gene wrote a song in Hamburg. November '63. 'You are the one that drives me crazy, Laten daten da da, Laten da da.' And so on. I never thought no more about it until a year ago (2007). I acquired a Gene Vincent box set. There on one of the CDs was our song. It said it was recorded at the end of '63. He went straight home and recorded it.

But my half was credited to his ex missus, Margaret Russell. Thanks again, Gene!

I nearly got Gene to sing on a Heads Hands & Feet record years later. It was when we were recording 'Warmin' Up the Band'. There was a line in it that went, 'Be-Bop-a-Lula tonight, Oh Mama, yer alright.' We were recording at Advision Studios and I knew just round the corner at the Marquee, Gene Vincent was advertised to do a gig, I said to Tony Colton (singer with H, H and F): 'Why don't I go round and bring Gene back to sing the line "Be-Bop-a-Lula?" I know he'll do it.' Tony thought it was a good idea, and off I went. Outside the Marquee was a notice. 'Owing to circumstances beyond our control Gene Vincent will not be appearing here tonight.' Apparently he was in trouble with wife maintenance and had buggered off back to America.

A few weeks later he was dead. I read in the paper one morning he died of burst ulcers. The end of another era.

Chapter 12

The Outlaws vs. The Beatles

We were Gene's backing band for about eight months, though through this period we were still doing our own Outlaws gigs and had built up a following. I can't remember how we split from Gene. I think we just drifted apart and went on the road as The Outlaws. Although we didn't have any hit records, the following we had was enough to pack out most gigs and we were earning money. I think that band would have made it big if it hadn't been for another band coming along to change the whole music scene. What band? The Beatles.

We'd worked with The Beatles earlier when we were backing Mike Berry. We did a week at the Cavern in Liverpool. I think it was 1962. The first time I saw their name was on posters advertising another act. The poster would advertise the act and in brackets underneath would be written '(Beatles style group)'. I mean, these bands were selling themselves on the fact that they were *like* The Beatles. So what were the real Beatles like? The first I saw of 'em was at a gig in Bootle. Mike Berry and The

Outlaws were topping the bill, The Beatles were second. We sat and watched 'em. We were reasonably impressed at the time. We weren't mad on 'em, but I do remember their high harmony vocals were different to any other band I'd ever heard.

Back in the dressing room, I was talking to 'em. I was talking to George. The door burst open and these birds came barging in waving autograph books. I stood up reachin' for me pen. They've screamed, but not 'Eeeeeeek, The Outlaws!' but 'Eeeeeeek, The Beatles!' They've grabbed George, ignored me, then run off to the rest of 'em, ignoring the rest of us. I put me pen away.

But The Outlaws, me, Ken, Mick Underwood and Ritchie were still doing okay. The Beatles had had a bit of a hit with 'Love Me Do', which I thought wasn't a bad record but no threat. The Outlaws were still packin' 'em in.

I remember one gig in particular where we couldn't go wrong. It was in Stourbridge and was run by Fred Bannister (who promoted Knebworth many years later). We'd arrive and there'd be queues outside the door. We were the kings! But on one of our return bookings we've arrived and no queue! Our first thought was, 'There's been a mix-up, and we've turned up on the wrong night.' But no. There were the posters. 'Outlaws, appearing by public demand. Here tonight.' Public demand? What public, where are they?

We've gone round the pub and got back to the dressing room about half an hour before we were due on. The hall must be packed by now. They probably all turned up while we were round the pub. We sneaked a look through the curtains. No more than two dozen people stood round the stage waitin' for us to go on. Something's definitely wrong, we thought, bad advertising or something, I mean they're usually spilling out the doors. Anyway, let's go and do our bit.

The Outlaws vs. The Beatles

The two dozen fans did their best to make us feel at home, but we had to get to the bottom of this. A few of 'em came back after to see us. 'Where is everybody?' we said. 'They've gone to see The Beatles. They're on down the road,' they said.

The Beatles. That band again!

Well, The Beatles were on their way and you don't need me to tell you how their career progressed from there. But The Outlaws' career moved just as quickly as theirs. In the opposite direction.

Everyone started to panic. Change this, change that. I thought we should have carried on regardless but I was outvoted. It was the 'Liverpool Sound' now. Dave Clark had got away with it, so Joe Meek thought, 'Why not The Outlaws?'

But it was outside of Joe's mode of thinking. He should have stuck to his guns too. At least he knew what he was doing in his own field. I mean, The Beatles were alright. The songs were good but we could *play* better than them. But Joe began asking us how the Liverpool groups got that sound. Joe couldn't make it out. They sounded like rough demos. But they were getting into the charts.

A half-hearted version of 'Shake With Me' was our attempt at the Liverpool Sound. We didn't like it. The other side, which was more us, was our consolation for letting that record out. It was 'Keep-a-Knockin'.

The solo Ritchie did on it was good. He got the idea from a solo Bernie Watson (the almost-Outlaw with the 'Diddly-Diddly' licks) had done on a Sutch record. Sutch's band had done some good stuff for Joe Meek. Ritchie took the idea and improved on it. Ritchie, as I said, didn't have a particularly good 'ear' for music. You'd sing him a line that he had to play and he was ages getting it off. But he was good in other ways. He had a good sound and a good technique. The solo he did on 'Keep-a- Knockin' was wild, but effective. But, apart from stories later that it was one of Jimmy Hendrix's favourite guitar solos, it went unnoticed and the band became disillusioned and skint. Ritchie left to join another band. I think he went to Germany. We needed a guitarist once more.

We got hold of Harvey Hinsley who became another good mate of mine. He's with Hot Chocolate now. (Note: in fact, just left, 2007.)

We went back on the road and had some fun but never made no money. The final straw was Ken Lundgren announcing he was goin' back to Canada. We got hold of Ed Hamilton to take his place and did a few gigs, but they got less and less. The spark wasn't there. The Outlaws were doomed.

We split and went our own ways. No more Outlaws.

A few gigs here and there and a few of sessions with Derek Lawrence, (a producer who much later gave me and Dave a free hand to do our *One Fing 'n' Anuvver* album) helped me to survive, just.

I started doing some demos with Micky Tinsley or Micky Dallon as he's known in the pop world. I'd first met Micky at the King's Head. He'd got a songwriting deal with some company and me and him would put down on tape demos of his songs. Mick was a character and had a good sense of humour. I didn't earn much from that episode, but learnt a lot and developed a talent for recording ideas. I was always interested in tape recorders and editing and overdubbing etc. Mick, on my suggestion, got hold of two Ferrograph tape recorders. I'd overdub between the two tapes – piano, guitar and whatever – then we'd add vocals. The demos we turned out were good.

Mick liked the glamour side of the pop world. I wasn't too interested in that. I was just into the music, but all the same

Mick, being a bit of a snappy dresser, came in handy one night.

I was round his house bungin' down a demo. We'd finished and I was about to go home. It was pourin' down with rain, I hadn't a coat to my name, but Mick's wardrobe was full of coats (or so he led everyone to believe).

'Do you wanna borrow a coat, Chas?'

'Cheers, Mick.'

Mick's come back with a coat. A sort of Executive Producer's special. Furry collar and the rest, made out of trendy nylon. Not quite me, but it was rainin'.

'Take care of it, Chas.'

'Sure, Mick. I'll let you have it back tomorrow.'

Tomorrow never came. Like I said, I wasn't mad on the style of it, but coats keep you warm. I kept wearing it. It soon got wore in. A couple of fag holes appeared down the front, the fur got chewed by our dog Mitch, and the linin' started to come adrift. Mick kept asking me, 'Where's my bleedin' mac?'

'I put it in the cleaners, Mick.'

I was just putting it off hoping he'd forget about it. I couldn't possibly give it back to him now. Once I knew it had gone so far, I lost interest in keepin' it in good nick. I wore it everywhere. Fishin', up the pub, in the garden. I meant to get it cleaned but I was kiddin' myself. It was too late. Mick still kept asking about his mac and I kept saying 'It's still in the cleaners, I'll bring it tomorrow.' In the end Mick got fed up askin' and I forgot about it, until, well, it wasn't really *my* fault. I didn't even know how it got there. Where? I'll tell you.

Mick's come round one night, the mac subject now forgotten. We're talking about a new song, how it should be done, etc etc. Mick's got up to leave at the end of the evening.

'I must have a slash 'fore I go, Chas.'

'Alright, Mick, you know where it is.'

I've carried on strumming my guitar. 'Fore I know what's happened, Mick's back in the front room, holding up something that resembled a reject from the rag man. My heart stopped as I recognised it.

'Is this my bleedin' mac?' Mick's gone. I didn't know where to put my face! Especially after all those lies about 'in the cleaners' and that. Mick took it well. He'd found it in the bathroom. As he was havin' a slash he was talkin' to Mitch the dog who was kippin' in the bath. Mitch's bed looked familiar. It slowly dawned on Mick it was his bleedin' mac!

By now I was courting seriously, and me and Joan were engaged to be married. I was doing a few gigs here and there, though nothing positive was happenin'. But me and Joan were a happy, optimistic couple, still are and always will be. We knew something would turn up, and it did. I remember saying to Joan, and I remember exactly where I was at the time – we were walkin' down Brettenham Road, Edmonton, goin' for a drink – 'D'you know who my favourite band is? Cliff Bennett & The Rebel Rousers. I got to know them in Hamburg. They are great!'

Chapter 13

Cliff Bennett
& The Rebel Rousers

A couple of days later, I think it was around the summer of 1965, I got a phone call. It was Cliff Bennett! Their bass player, Bobby Thompson, was leavin' to join The Rockin' Berries. Cliff had watched me with The Outlaws in Hamburg and liked my style.

'Do you want the job?'

Did I! My favourite band!

I'd had offers to join other bands that were earning good money, but the music didn't suit me. Cliff Bennett & The Rebel Rousers were not only my favourite group, but they were earning good money too. What more could you wish for? They'd just had a hit, 'One Way Love', and were managed by Brian Epstein, The Beatles' manager.

I'd passed the band's audition, but then I had to be interviewed by NEMS (Brian Epstein's company) before I could say I was finally in. Bennett suggested I get a haircut before I go 'cos the band's image was 'smart'. I bought some 'thinning-out' scissors and my Mum gave me a haircut. That and a new pair of trousers from Johnnie's Bazaar and off I went. It was like being interviewed for a job as a salesman or something. I was looked up and down, asked questions, and told I'd got the job but I must get a haircut. I didn't know what they meant by that! But I was in.

My appearance always did leave a bit to be desired. (I've tried to make up for it in later years!) I start off with the right intentions, pressing my trousers and all that, but no matter how careful I am, I always seem to spill something down 'em and I think, 'Sod it. Ya can't spend your life worrying about how you look. There are more important things to worry about.' I knew anyway that, once I was in, musicianship and enthusiasm would hold the job down.

The Rebel Rousers were a bunch of bastards, but a good band. As I was the youngest member they gave me some stick, and I soon learnt to fend for myself. After a while, we all got on alright, after a fashion. Cliff really held the band together. He made us work and the band stayed good because of it. They were a 'drinking band' alright. I liked a drink but I was a teetotaller compared to that lot.

The line-up when I joined was Cliff on vocals, Mick Burt drums (he's me and Dave's drummer now – I don't think of you, Mick, as being one of the 'bunch of bastards' but as part of the 'drinking band', well, you have been known to fit in there!), me on bass, Roy Young keyboards, Dave Wendells guitar, and Sid Phillips and Moss Groves on saxes.

Discipline was high in the band and anyone who couldn't maintain it soon got their cards. Dave Wendells was the first to go. He got the sack for being drunk and incapable. (In fact we both got drunk together, but as I wasn't incapable and a new boy, I got a second chance.) Instead of replacing him with another guitarist, Cliff talked Roy into getting a Hammond Organ. Roy wasn't too happy with the idea and was even less happy when he ended up getting one, 'cos no bleeder would help him carry it. We had one roadie and he couldn't manage it on his own. Roy got it sawn in half in the end and him and the roady carried a bit each. (I did help sometimes, honest!)

That bunch of bastards introduced me to poker too. Gambling in general, like horse racing and all that, never appealed to me, but I did get to enjoy a game of poker. I still do. Reading other people's minds, trying to work out what sort of hand they've got by the moves they made was interesting, and I paid dearly for it. But I was earning money. I saw me Mum alright and still had more than I needed. Save? Never entered my head. For the first time (or the second time if you count the Heinz management deal) I had more money than I knew what to do with.

I was rich in my books. By that I mean I didn't have to worry about money in regards to paying bills. That's being rich! I didn't appreciate it, though. Or p'raps I did in my own way. I just spent it, or gave it away, lent it, or it just dropped out of my pocket when I got my fags out.

I was getting something like £100 to £150 a week. In 1965 that was a lot of money. And of course it all had to go before next pay-day. Well, isn't that what I'd always done? It was what you did. You tried to last your money out 'til next pay-day and you were usually skint by at least the day before. If you did have any money left by the time next pay-day come up, you got rid of it quick in time for your new one. Saving didn't make much sense. If you saved, you saved to enjoy it later. Sooner or later, what's the difference? I wasn't one of those kids who saved his best bit of dinner 'til last. I ate the best bit first. While it was still there. Makes sense. Who knows what's gonna happen 'fore you finish your dinner? Some bleeder might pinch it!

It wasn't long after I joined Cliff Bennett that me and Dave Peacock became mates. It's funny how fate works. If it hadn't been for Joan going away, perhaps it would never have happened.

You see, at the time there was talk about a new Playboy Club opening in Park Lane. They were advertising for six girls to go to America to learn to be Bunny Girls, and come back to work and train the girls at the Park Lane club. Joan was doing fashion modelling at the time, but the work was not too plentiful, mainly because she had morals! She went for the Playboy job and got it. I was proud of her. From one thousand girls they picked six and Joan was one of them. I was pleased, but in another way, I've got to admit, I wasn't. I trusted her 100 per cent but I wasn't keen on other drunken geezers trying to chat her up when I wasn't around. But I knew she could look after herself and I felt it wasn't fair to stand in her way. She left for America around the end of 1965. I missed her like mad.

It was when I was courting Joan that I met Dave, not long before Joan went away. I always missed the last bus home after saying goodbye to Joan for the twentieth time! She lived in Enfield and me in Edmonton, about three miles away. Off I'd go, thumbin' a lift. One night, an old schoolmate pulled up. Brian Juniper. I used to have a bit of a Skiffle group with Brian back at Higher Grade School. He was in a band of his own now and the bloke who was with him was his bass player, Dave Peacock. On many a night after that, they'd see me thumbin' and give me a lift home. The conversation was always music. Back at my house, I'd bring 'em in for a cup of tea and we'd play records. Dave in particular seemed to like almost everythin' I liked. Jerry Lee, George Jones, pianos, banjos, family sing-songs. Then I'd end up on the piano doing me latest Jerry Lee bit, or my Earl Scruggs bit on the banjo. A sort of bond began to form and a friendship was struck up.

When Joan went to America, me and Dave started knocking around together. He used to come to the Rebel Rousers' gigs. On my nights off, we'd go and see a band. The Cooks Ferry Inn, Edmonton was always a good bet. If we weren't there with the Rebel Rousers, there was always a band worth watching. Zoot Money's Big Roll Band, Ronnie Jones with the Nightimers, John Mayall's Blues Band with Eric Clapton or Peter Green on guitar.

Me and Dave played there one night. It must have been the first Chas & Dave gig. We took our banjos down to 'Folk Night' at the Cooks Ferry. We went on as Stoker and Wart (nicknames from the Rebel Rousers) and did 'Grandfather's Clock'. It went down a storm! We started getting invited to parties and the playing partnership began, although we didn't realize this at the time.

The club scene was great in those days. I got to know Albert Lee from the Cooks Ferry. I had heard of him and first saw him play when on the same bill as the Outlaws in the early Sixties. He had a name among musicians. The first thing I heard him play on was a record called 'All Of Me' by Jackie Lynton (a mate of me and Dave's now and a great character with a lot of talent). Albert's guitar playing was superb.

Me and Dave, on one of my nights off from the Rebel Rousers, decided to go down the Cooks Ferry to see Chris Farlowe. Albert was with him. We were knocked out with his guitar playing and we went up and spoke to him after the gig. It turned out that Albert loved good C&W music like George Jones and Earl Scruggs and Jimmy Bryant. It was unusual for the time. Most people took the piss out of C&W music. There was, still is, and always will be a lot of duff C&W records, but the good ones among 'em are gems. It's a fact that they are few and far between, but the musicians who think for themselves, and don't go by what they read, will find 'em if they look for 'em. Me and Dave had found 'em and so had Albert. We introduced Albert to a good C&W band we knew who played on the Hammersmith circuit (the Red Cow, the Clarendon and the Red Lion). They were called Jamie, Jon and Jerry. 'Come down and see 'em, Albert.' Albert did and became a regular sitter-inner with the band. In between Rebel Rouser gigs me and Dave spent many a good night over Hammersmith watching Albert Lee.

In 1966, Cliff Bennett & The Rebel Rousers got offered a tour of Germany with The Beatles. We did it and it was an experience.

We opened the show. In fact Mick Burt did. We were announced one at a time and Mick came out first wavin' his sticks. Burty's claim to fame – 'Opens show for Beatles!' When The Beatles went on, they could have played 'Knees Up Mother Brown' for all the crowd knew about it. It was continual girls screamin' from start to finish. But they'd paid their money to enjoy theirselves and that was how they wanted to do it. By screamin' their bollocks off (well, you know what I mean).

One night The Beatles invited us to their dressing-room for a preview of their new album. As yet, it didn't have a title. A bottle of Scotch was offered to anybody who could come up with one. (So Sid said.) It ended up being called *Revolver*. (I don't know who won the bottle of Scotch.) It was still in the acetate stage.

Paul sat with me throughout the whole album. When 'Yellow Submarine' came on his eyes were on mine. How would I respond? On first time hearing how would you? Can't remember now how I did respond. If I did respond at all. It was a strange record first time around. When it got to the track 'Got To Get You Into My Life', Paul said, 'Listen to this, I think it would be a good one for your band.' He was right.

Mixing with The Beatles on that tour taught me a lot.

Here was a band that could pull the crowds in every country in the world. Sold literally millions of records, and yet, to hear them talk among themselves you'd think they'd only just started. By that I mean the 100 per cent enthusiasm for what they'd just done, and for what they were about to do. The so-called stars I'd met before that had all acquired an air of 'Now I'm rich and famous, I must act like a "star" and be blasé and matter-of-fact and wear expensive coats with hairy collars' and all that bollocks. Frightened to talk too loud about their next project, in case someone nicked it. As if anybody would! The Beatles were different. They had talent, and they knew it. They simply went out and did it. No fucking about.

I never spoke to 'em a lot while we were on tour. It wasn't my style. I watched the crawlers talkin' to 'em. I just listened. About how 'Yellow Submarine' was going to be a big hit with all the little kids all over the world (they were right), about how 'Got To Get You Into My Life' was gonna be a big hit for us (they were right). About the next album, about the next gig. They never sat back and rested on their laurels. That tour proved to me that The Beatles deserved everything they got.

But they couldn't *play* as good as The Outlaws, though. (Paul, you know I'm not including *you*. See Part Two).

When we got back to England, we went into the studio and recorded 'Got To Get You Into My Life'. Paul produced it and played the piano bit that leads into the solo. (He did it to cover up a duff spot.) I remember being impressed with the finished product.

It sounded like a hit, and it was. Life was good. Joan had come back from America and we had made plans to get married. I had proposed. At least I thought I did. Joan said I needed a bit of egging on, but I was a bit shy in those days.

The record was in the charts when me and Joan got married.

We got our picture on the front page of the *Daily Sketch*. REBEL ROUSER SAYS TO BUNNY GIRL 'GOT TO GET YOU INTO MY LIFE'. Dead right! I wasn't gonna let her go away again.

We moved into a flat in Cockfosters, and on 29 April 1967 our first daughter, Juliet, was born. I was a DAD! (Me and Burty had a drink on it that day in Edinburgh. Sixteen years later, me and Burty had another drink. Only this time we were in Germany. It seems to go in cycles of sixteen years that I'm not home for Juliet's birthday and I'm having a drink with Mick. Where will we be in another sixteen years, Mick? 1999! Summer season on the moon? Hope there's a night porter handy! [Actually, now I can tell you. Sixteen years later, me Dave and Mick were on the Isle of Wight. Just got the drink in in time. On 12 May 1999 I packed up drinking!]

The Rebel Rousers were still gigging, and although we didn't have any more hit records we had a good reputation and didn't need hits to earn a good living, unlike many bands then and now who are only as good as their last chart position. It was nice to have a hit but nevertheless our reputation for always being good on stage kept us in work. Socially, the band got on alright, after a fashion! Outside of music (and poker) it was a mixture of golf and fishing.

Chapter 14

Fishing Stories

In general, when we had time off on the road, Mick, Moss and Cliff would go golfing and me, Roy and Sid would go fishing. Me and Roy would keep our eyes open for trout streams when we were getting near to the gig or the hotel. If we spotted one that said 'Private Fishing', this was made a note of. If we had a couple of hours to spare before or after the gig then that's where we'd head. When you saw a 'Private Fishing' sign there was always a good chance of catching something. One day I caught a big 'un, and I mean a BIG 'UN!

Me, Roy and Sid all had our own individual styles of fishing. Roy was the sophisticated fisherman who reckoned he could fly fish. (Although I never saw him). I was the down-to-earth float fisherman, brought up on the oily canals of North London, and Sid just fucked about in general. If he never caught nothing after half an hour, he'd go and have a shit behind a tree then come back and started chucking stones in the water.

We came to a compromise in styles, though, when fishing for

trout. The method we all three decided on as being best was the plastic minnow. It was about three inches long with a treble hook attached to its tail. Three hooks, welded together, with vicious points and barbs on the end of each one. Couldn't fail to hook the fish once it got hold of it. You just cast it out and wound it in, hoping a fish would be fooled and have a go at it. Anyway, this big 'un I caught.

Me, Roy and Sid had homed in on this 'Private Fishing' trout stream. You found a likely spot, chucked your minnow out and wound it in a few times. If nothing was happening you moved on. (Before Sid started throwing stones in.)

Nothing much was happening that day so we decided to move on to another part of the stream. Off we've trooped in a line across the field. Roy leading the way, Sid next, and me behind. I've wound my little minnow in so that it dangled from the tip of my rod which I held out in front of me as we trekked across the field.

I'm looking about as I'm walking, daydreaming about catching the sort of fish that you only ever daydream about. Suddenly I've felt a tug. WALLOP! Fisherman's instinct, I've struck! 'OH! OH! OH! OH!' I've heard. It was Sid. I come back down to earth instantly to realize I'd hooked his earhole.

'What's the matter, Sid?' I said, not knowing what else to say.

'Something's stung my fuckin' earole!' said Sid. 'OH! OH! OH! OH! OOOH!'

Sid started running all round the field.

'Hold still, Sid, I'll see what it is.'

I knew what it was, but I didn't know how to tell him. I wanted to laugh but I daren't. He was bigger than me. He would have murdered me.

'I think I've hooked your ear'ole, Sid.' I said, as casual as I could.

'OH! OH! OH! OH! GET IT OUT, GET IT OUT!'

With mixed emotions of wanting to have a laughing fit and sheer terror of what Sid might do to me, I shouted at Sid like a Mum might do to a kid who's having a tantrum round the shops.

'Sid!' I hollered. 'Calm down!'

Sid stopped running round the field.

'Right,' I said. 'Let's have a look, I'll soon get it out.'

But it was stuck in fast. In the hard bit, at the top of the ear'ole. Right through past the barb. No chance.

'Well,' I said, with an air of 'You brought it on yourself' (bit of a cheek, I know, but it worked), 'we'll have to get you down to the hospital.'

I led Sid to the car, moaning and holding his ear'ole. Every now and then willing myself to *not* see the funny side of it. Especially when we had to stop to ask directions to the hospital and Sid did the talking. The plastic minnow dangling from his ear.[1]

It was funny enough, but ain't things always funnier when you know you mustn't laugh? Roy never saw nothing funny in it, though. He had a fixed, wide-eyed and worried look all the way through the episode. At the hospital, they sorted it. From the receptionist to the nurses to the doctor who finally disgorged Sid, they all fell about. It was such a relief. Even Sid managed a smile.

Like I said, if we saw a 'Private Fishing' sign, we homed in. They didn't put up those signs for a laugh. Here was a stretch of water teeming with bored fish just waiting to have a go at

---

1 Nothing unusual today. But this was 1967. Well pre-punk. A man like Sid in cavalry twill trousers, tweed jacket and snooker player's haircut, would not have thought a plastic fish hanging from his ear to be a nice finishing touch to his appearance before a night out.

someone's maggot. But fishing in these places had its drawbacks as well. Fishing is supposed to be a relaxing pastime, but we had to be on the alert all the while. We done a 'runner' on many occasions. Not that I was particularly bothered about that side of it personally. I quite enjoyed it really. There was something exciting about being chased across the fields, hearing 'Oi! You!' behind you in the distance. It took me back to my scrumpin' days. Nevertheless I think I was on my own in this respect. Roy was a bit older than me and got puffed out easier. He devised a plan that would mean if we got caught we wouldn't have to run.

'It's simple,' Roy said. 'What we do is, if we get caught, we pretend we're foreigners and don't understand a word their saying. They'll get fed up trying to get through to us and just tell us to bugger off.'

'Roy, you're a genius! We'll be Germans.' We'd been to Germany. 'We can convince 'em with a couple of "Jas" and "Neins", and we'll be able to move off peacefully.' So that was the plan.

A 'Private Fishing' sign was spotted and we were there. This time Sid wasn't with us. He'd traded his fishing tackle in for a set of golf clubs. (Gawd help Mick, Moss and Cliff!) Tony Dudley, the new trumpet player in the band, decided to come along with me and Roy. Tony at the time was into neither fishing nor golf, but the basic fishing equipment (a stick and a bit of string) was cheaper than a set of golf clubs, so Tony came fishing.

We'd been fishing for about an hour, me and Roy with proper rods and reels and Tony with his stick and a bit of string, when we spied these two geezers walking towards us along the bank. You could tell by their faces they meant business.

'Don't forget we're Germans,' said Roy, looking down the

Top: A photo of my dad (*second from right*) with his mates just after the war.

Above right: Mum and Dad on Southend Pier in 1938.

Left: Charles Nicholas Hodges, aged 14 in my high-school photo from summer 1958.

Bottom right: Uncle Will always took good photos. He would say something funny and catch the moment, as he did here in this picture from Mum's second marriage. These ladies are (*l-r*) Aunt Lil, Aunt Anne, Mum and Aunt Lizzie Pine, and in the front row are my brother Dave, me (aged five) and Jennifer Pine.

Top: Posed photo with Danny
Rivers and Reg Hawkins at
Butlins, 1960.

Above: On the 1963 Jerry Lee tour.
(*Left to right*) Ritchie Blackmoore,
me, Jerry Lee, Ken Lundgren and
Mick Underwood.

Right: Me and Mum at the Welsh
Harp pub in Waltham Abbey, 1965.

Top: Mike Berry and The Outlaws, 1961. We're pictured on the Forth of Firth ferry. (*Left to right*) Ken Lundgren, Mike Berry, 'Scratch and Scrape Bailey' (Roger Mingaye) and me. Don Groom, our drummer, took the photo.

Bottom: A publicity picture for Heads Hands and Feet showing (*l-r*) Pete Gavin (drums), Mike O'Neil (piano, who was also the Nero of Nero and the Gladiators), Tony Colton (writer and lead vocalist), me (bass), Ray Smith (writer and guitarist) and Albert Lee (guitar).

A 1968 publicity picture of The Rebel Rousers. (*Left to right*) Moss Groves, Harvey Hinsley, Roy Young, me and John Golden. Him with the sunglasses squatting? Mick Burt.

Top left: On stage in Ware Cinema with The Stormers, Tony Ollard, me and Albert Dust, 1959.

Middle left: Jerry Lee and me at the Hamburg Star Club, 1963.

Top right: I sent this picture home to Joan from Beirut in 1968. Note the stereo jack plugs, which I fitted myself: two amps, one bass and one twangy.

Above: November 1963 – Gene Vincent and The Outlaws at the Star Club in Hamburg. *From left to right*: Richie Blackmore, Mick Underwood, me and Gene Vincent.

Fred and Chris Cooke's pie and mash shop was the best in London. Me and Dave became great friends with them over the years.

Top: The *Rockney* album launch, where the eels were served with champagne. Lovely. (*Left to right*) Dave, Tony Ashton, John Darnley, Bob Mercer and me.

Bottom left: This picture went on the cover of the *Rockney* album.

Bottom right: Dave and I with my brother Dave, summer 1979. The place is a Chinese restaurant now.

Left: A piece of history. These are the original lyrics to 'Gertcha!' which was Chas & Dave's first top twenty hit.

Below: Celebrating a quarter of a million sales of 'Rabbit.' (*Left to right*) Dave, our engineer Andy Miller, me, Bob England, Mick Burt and Terry Adams.

① When the kids are swinging o the gate.
When the paper boys half an hour late.
When the pigeons are a peckin at his seeds
When the banker starts diggin up his beans

② When the dogs left a message on step.
Lester Piggott, lost it by a neck
When the kids are bangin on his door.
When the barman won't serve him anymore

Barstool preachin thats the ale mans game.

③ When me rock n' roll records wake him up.
" the Polish knocked England out the cup
When me brewer ruined his new shoes
When the housefly are are flyin round his food

Top: The wives have it. Joan and Sue in outfits they made themselves for the launch of *One Fing 'n' Annuver* on HMS *Belfast*.

Bottom: 'Over to you, Dave'.

bank at the geezers, with a big daft foreigner's grin on his face.

'Guten Tag,' said Roy, as they approached, still grinning like a nutter. 'Oh, no, he's overdone it,' I thought. But no, they hadn't sussed. They hadn't quite caught what Roy had said, but they sensed we weren't locals. At this point they probably figured we were from the next county.

'Guten Tag,' Roy said again, showing all his teeth. He had a lot of teeth too.

'Look mate,' said one of the blokes, 'this is private fishing here and you're coming with us to the police station.'

'Ja?' said Roy, still grinning. I thought he was overdoing it but it convinced 'em.

'They're fuckin' foreigners,' said the other bloke. 'Cheeky bastards.'

I realised then that although Roy was right in the fact that we could convince them we were foreigners, he was wrong in the idea that we were going to get off light. It was obvious that they didn't like 'fuckin' foreigners' who come over here and think they can do as they fuckin' well like!

'Look,' said the first bloke to Roy. 'You' (pointing at Roy) 'are fishing' (making casting-out movements) 'in *private*' (doing some other movement) '*waters*' (pointing at the river). He looked at his mate, satisfied with bilingual talents. 'You,' he said again, pointing at Roy, 'must give me your rod. I take it away 'cos you break the law' (making 'gimme-that-here' movements towards Roy's rod).

'Oh yah, yah!' Roy's away. 'Mein rodden ist gut! Glassen fieber! Eine guten Deutsche rodden. Danke Shoen! Eine Hundert pounds,' said Roy, offering it to the bloke but keeping a tight grip on it.

'Oh for fuck's sake', said the geezer to his mate. 'He thinks I want to buy the fuckin' thing.' Up 'til now, me and Tone have kept a low profile. There wasn't much point in joining in, Roy seemed to be doing alright. But they weren't getting through to Roy. I should have been ready for it, but I wasn't.

'Do you speak English?' they said to Tony. Tony shit himself. 'Owgli mumpa shlafen,' was all he could muster up.

It didn't mean fuck all but they were none the wiser. I was watching Tony, wondering what noises he was going to come up with next when they turned to me. I was taken by surprise.

'What about you. Do you speak any English at all?'

I put myself right in it. 'A leetle,' I said, making a finger-and-thumb movement. What a stupid git! I was now the bloke to talk to.

'Thank Christ for that.' They said, and he began to explain the Private Fishing bit and the rod confiscation bit all over again to me. I had to nod in a knowing way and try to explain to Roy what he was on about. It wasn't easy with Roy grinnin' at me like a nutter. Tony hid behind a tree. I knew he was quietly having hysterics. This didn't help matters. I had enough to contend with. What with Roy's nutter face, which he nodded every now and then, I really had to think of horrible things in case I laughed and ruined everything.

Roy did help me out in the end. When he felt like I'd got to the punchline of all the bollocks I'd been rattling off as an explanation, he took on a concerned look. For the first time he closed his mouth and hid his teeth. He *did* look concerned. He began making apologies in German of course but they seemed to suss what he was on about. They weren't particularly impressed, but by now they were getting fed up with the whole thing. 'Go on, bugger off,' they said, resigning themselves to the fact they weren't getting anywhere.

Thank Christ for that I thought. It's over. We don't do *that* again!

Now there's an old saying that all's well that ends well. But for us it hadn't ended. Let alone well! We all three made our way to the car, not daring to look at or speak to each other. We each knew what the others were thinking. As soon as we were in the car and on our way, are we gonna have a good laugh or what!

'Quick, gimme the key,' said Roy, quietly.

'I haven't got the key,' I said.

'Yes, you have,' said Roy. 'You got the rods out of the boot.'

'Oh yeah, you're right, they're in the boot,' I said.

'What!'

'They're in the boot,' I repeated, wondering what the raised voice was all about. All he had to do was turn the knob that opens the boot and get 'em out. Let's go!

But no. Roy had a new Ford Cortina. The boot worked in a different way to my old 1100. The key opened the boot, but the boot locked automatically when you shut the lid down.

Worse was to come. Not only had I locked the key in the boot, that was bad enough, but the two bailiff geezers were waiting in their car for us to get out of the way. We were blocking their path.

'What do we do now?'

'You'll have to go and tell 'em what's happened,' said Roy.

'Hold up a minute. How do I explain this? I'm supposed to be German. I can't talk English.'

'You told 'em you speak a "leetle".'

'Yeah, but I don't *wanna* talk to 'em anymore. Why can't Tony go?'

'Chas, don't be daft.' I knew he was right. There was no way out. The two geezers were looking more and more impatient by the minute. I went over to their car and explained what happened. I must have done it alright. They didn't suss.

'Okay,' they said (muttering 'fucking foreigners' under their breath). 'Come with us to the police station and we'll get you another key.'

I froze. I realised in an instant what would happen. There's bound to be some cocky copper there who speaks German and I'm fucked. Roy, in fact, could speak quite good German. He'd spent more time than us in Hamburg. Roy was the one who should go with them. At least he can get away with it if someone starts spouting off in German. Roy's going whether he likes it or not. Anyway, it was his idea to be Germans.

I explained in the best way I could that instead of me, my friend will go with them to the station.

'No, we want you to come. He can't speak English.'

Oh Christ! 'Eine moment,' I said. I wanted to jump into the river, but I walked back to the car. Roy had now developed, once more, his irritating daft foreigner's grin.

'Roy,' I said, between my teeth, 'you've got to go with 'em to get a key. They want me to go, but I'm not gonna risk it. I don't care what they say, I don't care if I have to own up, but I'm not going with them to the police station. If I have to talk German to a copper, I'm gonna blow it. You can speak German. There's bound to be a copper there who speaks it a bit. I'll be sussed out in no time. I *refuse* to go.'

'Alright, alright,' said Roy, 'I'll go.'

Off he's gone. I see his head nodding and his hands waving about as he's talking to 'em. I see their heads shaking and waving their hands about as they're trying to answer. In the end they all nod and Roy gets in, looking round at us. He still had his fixed foreign nutter's grin but it didn't seem so irritating this time.

They arrived back an hour later. No luck with the key. Roy had an entertaining time, though. He didn't meet up with any

German-speaking copper, but he enjoyed himself listening to what they were saying about him. 'German bastard!' 'What are we helping him for?' 'Fuckin' well go back where they come from.' 'Coming over here thinking they can do as they like!'

We ended up ripping the lining out of the inside of the car to get to the boot. The next time we got caught fishing in 'Private' territory, we took the easy way out. We run.

Chapter 15

Cliff and the Rebs Split

Roy Young, who fronted The Rebel Rousers when Cliff wasn't singing, had a great Rock 'n' Roll voice. Many people preferred him to Cliff. In fact, for out-and-out Little Richard-type Rock 'n' Roll, Roy was better, but he wasn't quite as versatile as Cliff. Cliff had the 'Soul' thing together, and kept the band in shape. I sang a bit, but reluctantly at the time.

Around the beginning of 1968 (I can't remember how it came about, I think we just wanted a change), The Rebel Rousers split from Cliff Bennett to go on their own. In theory, the idea was good. It could have worked. Trouble was, none of us had any real business sense. We thought we'd go straight back on the road earning almost as much money as we did with Cliff. I knew the band was still good and thought that would be enough, but promoters weren't as enthusiastic about booking us without Cliff. The gigs got less and so did the money.

Sid got fed up being skint and went back to his old job as a typewriter mechanic. The rest of us, me, Roy, Mick, Moss and

John Golden (the new trumpet player who replaced Tony Dudley towards the end of the Cliff Bennett era) knew we had to get some work quick.

We got offered a couple of weeks' work in a club in Munich. The money wasn't good but it was better than nothing. Harvey Hinsley, my old guitar-playing mate from The Outlaws, came with us too. He'd come to see us on a gig just before we went and we wanted a guitar player. The prospects weren't exactly fantastic, and Harvey had now settled in a 'proper' job, which he went back to when The Outlaws split up. But Harvey fancied the idea. He threw his job in and was on the road again. Germany! We had a gig!

We arrived at the PN Club, Munich, tired but eager and ready to go. We found out that we had to play for about five hours a night. Great! Perfect for whipping the band into shape. There was a small obstacle to overcome, though. We only had two hours of material. 'Well, we'll have to do "special requests" or songs we've done earlier, plus double or triple solos for everyone in each song, and don't forget Burty's drum solos are quite long. You can even make them a bit longer, Mick. Throw everything in.' He did.

Mick played his solo, tapped all up and down the mike stands with his sticks, got up from his drums, tapped all round the stage, all round the club, on people's beer glasses, people's heads, back on the stage, stood one-legged on his tom-tom while still playing it and finished off telling a joke on the mike. It killed a lot of time. But not enough.

It was the first night. After a couple of sets, we worked out we were still gonna be short. Something had to be done. But what? Half-way through the night I was stuck. We'd done all the requests, except – it suddenly came to me!

'Ladies and Gentlemen,' I said. 'We have a special request for Mick Burt to do his solo again. '*Way you go. Mick!*'

Mick looked at me daggers, but he was a trooper. Off he went. Boomp...boomp...boomp, all round the stage, all round the club, back on the stage, did the one-legged bit on his tom-tom and told a joke (the same one). He went down a storm! Mick cheered up a bit. We were in shape so far and winning. We only had one more forty-five-minute set to go.

We got through the first half hour somehow. Just fifteen more minutes. But now we were well and truly stuck. We'd done requests three and four times, and three and four piano and brass solos in each. We've got to think of something. There was nothing else for it. 'Ladies and Gentlemen. In response to many requests, Mick Burt is going to do you another drum solo!'

'No, Charlie, I'm not,' said Mick, through his teeth.

'You've got to, Mick,' I said, trying hard not to let the crowd know what was happening. 'If we come off early we might get knocked. We've done everything else three or four times. We've only done the drum solo twice. Do a short one.'

'Here he is, Ladies and Gentlemen, *Mick Burt*!'

Boomp...boomp...boomp...boomp... Off Mick's gone looking even less happy this time. But he did shorten it. He didn't tap all round the stage. He didn't tap all round the club. He didn't tell a joke. He never got that far. He only got as far as his one-legged tom-tom bit.

I swear to this day, Mick, as far as I know, nobody tampered with your tom-tom. Mick was there, on one leg, on the tom-tom, playing it at the same time. One of the tom-tom legs collapsed and threw Mick into the crowd!

'You bastard, Charlie!' he shouted from the club floor. 'You wait 'til I fuckin' get hold of you. You fuckin' loosened that tom-tom leg!'

'Mick, I didn't. Honest!' I didn't either, honest! But because I laughed, he wouldn't have it.

He didn't really hurt himself, it was the shock really. He grazed his shin a bit, that was all, but he wouldn't have it that I didn't do it on purpose. I have been known to play tricks, but I wouldn't do one that would hurt anybody[2].

It was funny though, Mick. And you did get us through to the end of the night!

We started rehearsing in the daytime to get a few new numbers off. The band got better, but it was never very disciplined. Perhaps it was the years spent before under the iron hand of Cliff Bennett, with fines for drunkenness and all that. The New Rebel Rousers had no such rules. The last set was always a free-for-all. By that time, a few pints of German lager had been sunk. Moss and John would decide that 'Gambols' (Moss's word) was a good idea. 'Gambols' was Moss and John running up and down the club floor doing somersaults, and John, every now and again, chucking his trumpet to Moss, and Moss missing it most of the time. John's trumpet ended up looking like a little brass concertina. How he still managed to play it, I don't know, but he did.

One night, after doing our first couple of sets, we were told that there was a couple of geezers in the club that wanted to buy us a drink and have a chat to us. We all went over and it turned out they wanted to book us to play in Vienna. They were starting a club there and wanted us to open it. (They caught us at the right time. The first couple of sets were usually pretty good and we were reasonably sober.) We talked money and it was good. Much better than we were getting in Munich. The deal was done on the spot. We were to open their club about a month later, and were to play there for three weeks. Great! We shook hands on the deal and carried on talking socially. I did notice that the two blokes

2 To this day Mick says I loosened that tom-tom leg. Mick. I honestly didn't.

kept calling Roy 'Cleef' all the time, but just passed it off as getting names mixed up. As people often do.

They got onto the subject of our past visits to Germany. The Beatles tour and that. 'Cleef Bennett and The Rebel Rousers for a long time have a good name in Germany. We notice you have not done 'Got To Get You Into My Life' yet. Will you do it, Cleef, when you go back for your next set?' Suddenly it dawned on me and Roy at the same time. It wasn't just a simple case of getting names mixed up. They thought Roy was Cliff Bennett!

I was just about to speak when Roy gave me a look of 'For fuck's sake don't say nothing'. I didn't. I left it to him. He mumbled something about 'haven't done it for a long time' and we went off to do our next set. At long last, we finished the set. I was dying to find out what the next move was gonna be. We met over the road at the pub.

'Roy,' I said, 'what the fuck we gonna do? We've got to tell him!'

'We'll worry about that later,' said Roy. 'We can't tell him now, we'll blow the whole thing. We need the money. Once we're there, even if he does find out, it'll be too late for him to find another band. He likes what we're doing anyway. He won't be able to find a band good enough to replace us. We can laugh it off as a misunderstanding, but we'll be there! Earning the money.'

'Roy! Once he finds out it's not Cliff Bennett & The Rebel Rousers, he won't want to know. All the punters will be asking for their money back. Let's laugh it off as misunderstanding now and take a chance.'

I was still slightly in two minds, and if Roy had come up with an answer to this, I would have gone along with it. We all needed the money but we decided to come clean. We went and sat with them after the next set.

'Chas seems to think that you think I'm Cliff Bennett,' said

Roy, trying to smile casually through a face that I could see was full of panic. We waited for the answer. Our immediate future rested upon it.

'You are not Cliff Bennett? I must say I thought you were.' (Here it comes.) 'No matter. You are better without him.'

We all laughed. A bit too heartily for what the remark called for. But the Austrian chap was pleased with himself. He liked our sense of humour, and he was looking forward to seeing us in Vienna in a month's time. 'So long, Cleef,' he said at the end of our talk. We all laughed again.

As I said, the money was good, better than Munich anyway. We decided we could afford to bring our wives and kids over with us. They hadn't had much of a time, not much money and all that. It could be a bit of a working holiday for all of us. Roy was in touch with Lippy (the main Austrian who run the club) in the few weeks that preceded the gig, sorting out hotel arrangements, arrival times, etc. Roy suggested to me that, rather than stay in a hotel, why don't he get Lippy to fix up a flat for me and him and our wives and kids. Somewhere we could cook for ourselves if we wanted to. It would save a lot of money. Good idea! Roy fixed it up with Lippy.

I was looking forward to it. So was Joan. Juliet was about a year old at the time. We all went in our own cars. I kept my fingers crossed my old 1100 would make it. It did. We arrived about midnight on the night before we were due to play. Me and Joan were dog-tired and ready for bed. Juliet, like kids are, was wide-awake and ready for action. But then she'd been cooped up in the back of the motor for hundreds of miles.

'Let's get to the flat quick,' I said to Joan. 'And we can let her loose to crawl about all she wants. When she's had enough, we can put her to bed and we can just flop into ours.'

We found the club and I went to find Lippy. Roy was there

all smiles. He'd arrived about an hour earlier. He was with Lippy.

'Good to see you, Chas,' said Lippy.

'Lippy's gonna show us where the flat is,' said Roy.

'Follow me' says Lippy. Out into the street we've gone and followed Lippy's car all round the back streets of Vienna. We finally come to a stop in some little street.

'There's the flat' said Lippy, pointing to a dingy doorway, 'and here's the key. Sleep well. I look forward to seeing you tomorrow.'

I didn't take too much notice of the look of the outside. I didn't expect a mansion. Roy opened the door and went in. The passageway was a bit dismal, but nobody said nothing, we were too tired. We woke up when we saw the actual flat itself though! Talk about a khasi! My Nan's coal cupboard back at 11, Harton Road was cleaner!

'Fuckin' hell!' said Roy quietly. I don't think I said anything, I just looked.

'Fuckin' hell!' said Roy again, a bit louder. I still don't think I said anything. I was trying to will myself into thinking it wasn't too bad. I was knackered.

'Fuckin' hell!' said Roy, loud and positive. 'We ain't staying here.'

I knew he was right. We'll all end up with the plague.

'I'm getting on the phone to Lippy,' said Roy, and so he did.

Lippy came down and looked concerned. He knew full well what it was like all the time, crafty bastard. 'I am sorry I was assured it was a clean flat.'

'Clean flat!' Juliet escaped our clutches once or twice and crawled about the floor. She had a snow white Babygro on when we arrived. Now she looked like she'd been up the chimney.

'I fix you up another flat tomorrow.'

'Fair enough, but what about tonight?' said Roy.

'Okay, I find you a hotel.'

A hotel was found and Lippy promised to sort us out a flat as soon as possible.

When the news got back to the band, certain members (who shall remain nameless until about two paragraphs' time) interpreted this episode as 'special treatment' from the promoter. 'Unfair! Staying in a posh hotel while we stay in an ordinary one.'

A couple of days later, me and Roy and our families were still staying at the hotel. Lippy hadn't managed to find us a flat yet. On the third day, Lippy found us a flat. He also fixed up a gig on the same day, supporting Bill Haley at the big concert hall in town. The plan was to rehearse for the concert in the afternoon.

By the time me and Roy had checked out the hotel and moved our families in, we'd gone well over the call-time for rehearsal. In our absence all this unrest in the band about me and Roy getting 'special treatment' (they were convinced Roy was at the bottom of it) had come to a head.

Mick and Moss, fed up with waiting, decided to go to the local bar and air their grievances over a bottle of whisky. By the time me and Roy arrived, three hours later, Mick and Moss were back in the dressing-room, hardly able to stand, and were *mad*! They had decided Roy was well in with the promotor and had taken Charlie along with him for credibility.

'Staying in posh hotels, probably getting free dinners as well. *Special treatment*! Who the fuck does he think he is?'

At that moment me and Roy walked into the dressing room. 'Sorry about being late' said Roy, genuinely, but unfortunately he sometimes had a way of making himself seem really 'showbizzy', a bit patronising. Mick became a wild man.

'Sorry about being late! We've been stuck here three hours waiting for you while you've been enjoying yourself having free dinners and everything else.'

'Mick, take it easy man.'

That done it. '"Take it easy man?"' said Mick. 'I'll show you how to take it easy. Cunty!'

With that, Mick's gone at Roy with a snare drum stand. He was gonna hit him on the head with it, and he meant it.

Crash! The drum stand misses Roy's head and embeds itself in the dressing room door. Mick's gone for Roy. Roy's dodged him. I've grabbed Mick. 'What's the matter, calm down, Mick!'

'I'll fuckin' have you cunty!' Mick's *wild*!

'It's not you Charlie, it's him! I know what he's fuckin' like. You bastard, Youngy, I'll fuckin' have you! Crawlin' around the promoter's arse, havin' free dinners and that. *Cunty*!'

'Mick,' I said, holding him back with all my strength. At that moment Lippy slung his head in the door.

'Boys' You're on now.' Duty called. All was forgotten for the minute. The magic words had been said. 'You're on.' And out we went. To perform the worst show we'd ever done in our lives.

Lippy had arranged as a 'show stopper' for Moss and John to chop up a piano halfway through the act. Halfway through the act? We were lucky to get through the first tune. Burty played like the wild man he was. Keith Moon wasn't in his class. It might have been good, but it was fuck-all to do with what *we* were doing. Then the two axes were passed to Moss and John to do their bit on the grand piano.

It was a real grand piano. Shame really. It was a better one than we had. Moss and John laid into it. Two wild men, both pissed. They managed to wreck the piano, narrowly escaping chopping out each other's knee caps. Moss, now drunk with power too, decides to finish off with a duck walk along the edge of the stage, blowing a sax solo at the same time.

A good idea in theory, but in Moss's state his sense of balance wasn't quite up to par. He teetered a couple of times but managed to right himself. It was a high stage, about ten feet. Quite pretty too. It was surrounded by ferns and little trees in pots. Bracing himself for his final blast he let go with a high pitched '*wheeeee*', teetered, and almost like it was part of the act, disappeared off the edge of the stage. The ferns parted and came together. Then they were still. I watched the ferns. As I walked to the edge of the stage, the ferns started moving again.

They began to wobble and a couple fell over. Thank God. Something was happening down there. Two little hands appeared over the edge of the stage, then a face, with a stupid grin on it. The next minute Moss, helped by other willing hands from the front row, was back on stage in a heap.

He wasn't gonna be beat, though. He was up on his feet ready to finish the round. He grabbed his sax, closed his eyes and went for it. He was gonna finish his solo in style. Only he couldn't get his mouth round the mouthpiece. No wonder. You see, the sax broke his fall. The mouthpiece was the bit that hit the floor first. It was now bent round in a U shape, instead of being stuck out in the usual way at right-angles. Moss opened his eyes, studied his sax for a bit, figured out that the only way he could get at it was to turn the sax upside down, did so, closed his eyes again and away he went. It was a sight to see.

We got a write-up next day in one of the Austrian papers. I don't know what it said, but were advised, 'It is best you do not get this write-up translated into English.'

After the Bill Haley concert, we had to go back to the club. We had another show to do and Moss wasn't finished yet. Mick's drum solo had now become a featured part of the act. It was particularly liked by a bunch of geezers who came to the club every night. They were sort of well-to-do hard nuts and were well respected by the club owner (I got the impression that their line of business wasn't the type of thing you'd find advertised in the Yellow Pages). They showed their appreciation of the songs they liked by chucking screwed-up bank notes onto the stage. Burty's drum solo attracted notes like a magnet. The more he banged the more them notes flew up. He was like a man possessed! That night the inevitable drum solo was requested by 'The Boys'. 'Bang' and 'Zip'. A note flew up and landed on his snare drum, '*Wallop*!' went Mick and two more bounced off his tom-tom, '*Boom-boom-boom-boom*!' Mick went mad. Notes flying all over the place. No more did he moan about doing a solo. In fact he was a bit choked that we now had a reasonable repertoire, which meant he only had to do one solo a night.

Then, 'Boom...Boom...B-B-B-B-B-BOOM!' Mick played a pattern that sounded like it was our cue to come back in, I realised by the look on Mick's face that he hadn't meant to do it. So did everybody else. Except Moss.

No amount of arm waving and shaking of heads was gonna convince him. He'd heard the cue and that was it. Everybody else was wrong as far as he was concerned. He leapt in for his final 'Toot-toot-toot-ta-ta-toot-toot-toot'. But he never got as far as the first 'Toot'.

He had that Rock 'n' Roll sax player's style of leaning back when he went for a note. It worked well when he was sober. But he wasn't. He leant back raising the sax to his lips. But the sax never reached his lips. He just kept leaning back.

One minute Burty was looking at the back of Moss's head. The next minute he was looking at Moss's face, at his feet, upside down, still trying to 'toot'. Moss had fallen backwards into the drum kit, the drums scattering in all directions like they'd been blown up. Burty stood up and bowed drunkenly to his fans. Needless to say, the number ended there, the rest of us trying to play some sort of Rock 'n' Roll fanfare as if the whole thing was planned.

Screwed up notes began to shower the stage.

A couple of the well-to-do hard nuts rushed the stage and hoisted Burty bodily over the debris and plonked him down on their table. They poured him drinks and patted him on the back and stuffed screwed-up notes down his shirt. They thought it was a tremendous finish. We left Mick among the hoods, grinning from ear to ear, while we escorted Moss back to his hotel. I didn't envy the aches he was gonna wake up with in the morning. From the head downwards.

Apart from the 'odd occasions' which I've just mentioned, the Viennese gig was successful. The club owner was well pleased with the band(!) and we left for home with a few bob in our pockets.

The next gig we got offered was six weeks in Beirut.

Beirut, at that time, had more clubs in one square mile than anywhere else in the world. I enjoyed it there. It was the first time that I felt like I was in a real foreign country. Things like pomegranates growing (my favourite fruit) and locust beans which I lived on when I was a kid (my own kids don't like 'em, though; I bought some a while ago and they said they made 'em sick).

Also, it was the feeling that Jesus in his day used to lig about round there. I am a fan of Jesus. Don't get me wrong that I mention Him so lightly, I mean it. He probably ate locust beans and pomegranates. I wonder if he swallowed the pips or spit them out? Some people do and some people don't. I always spit them out. My Mum said you get consumption through swallowing pomegranate pips. Can't see it myself but that's what she said.

I visited Sidon while I was there. That was where Jesus performed one of His miracles. A woman came up to Him and said her son was ill. 'Go home and he'll be alright,' He said. And he was.

I went to Byblos too. The word 'Bible' comes from the name of that city. I know quite a bit about the Bible. More than Dave anyway. When Dave says he was 'well pleased' and I tell him that the Lord said that in the Bible about Jesus, 'My son in whom I am well pleased' – he thinks I'm having him on. He thinks it's a Cockney saying. Coined by one of the Krays. 'In you I am well pleased, my son, you are on the firm.' I'm not saying they didn't say it, I'm just saying that the Lord said it first. I browse through the Gideon's Bible when we're staying in hotels. But I often think, if there really is a god, why didn't he let me know that Piano Red was down the 100 Club in 1978?

The Beirut club was a typical sort of disco effort that you'd find anywhere in the world. It was called 'La Locomotive', and we were to open it. Perhaps our reputation for 'opening' clubs got round. It was a bit weird at first. Although night clubs are basically the same wherever you go in the world (they're all based on American clubs), the punters are always different. At least they look different. They always act the same once they know what they are supposed to be doing. But a club full of Arabs, most of them with their headgear on, seemed to present a bit of a challenge from the off. What do we do? Arabic music always seemed to me to sound like western music played backwards. But after a couple of nights I realised I was thinking too ethnic. All they wanted was western style 'Git-up-and-down-with-it' disco beat funk. Just like everywhere else. And they danced just as bad.

The disc jockey, George (couldn't have been his real name), done his best to guide us. 'I naw vot zer pipple vont. You do ze slow vun so zey ken grop itch udder and zen zer fonky fing.'

Alright, George. We did our normal set and they liked us. Why not? It was good and we now kept reasonably sober. Roughly towards the middle of the night, we did what we always done, the 'Rock 'n' Roll Show'. It was my favourite part of the night. Roy Young did his Fats Domino and Little Richard bit and I did my Jerry Lee bit. We did it well.

But the punters didn't like it, said George.

My back was up. Stupid bastards don't know what they're listening to. This was Rock 'n' Roll! Played from the heart! George'd say, 'Do not play ze Rack 'n' Rolly. Play ze funky fing. Zer pipple do not understand. Zay nat know zer rack music.' It dawned on me that it was strange to them because they had never heard it before. It never reached Beirut in the Fifties. Well ain't it about time it did, then?

We persevered under pressure. The Rock 'n' Roll got better for it. It became an obsession with me. I was sure it would get through in the end 'cos it sounded so good.

I remember upsetting Harvey one night. After the end of the show he came up to me and said, 'I think we ought to cut out the Rock 'n' Roll bit.'

'Why?' I said. I knew he enjoyed it.

'My girl don't like it.' he said.

'Fuckin' hell! You wanna stop playing Rock 'n' Roll just 'cos some stupid bird don't reckon it? Bollocks!' P'raps I did upset him and it might have been an insult to his bird, but to me giving up Rock 'n' Roll was like putting your Dad in a home.

Me and Rock 'n' Roll won in the end.

The Little Richard bit, the Jerry Lee bit, the Fats Domino bit. People began asking specially for it. Even George. 'Do zer Rack 'n' Rolly. Zer pipple love it!' By the time we left, it was the most requested part of the act. Rock 'n' Roll will never die!

We left for home just before Christmas with a welcome bit of bunce. Them club gigs abroad paid alright really. Trouble was, the long gaps between used up any money we'd saved. We tried, in the best way we knew how, to get back into the recording scene, but nobody really wanted to know. We did manage to get one record out, 'Should I Or Shouldn't I?' It flopped and that was that. Doing the clubs abroad was the only way we could be certain of making a few bob. We'd save as much as we could and hope the next gig come along quick. I had a good Christmas that year but by January I was skint again.

Chapter 16

Now What Can I Do To Get Some Money?

I did a few sessions and a few gigs here and there, but it wasn't enough. The Social Security were highly unsympathetic. The first and the last time I shall ask for their help. Me and Joan and Juliet were evicted from our flat. My old 1100 was nicked by the bailiff – the scum of the earth, who can only answer, 'Somebody has to do it.'

Joan's Mum and Dad were great. They didn't have much room, but they took us in willingly. I think Joan's Mum had as much faith in me as Joan did. I was encouraged to stick at it. There was never so much as a mention of getting a 'proper' job. The worst of it was, I knew I was good at what I was doing but, at the time, I didn't know what to do with it. Like I said earlier, all thoughts about doing your own thing go right out the window when you're skint. I felt guilty about being skint and all I could think about was where the next bit of money was coming from. The club thing seemed the only sure bet for some money. We just had to work on getting them more regular. Me,

Joan and Juliet were still living with Joan's Mum and Dad (Doris and Doug) and her brother Bruce when the next club gig came up. It was in the Bahamas.

Sounds great, don't it? But it ain't. It's a horrible place. Some people might like it, but I don't. It's too fuckin' hot. I spent all my spare time with my head in the air-conditioning system in the flat. Mind you, we did go over in the height of summer. I've not been over in the winter. Perhaps it ain't so bad then. But the money was good – the main thing. We had a free flat, free drinks, and all we had to buy was our food, which we cooked ourselves, so it didn't work out too bad. But I was getting in a rut. Here we go again.

Earning alright, sure, but I was bored. Once again the punters only wanted music they could dance to. There's got to be a way of earning money by playing what I wanted to play, but I wasn't sure what I wanted to play yet. I knew it wasn't this. Playing music just so's people can dance, or wriggle about like cunts. The band began talking about, and doing, anything that wasn't to do with music. Football, fishing, these all began to sound more interesting than music. Something was wrong.

Music had always been my first love. I used to drop Dave Peacock a card now and again. I'd tell him all about some great Rock 'n' Roller or C&W artist I'd just seen on this new American TV programme, *Hee Haw*. I was into music. This was all I wrote about to Dave. We had the same views on music. It was obvious that we should be making music together, but I never realised it then.

When we came back from the Bahamas, Roy left the band. He wanted to go out on his own. We got another singer for a while, Mike Stevens, but, although he wasn't a bad singer, the band's morale was sinking fast. What little spark was left soon died. In the winter of 1969, The Rebel Rousers split up.

Now What Can I Do To Get Some Money?

I began doing a few more sessions with producer Derek Lawrence. I told him about Albert Lee. Albert became a regular. That suited me. I loved Albert's playing. He played *real* notes. Unlike many of the popular guitar heroes of the time. An Albert Lee album was got together, but was never released.

We did another album with a black soul singer, Earl Jordan, featuring guitarists Ritchie Blackmore (who had now made a name for himself with Deep Purple), Jim Sullivan, and Albert Lee. The album was called *Green Bullfrog*. Lawrence had a thing about colours. He had a hit called 'White' something or other with some bird. That was it! Every record he put out after that had to have a colour in it. He suggested a number for me to record that this new American group, The Band, had out on an LP. They were good.

We recorded the song, 'Across the Great Divide'. I didn't think it was bad, but it wasn't as good as their version. It was recorded with session men but Derek wanted it to be put out under a band name.

Jerry Reed had an instrumental out called 'The Claw'. I thought this would be a good name for a band. Del thought so too, but he had to get his colour into the name. After going through more colours that there are in the rainbow, we came to a compromise. I liked 'Black'. Derek argued that black wasn't really a colour, and as the whole of point was that colours were lucky to him, we couldn't have it. When I pointed out that 'White' wasn't really a colour either, which was his original lucky colour, 'Black' suddenly became the colour. Why didn't he think of it before? 'Black Claw' became the name of the band, and the record was released. It didn't do fuck all. But a band called Black Claw was formed just the same, with the idea of making more records. The band members were me (piano, doubling on guitar), Dave Peacock (bass), Mick Burt (drums) and Harvey Hinsley (guitar). We began doing gigs. Not many, but the ones we did went down well. The music we were making was good, and above all we were enjoying ourselves. Music was number one again. We accepted anything that was put our way. We just wanted to play.

We knew we had something, but it was gonna take a time to get it off the ground. We tried as best we could. We made an album and got about thirty quid each. It was done in three hours. It wasn't a bad album either, It was called *Country Pie*. We did it 'on the side' for another company. It's still around today. I've seen it on sale in Tesco's![3]

Harvey wasn't on that album. I overdubbed the guitar. Me, Dave and Mick. The line-up we have today. That was our first album. We had a disastrous trip to Berlin and a few more gigs here and there, but it wasn't meant to be. The band was short-lived.

That old enemy, poverty, began to rear its ugly head once again.

Then I got a phone call from Albert Lee. He was joining a new group called Heads Hands & Feet. They needed a bass player and he recommended me. I didn't want to leave the band 'cos I was happy, but I was skint. It was a hard decision to make, but all agreed Black Claw's future looked dim without money behind us. And money was non-existent. Harvey joined Hot Chocolate, Dave joined a country and western band and Mick went back to his old job, plumbing. In 1970, Heads Hands & Feet were formed.

---

3 You can get it on CD on Sanctuary Records. *Chas'n'Dave, the Early Years.*

Chapter 17

Heads Hands & Feet

The line-up was me (bass), Albert Lee (guitar), Tony Colton (writer and lead vocalist), Ray 'Smiffy' Smith (writer and guitarist), Mike O'Neil (piano) and Pete Gavin (drums). We were managed by Danny Secunda who had great hopes for the band.

At about the same time, me and Joan got offered a council flat in Edmonton. It wasn't what we would have chosen for ourselves, but it was brand new and it was a place of our own. True it was a tower block and we were on the twenty-second floor (frightening! I'm not mad on heights), but we, forever optimists, moved in and made the most of it.

That band had ambition. Not only to play good music. It also had plans to become world-famous. I'm not saying it couldn't have been. There were plenty of world-famous bands that were duff and we could *play*, so it didn't seem that unlikely. I wasn't so sure that I wanted to be famous with *this* band, though. I realised, then, that you have to live with whatever makes you famous.

I liked the band and most of the music. But not *all* of it. Working with 'em taught me a lot though. It proved once and for all that no matter what talent you've got, you can't sit around hoping that people are going to recognise it. You've got to *work* at it and put yourself about. Talent plus hard work leads to success: '10 per cent inspiration and 90 per cent perspiration'. A good adage.

In 1970, guitar heroes were still very much in evidence among the 'world-famous' bands. But we had Albert Lee. My favourite English guitar player. My only reservation at the time was that perhaps he's too good. Most of the famous ones at the time I didn't think were all that. Perhaps you had to be bad to be famous? No, that can't be right. There were one or two I liked. Albert can do it! In England at the time Albert was known, or heard-of anyway. But the Trendies weren't particularly impressed. He wasn't loud enough, he wasn't distorted enough and never set light to his amp. On top of that, he liked Country and Western music! I mean! The Trendies read music papers. Music papers always take the piss out of Country & Western music.

He can't be any good.

No, the music papers never took a lot of notice of Heads Hands & Feet. 'Old Albert? Yeah, we know him. Plays all that cowboy music, don't he. Now ol' Nobby Rotten bollocks, now there's a *guitarist* for ya! Plays two notes at once! And farts in the pick-up to create a minor third. Fabulous! He makes the guitar sound like the Hallelujah Chorus.'

Then we took a trip to America. We went to Los Angeles to do the Troubadour, shortly after we got together. We went down great. The Yanks saw the band for what they were – good. They became interested in us in the States. We talked to

Mort Lewis who wanted USA management. (He managed Simon and Garfunkel at the time.)

The news filtered back to England. Suddenly the press were interested.

HANDS & FEET GO DOWN WELL IN AMERICA
ALBERT LEE IS ACCLAIMED AS A GREAT GUITARIST!
ANOTHER ONE OF OUR GREAT ENGLISH GUITARISTS
KNOCKS THE YANKS FOR SIX
SIMON AND GARFUNKEL'S MANAGERS LOVES THE BAND
WE ALWAYS KNEW YOU'D MAKE IT ALBERT!

And quotes to that effect. The Trendies began to like Heads Hands & Feet. Yes, we *had* gone down well in America, and if I generalise, the Americans use their ears more than the English. This is not being fair on the real English punters, but remember I'm generalising. A lot of music in England is judged with the *eyes*. Seems daft, don't it? But it's true. If they read something is good, then it is. If they read something's bad, then it is.

In America they go more by their ears. Music is important to them and is there to be listened to and not read about. Frank Zappa said English punters are more interested in what the bloke in the next seat is wearing rather than who they are about to see. There are exceptions but he wasn't far wrong. I'm still not sure, though, how the same country that produced the likes of Big Bill Broonzy, Hank Williams, Ray Charles and Jerry Lee Lewis, suddenly went mad on Herman and the Hermits. But there you are.

The Americans did like Albert's guitar playing. They knew he was good. But then their country was brought up on the guitar. It's in the blood. They were good judges. If the music you're making is good, whatever style, they'll like it, and they'll show it. Me, Dave and Mick went over to New York in 1980 amid cries from some people in England of 'Chas & Dave? You're too English. They won't understand you.' But they judge America from their front rooms. They haven't been there, playing to the people.

Chas & Dave went down great. They copped hold of the feeling of the music. The only thing that matters. The way we sang was fresh to them. You can tell when people come up to you after the gig. You can see it in their eyes if they're just being polite. If they really like you, they can't hide it. They liked Chas & Dave. 'Understand them? Why ask that question? We enjoyed it!' Why all this shit about understanding? Did the cave man understand it when he was having his first bunk-up? It didn't matter. He knew he was *enjoying* himself!

Heads Hands & Feet came back from America to a bit more receptive English audience. Our first album was well received in an underground sort of way, and we started doing the rounds of the colleges and universities. The first album was a double album titled *Heads Hands & Feet*. (It was released as a single album in England, a compilation of the two.) Our second album was called *Tracks* and on 19 June 1972 we went over to the States again for an eight-week tour. It was an experience. I loved it.

Just before we left, me and Joan moved from the tower block in Edmonton. We managed to get our own place. A little bungalow in Broxbourne. It was heaven. Me, Joan and Juliet and our new addition to the family, Katie.

The tour was pretty well organised. It all went smoothly considering we were jumping from tour to tour. We worked with people like Procul Harum, J. Geils, Humble Pie, Jethro Tull, Edgar Winter and others. I'd watch 'em from the side of the stage. They were all good in their own way, but I had my favourites.

For sheer Rock 'n' Roll/Rhythm and Blues, it was J. Geils. For good tunes, Procul Harum. Excitement, Humble Pie (with Stevie Marriott). Jethro Tull put on a show and had a good sense of humour. Edgar Winter? Not my cup of tea really, but he did have something and I could see why he was liked. We got about a bit, too, on that tour. Los Angeles, Alberquerque, Houston, Chicago, New York, St Louis, San Diego, Oklahoma, Denver.

I remember Denver!

We stayed at the Holiday Inn (where else?). We went through the normal routine on arrival. Check in, chuck the bags in the room and meet in the bar. I was first down. There at the bar, looking like they was really having a good time was the scruffiest, filthiest couple of characters you ever saw. At their feet was this little scruffy dog. They thought the world of it and with every round of drinks they would order it up a steak sandwich. I got talking to them and it turned out they were hillbillies. They'd come from the hills just outside Denver. I didn't ask questions as to how they come to be here, or, more to the point, how they didn't get thrown out. They were treated with respect by the staff. It was obvious to me, they must be a couple of gold prospectors and had struck it rich.

The rest of the boys came down and when the hillbillies found out we were musicians, they decided to throw a party that night. Drinks on them! Not only for us, but the whole of the hotel was invited. After the gig, we all met in this big room. The two hillbillies were the life and soul of the party. Someone somewhere had given one of 'em a Margarita. (In case you've never had one, a murky sort of cocktail, a lady's drink really; the rim is dipped in salt and it's drunk out of a dinky glass.) They'd never seen anything like it before in their lives; but they were gone on it!

'Margaritas for everybody!' They shouted. 'And another

steak sandwich!' (For the dog!) Me and Albert homed in on the grand piano and we Rock 'n' Rolled 'til the sun come up. Every now and then a couple more Margaritas arriving.

Next day, we all met by the swimming pool. There they were. Still drinking. Only now it was beer. (The salt in the Margaritas must have given 'em a thirst!) The old dog was now a-kip on a sun lounger. He was wet so he'd obviously been having a good swim around the pool. They livened up when they saw me.

'Hey Chas! You and Albert played great last night. What d'ya wanna drink?' Drink? How do these boys do it? 'I'll just have a coffee, if that's alright.'

'Sure, whatever you want. Hey, waiter. Bring our friend a coffee.'

'Hey, Luke!' he said to his mate. 'This little ol' piece of plastic can get us a plane ride!' He had in his hand a credit card. 'Ain't it amazing? No one needs money anymore. You just carry one of these little pieces of plastic, and you can get anything you want! I just been told we can fly to Hawaii just by showing the right person this little card. It sure was a lucky day for us when we found this!'

They'd found it! The hotel room, drinks, steak sandwiches for the dog, Margaritas, had all been down to this credit card they'd *found*.

'Finish your beer, Luke, c'mon, let's go!' They whistled the dog, and off they went. Presumably to have another party in Hawaii.

It was that tour of America that got me thinking about a definite new direction.

I had always sung (in all the bands I'd been in) with an American accent. Nothing strange in that. All English pop bands did. I began to have this niggling feeling, though, that there was something not quite real about it. Now I didn't want to forsake the Rock 'n' Roll feel that I had, but at the same time

I didn't want to be looked upon as a Rock 'n' Roll revivalist. There must be a way of keeping the feel, but singing in my own accent. About things I knew about.

I tried writing a Cockney song with Tony Colton for the *Tracks* album, but it never really come off. We ended up using just the intro to it as an introduction to 'Hot Property'. But it was a start.

When I began working in the States, I realised that although that particular effort at a Cockney song didn't really come off, the idea was right. When I got up in front of them American audiences singing things like 'Oh Mama, ya alraht,' and 'The boy cain't even daince', I felt such a fraud. It didn't seem so bad doing it in England. At home it sort of felt like you were giving 'em a taste of what you thought a good American band would sound like. But here we were, in America, showing 'em what a good English band sounded like. But we were singing in their accent!

Jerry Lee, Little Richard, Fats Domino sang in their own accents. That's why I liked 'em. They were real. It suddenly became so obvious. Everybody should sing in their own naturalised accent. Whether you're from Memphis, New York, Newcastle, Glasgow. It's what you should do and it's what I've got to do.

I began changing a few words. I'd sing 'Oh Muvver' instead of 'Oh Mama'. Daft, I know, 'cos the lyrics didn't translate properly. But I felt better doing it. I began to feel a bit more real. All that needed to be done was to write a song thinking in my own accent. That's it! The idea became an obsession. I had found my direction. It wouldn't be easy, but I had the feeling that it would work. I began making mental plans.

But in the meantime, while I was in America, I was gonna enjoy myself. It was the Land of Music as far as I was concerned, and I wanted to see and hear as much of it as I could.

The tour was strenuous. A different place every night and, America being the size it is, we flew everywhere. We had to be up early most mornings to catch the plane to the next town. I vowed every morning (you know how I love mornings!) that after the gig that evening I'd get an early night. But that night we'd be somewhere like St Louis. For one night only! How can I go to bed knowing there's probably some fantastic band playing in some club just around the corner? I couldn't do it. We'd be gone next day. I'd get no second chance.

Me and Albert would ask around after the gig where the music was, and off we'd go. If we got to sit in with the band, which happened most times (we made sure of that), our night was complete. Or almost. We usually ended up in the guitar player's or the banjo player's hotel room, singing and strumming 'til it was time to catch the plane to the next town.

If we had any time off, and we did get one or two days, it was spent in LA. That was where we were based. There was always someone to see in LA. I went to see James Brown at the Forum. He was great. So was the black comedian on before him. The audience, mostly black, were falling about in the aisles. Their laughter was infectious, I was laughing with 'em. I couldn't help it, though didn't understand a word he was on about!

A late night club in LA was the Palomino. It was a C&W club. I saw Doug Kershaw there. A wild fiddle-playing Cajun. I loved it. I was playing a bit of fiddle in the act with Heads Hands & Feet. We found out he was staying at our hotel and that night me and Smiffy (Ray Smith) had a fiddle-playing, guitar strumming session in his room. I remember writing a song with him. Though I can't recall the tune.

The next day we were playing at the Whiskey, and Doug Kershaw said he was coming down. That afternoon I got my fiddle out for a bit of practice. There was a knock on the door. I put my fiddle down on the bed and went to open it. It was Smiffy.

Now Smiffy was having the time of his life in America. He loved Hollywood, he loved the film stars, he loved Tequila Sunrises and he loved the girls. He was convinced that oysters kept him in shape. He had 'em for breakfast, dinner, tea and supper. Smiffy threw himself hook, line and sinker into whatever part he was playing.

The part he was now playing was 'The English Rock 'n' Roll Superstar'.

Not long after we arrived in the States he said to me, 'Someone told me, Charlie, that in America they spike your drinks with LSD and that.'

'I've heard that, too, Ray,' I said.

'Well,' said Ray, 'at that party the other night, I went round all of 'em and not one of 'em was spiked!'

I laughed, and so did Ray – but only after I laughed. He meant it.

Smiffy wrote great songs and was one of the nicest blokes you could ever meet. He was also one of the clumsiest. John Wayne was his favourite actor and he loved Elvis and Stanley Matthews the wizard '50s footballer. He hit on this idea that he reckoned would improve his stage image. He was gonna stand and 'look about' like John Wayne, while using the legwork of Elvis and the footwork of Stanley Matthews. The result was fantastic!

'Ray,' I said, 'you've hit on a gimmick that someone like Jerry Lewis would give his right arm for.'

'Jerry Lewis? Don't you mean Jerry Lee Lewis?'

'No. Jerry Lewis. I love him, and what you just done was as funny as anything he's ever done.'

Ray dropped it. He hadn't meant for it to be funny. His new

American image had to be cool and moody. They didn't know he was clumsy. They didn't know he was an ordinary bloke who liked a laugh. It was his big chance to put over the 'Ray Smith he wanted to be'.

'Stars' had a reputation of being able to pull any bird they wished. Ray set to work. He decked himself out in velvet trousers and five inch high heel boots (which gave him a 'here's me head, me arse is coming' walk) and away he went. He planned a line of chat that was unique. He'd swotted up on phrases that sounded deep and poetic (all nicked from somewhere or other). The idea was to let 'em loose when the timing was right. There he'd be, in the foyer of the Continental Hyatt House, LA (the groupies' paradise, and Smiffy's) looking about, all John Wayne cool.

'Hey! Aren't you with that new English rock band?' A dodgy bunch of groupies had homed in on Ray. They needed an 'in'. Someone to get 'em past the doorman.

'Yeh!' That was enough. No questions about 'What new English rock band?' in case it was the wrong one. 'Care to join me for dinner, girls?'

Smiffy was there! At the dinner table surrounded by admiring birds! Weyheyyy! Long live Elvis and John Wayne and Hollywood and America and...but hang about...don't go too mad yet. Play it cool, Smiffy boy. Ray goes into a theatrical pose and gazes into the distance. It was time for his pulling plan to be produced with a flourish out of the bag. Smiffy had set up a pregnant pause and was about to give birth.

'Far be it for me to gander into a ladies' chamber, but sail on silver silver!' A sort of mixture of Shakespeare and Simon and Garfunkel. It worked! The one he fancied was impressed.

'Hey, Ray, did that just come straight off the top of your head?'

'Pardon, Mam? Oh yeh, I'm sorry, just thinking out loud.'

'That was great! It sounded like a line out of a great song. Couldn't you use it?'

'Well, it could be tidied up a little. Hey waiter! Tequila Sunrises all round and a plate of oysters.'

Ray was away! What could possibly go wrong? But it was Smiffy playing a part. You knew sooner or later the real Smiffy was gonna reveal himself. Looking her straight in the eyes he's gone:

'How about making it with me down to the gig tonight? Ahh! Here's the drinks. Thanks, waiter. Here, keep the change.'

'But it's a $100 bill, sir.'

'Is it not enough?'

'More than enough, Sir!'

'Keep it!' says Ray and with a smile and a sweep of his arm, meant to convey to the waiter that money means nothing, manages to sweep the drinks, trays of hamburger relish, tomato ketchup and anything else that was in his path, off the table and all over the birds.

The real Smiffy had arrived, bless him!

Ray's got up. 'You alright, love?' Trying to brush off tomato ketchup from some bird's dress with a dirty hanky he's just pulled out of his pocket. 'I'm sorry, love, let me...'

But it was too late. They were all up now, backing away from Smiffy. Smiffy blew his nose, which he did continually as the real Smiffy, leaving tomato ketchup on the end.

'Girls! Do you still think any of you might be still coming to the gig tonight?'

They were gone. To the powder room to get cleaned up. The odds were they weren't coming back. Not to Smiffy's table anyway. Smiffy's sat there with a furrowed forehead. But only for a minute.

'Charlie!' He's spotted me across the restaurant. 'Charlie! Weyheyy!' His big Smiffy grin taking over. 'Where's Albert? Are we going clubbing it tonight after the gig, or what? There's a Country & Western club just off the Strip. We'll take our guitars. I got this new tuning worked out. Let's go to the bar, I want to tell you about it.'

We go to the bar. 'Ray, you've got tomato ketchup on your nose.' 'Where?' He gets his hanky out. 'Is it gone?' 'Yeh.' Smiffy stuffs his hanky back in his pocket. The bit of ketchup is now on his moustache. 'What I was thinking was, if you tune your G down to F and your D down to D flat...'

Well, this was Smiffy. Now you've got the picture I'll go back to what I was telling you. I bet you guess what happens. I'll recap. There was me sitting on the bed practising my fiddle, hear knock on door, lay fiddle down, open door. It was Smiffy.

But just to be fair, and I wont keep you in suspense much longer, I wanna get across to you that what was about to happen was entirely my fault. Although Smiffy did it. Now, if you've got a dog that you know likes chewing your boots up, well you don't leave 'em about, do you? You put 'em away, out of his reach. Also, if you've got kids that are in the toddling stage, then you don't deck out your house with breakables that they can get their hands on. If you do and they break 'em, or you do and your boots get chewed up, it's your fault. I know what dogs are like. I know what kids are like. I wouldn't want 'em any other way. I knew what Smiffy was like, and I wouldn't want him any other way. But as soon as I saw his face at the door, I should have reacted instantly. I should have barred his way and grabbed that fiddle. It was only the difference of a fraction of a second. But it was long enough for Ray to get past me and into my room.

'Ray! Don't sit...' Too late. CRACK! You've guessed, ain't you? It don't take much figuring out. I was gonna say, 'Ray, don't sit down on the bed.'

It don't matter though, I shouldn't have left it there. Ray knew what he had done, but he didn't move. He just sat there. He didn't want to get up and see it. He just looked up at me with a 'Done it again' expression on his face.

'Get up, Ray,' I said quietly.

Ray got up. Still not looking.

There it lay and, surprisingly enough, it didn't look as bad as I thought.

'It don't look too bad, Ray.' But I knew I was kidding myself. I'd heard that crack.

'It's alright, Charlie,' said Ray, making a grab for it.

'Don't touch it!' I panicked, 'leave it to me, Ray!'

The angle of the fiddle's fingerboard in relation to the body didn't look quite right. I picked it up. The only thing that joined the top bit to the bottom bit was four slack strings. He'd broke the fuckin' neck off.

'I'll get it fixed for you, Charlie.'

'Ray, we're on stage in an hour.'

'I'll get one, don't worry.'

He was gone and back in five minutes.

'I've just been up to Doug Kershaw's room. He said he'll lend you his.

It was a nice thought and I was tempted, but the thought of Smiffy treading on Doug Kershaw's fiddle brought me out in a cold sweat.

'No, Ray, we'll have to get one from somewhere else.'

We hired one and the gig went off okay. Doug Kershaw turned up and was impressed. Smiffy was happy. 'Weyheyy, Charlie!!'

All's well that ends well. Smiffy got mine fixed next day. Bless him again!

Chapter 18

HH & F – RIP

Back home in England we carried on gigging, but I was becoming increasingly dissatisfied with what I was doing. I appreciated that it was a great band in a lot of people's eyes, but it wasn't *my* ideal band.

I was ready for the change, but I suppose I was waiting for the right opportunity. I began playing from the head rather than the heart. It was interesting but the buzz was different. The heart must come first. The head works out all manner of clever and important things, but the heart must be the governor. Festivals began to be the most coveted gigs. You could get across to thousands in just one performance. It would take at least a dozen or more normal gigs to cover the same amount of ground as one festival gig. I weighed it all up in my head and it made sense. But after doing a few I wrote a poem from the heart. This poem was based on a true event. Heads Hands & Feet at Weeley Festival about 1970. I wrote it soon after the gig.

Festivals

Now Rock 'n' Roll festivals might seem exciting events,
But don't ever play on 'em, if you've got any sense.
I've bin in a few bands and done gigs big and small,
But them Festivals, well, they're the worst of 'em all.
Thousands of people all acting the cunt,
Specially the ones who stand round the front.
Shovin' their heads in the PA stacks.
It's a wonder they all don't get heart attacks.
Now this one I'm on, and there's no doubt about it,
On hindsight I could've well done without it.
But I agreed to the gig and I'm doin' me best,
To gee meself up, though not too much impressed.
'Not long to go now,' I'm starting to think,
'Soon be back in the caravan, having a drink.'
Then the singer, like he's just escaped from a cage,
Decides to start jumpin' all over the stage.
Just as the fat geezer (who's runnin' the show),
Shouts out, 'You've got one more number to go!'
'Fank Christ!' you say, 'cos it's startin' to rain,
And you long to be back in them pubs again.
Then your amp packs up 'cos the rain's got in it,
'Oi! Roadie!' You shout, he says, 'Hang on a minute!'
He finally comes on and gives it a thump,
I'll bollock him later. I've right got the hump.
'It's knackered,' he says. What a smart observation!
'I'll get you a lead from the 'lectric Ovation.'
'That's no good, dozy git! It's me AMP that's gone!'
But he ain't took no notice. 'For Christ's sake, COME ON!
HURRY UP! I'm comin' up for me bass solo!'
And the stage is more suitable for playin' water polo.
Then me amp's getting wetter, and sparks start to fly,

And I think, 'In a minute, we're all gonna die.'
I shout to the Roadie, 'Hurry up! 'Fore it blows!'
But he's too busy snorting some stuff up his nose.
Now the singer's gone spare, starts revolvin' his head,
Don't even notice me amp's gone dead.
He decides he's gonna start climbin' about,
Climbs up the PA, and starts to shout out.
(He's stood there, balanced on this little shelf.
He don't know he's makin' a cunt of hisself.)
'All clap your hands!' He says, 'Like me!'
'What a wanker!' The crowd all think, generally.
He shouts to 'em all, 'Can you hear me out there?'
'All clap your hands and all shout 'OH YEAH!'
And the rain's pourin' down, and the wind is a-blowin',
But the singer's determined to get 'em all goin'.
He jumps down and starts sliding all over the deck,
Then goes arse over head, nearly breaking his neck.
But up like a shot and, 'Oh no, here he comes!'
He picks up a stick and starts banging the drums.
The drummer gets humpy, shouts, 'Leave 'em alone!'
But the front man, well, he's in a world all of his own.
Then the fat geezer (him, who's runnin' the show),
Shouts, 'COME ON, GET OFF, WE'VE GOT TEN
GROUPS TO GO!'
Then we all go mad, and we all jump about,
And hit the last chord with an almighty clout.
And run from the stage to get out of the rain,
And I think, 'I must be outa me brain!'
Then the singer says, 'We had 'em goin' in the end!'
I nod, but think, oh well let him pretend.
'Cos the crowd, they just sat there as wet as can be,
And it all seemed a load of old bollocks to me.

But tho' they never cheered, nor hollered and hooted,
Hooray! I'm HERE! I never got electrocuted!

Well, take from it what you will. It's basically true. My summary of all the festivals I've ever done. But it's all experience ain't it? (Mind you, I had yet to experience Glastonbury! That hadn't happened when I wrote this of course. What a treat I was in for!)

Heads Hands & Feet were getting a name, but we weren't getting in the Charts, It was decided that we needed a single. We did one. It was a good one too, as far as singles go. I got credit for a share in the writing. My only contribution was telling Ray and Tony the bits I liked and the bits I didn't like. The bits I liked they kept in, and the bits I didn't like were dropped. Not enough in my book to be credited with part of the writing, but, nevertheless, full credit to Ray and Tony, they gave me part of the song.

I found out later, though, that although I felt I didn't deserve it, my contribution was a lot more than some famous 'writers' had done. If ever I saw one name under a song title, to me it was obvious. He wrote it. Two names? Okay, one wrote the tune and the other the lyrics.

Three names? A bit more difficult. Possibly the third helped with lyrics and tune. Not being experienced in songwriting, this is how I thought it went. Perhaps it does in some cases. But sometimes I'd see a song credited to three or more writers. How the fuck did this work? Oh, yes. They all wrote a bit each. But no. I found out that a lot of my favourite songs were 'written' thus.

For example, a song is credited to six people. First person actually wrote the song. All of it. Second person was a publisher whose only part was to get the song to the artist. Third person was a publisher's partner who had to have a bit if his mate got a bit. (This is a fact, even though it sounds daft.) Fourth person was the artist whose part in writing the song was singing it. (If he didn't want to sing it, the song never got recorded.) Fifth person was a producer. (I mean, he did get a commercial sound on the record. His normal percentage hardly pays for the petrol in his fleet of Rollers.) Sixth person was the DJ. (I mean, how the people gonna hear it if he don't play it!)

On top of that, the actual percentages had to be negotiated sensibly. The writer only wrote the song. Who the fuck knows him? They know the publisher (had many hits), they know the artist (had many hits), they know the producer (had many hits), they know the DJ (plugs all the hits). The songwriter? Well, who's heard of him? We might do soon, but we're giving him a chance. Let's grab the bunce while we can! Before he cottons onto our little game. Give him 5 per cent, that leaves us 95 per cent. Five into ninet-five goes nicely. Exactly 19 per cent each.

This sort of thing went on. Probably still does. But it didn't go on with HH & F. I was given part of the writing royalties simply because I genuinely helped with the song. I appreciated that. But I still felt I didn't merit it.

The song I'm talking about was 'Warming Up The Band'. It didn't do what we hoped it would. It got the plays and everybody said, 'Why ain't this record a hit?' But it wasn't. The people just didn't buy it. They all liked it, sure, but they didn't buy it.

'I like your new record,' is often said to me and Dave. Great. But the test is to ask, 'Have you bought it?' 'Yes' was the general answer to 'No Pleasing You'. 'No' was the general answer to 'Miserable Saturday Night' and 'Poor ol' Mr Woogie'.

You know where you are with the people. The *people* didn't buy 'Warming Up The Band'. Everybody said it should have been a hit, but it wasn't and that was that.

Things began to go wrong. Reasons why the band weren't

making it were put forward. Now that the band were on the verge of making it, more and more people began slinging their oar in. The same people who, at the beginning, took no notice.

Somehow or other, Danny Secunda, the manager, got aimed out. The man who got the band off the ground. Who had faith when no one else did. The band, instead of being a unit, began to be, once more, just a bunch of talented musicians with no leader and therefore no positive goal. Unrest began to settle in the camp.

It's the same with any team of people who make up a unit. A band, a football team. The talent may be there, but they need a figurehead to be the boss. A father figure. Perhaps it's instinct. It's like a family. You all work together, but you know Dad is the Governor at the end of the day. How many times have you seen a football team fall by the wayside because they've lost their manager to another team? They are still the same bunch of geezers, but they've lost a leader. Someone to work for. Like a Dad. They may not always agree with their manager, like sometimes you might not agree with your Dad, (I'd liked to have had the chance to, though I can empathise) but you respect him and inwardly feel that at the end of the day he is always right. A bunch of talented footballers or musicians can play well, but they need that extra push when under pressure. A good manager gives this. But Danny Secunda got the push, and Reggy Lock took over.

Reggy Lock began acting as manager under Tony Colton's direction. No doubt this suited Tony. But he was also the singer, the songwriter and the producer of the band. Reggy suited him perfectly. He acted out TC's orders. Just like the board of a football club who try to run their team through the manager. It might sound good in theory, but it don't work.

The band had lost its figurehead. Someone who would be

impressed by, and work creatively with, the band product. Putting forward constructive criticism now and again, knowing from the heart what the band has got and only wanting the best out of them.

I began to lose interest. I liked Reggy Lock, but as a tour manager. Not a band manager. Tony Colton has talent but he wanted to do too much. A great songwriter and a great producer but he should have stopped there.

Me and Albert started making plans for a new band. One more album was made with Heads Hands & Feet, *Old Soldiers Will Never Die*, but me and Albert had decided. We wanted to leave and form our own band. We announced our decision.

It was to be the band we'd often talked about. Me and Albert were really close in our likes and dislikes in music. I was enthusiastic. I wanted to get a band going. I wasn't interested in the fame and glory, I just wanted to be part of my ideal band. So did Albert. But the record company thought different. I don't know why I didn't see it at the time. But now I do. I was blinded by my love of music. The record company saw Albert as the new guitar hero. As long as he was up front making a guitar noise, they saw money. They weren't interested in the type of music we were gonna play.

The new band was formed, but it never felt right from the start. From the off we wanted it to have a new name, but the record company talked us into calling it The New Head Hands and Feet. The line-up was me, Albert, Dave Peacock, Ian Wallace and Steve Simpson. All good players. But it was a rehash. We did a few gigs and went down alright but there was no real spirit there. The record company was pushing Albert up the front which he didn't really want. They were turning up on gigs, reporting back on the 'goods' and the 'bads' on everything we did. Fuck it! Here we go again. This is not how we meant it to be. What happened to the band we'd talked about? We wanted to play again and not be judged on 'Hit Potential'. We had more to offer than that. But I felt that it would be, in the end, up to us and I was willing to give it a real go. This was my ideal way forward. Form a band that would eventually achieve pulling power on the road. Didn't care how long it took. Talent will out. Any hit records being a bonus. If it didn't work, then it wouldn't be for want of trying.

But it never got that far. One night, three or four weeks after the new band had formed, me, Dave and Albert went for a drink down the Speakeasy in the West End. The favourite musicians haunt. The Crickets were playing. They asked Albert to join 'em and he did.

I don't blame Albert. It was what he wanted to do. I admit it was a disappointment at the time. All them months we'd talked about our 'Ideal Band' together. Now I knew it was never going to be. But ain't it strange how things work out? Or is it?

I remember my Mum saying, 'If you bank your hopes on anything in life and it don't work out, don't sit there grieving about it, get out and do the next best thing. Quite often you'll find that the next best thing turns out to be what you should have done in the first place.'

She was right.

The next best thing was getting together with my mate to form a duo called Chas and Dave.

The Meeting

It was a cold night in the early '60s. Once more he'd missed the
late bus home. Time flew by when he was saying goodnight to
his girlfriend and half an hour always seemed like five minutes.
Home was about five miles away, but never mind, he didn't
mind a walk. It was a cold night but quite pleasant really. In fact
he quite liked winter nights. Nice pacey stride. That'll keep him
warm. Not gonna run like he did the other night though. Got
stopped by a copper who thought he was up to no good. Nice
cup o' tea and a fag soon. Lovely. Oh, what a git! Out of fags!
But no worries, half a crown in pocket and pass a fag machine
on way home. Ten nice cold Senior Service. Then home. Kettle
on, get light off the gas stove, then with ear close to record
player so no bollocking from those sleeping, listen to Jerry Lee's
latest single another twenty times. But he's thinking ahead. He's
still got three miles to go. Here comes the fag machine. In goes
the half crown, out comes the…Bollocks! The fuckin' drawer's
stuck! No fags! No amount of slapping and banging produces
any sort of result.

So. Fuck it. Put the kettle on and go round the ashtrays.
Everyone smokes so no lack of dog-ends. Nan, Grandad, Mum,
stepfather, brother, sister. And Grandad's fag papers. Plenty
good smoke ahead! Couple of miles to go on the lamplit high
road. Starts thumbing. Car passes and pulls in. Could this be a
lift? Stride up to, positive. Driver has opened the passenger
door. Driver's face is familiar. 'Brian! Brian Juniper! Ain't seen
you since schooldays! Nearly five years ago!' 'Jupes' as he was
known as and still is, grunted something and the passenger got
in. 'Chas!' says Jupes, 'You're doing alright! Heard your new
record with the Outlaws on the radio today. Great bass sound!'

'Cheers Jupes. What you up to?'

'I gotta band. That's my bass player in the back.'

'Pleased to meet you,' says Chas, 'I'm Chas Hodges.'

'Pleased to meet you too, I'm Dave Peacock.'

They get to Chas's house. 'Coming in for a cup of tea?' says Chas. Kettle goes on. 'Heard a great record today,' says Dave, 'Gonna get it tomorrow. Jerry Lee's latest.'

'Got it here!' says Chas.

'Don't believe it! Put it on immediately!' says Dave.

Tea's poured, Jerry Lee's playing.

'All I need now to make it perfect is a fag,' says Chas.

'I got a packet of Senior Service. Any good?' says Dave.

'I got a feeling me and you are gonna get on well!' says Chas.

PART TWO

THE CHAS & DAVE STORY

Chapter 19

The Beginning

Well, here I am over twenty years later writing the next part in the life of Chas Hodges.

'All About Us' The Chas & Dave Story. So what kept me so long? Well perhaps timing.

When I finished Part One, 'Chas before Dave', Chas & Dave had only been together for about thirteen years. Perhaps my subconscious told me to wait, (that happens to me sometimes) until Chas & Dave had been around a few more years to make the book look fat enough. We've now been together thirty-six years.

That's fat enough I'd say!

It was around the end of 1972. The idea of me being myself and not wanting to sing in an American accent had become an obsession. I spoke to Dave about this. I'd just come back from a tour of America with Heads Hands & Feet.

That's when the seed was sown. I felt a fraud singing in an American accent over there. It seemed okay at the time singing in an American accent at home 'cos you were sort of playing a part. 'This is what American music sounds like, and it's good.' It was too. But singing like that in America? Hold up! Here's the real thing here all around us!

And I wanted to be the real thing wherever I went in the world from there on in. My ambition before I'd even spoken to Dave, was to write and sing a serious song in my own accent. For the want of a better description, Cockney. It had never ever been done before. Funny Cockney songs yes, but serious? No. 'Ain't No Pleasin' You' was the first one to fulfil that 'serious Cockney song' ambition, with of course the 'Gertchas' and 'Rabbits' Rockneying nicely along the way. But whoa back a minute! That's getting on for something like ten years later in the Chas & Dave story! I'll tell you more about them later when we get there.

Back to 1972. Back in England I spoke to Dave about getting together with these ideas in mind. He was with the Mick Greenwood band at the time, had also been to America and the band looked like it was winding down. He was ready for something else. I was also ready to give up bass and take on piano (my favourite instrument) as number one. I know this must have pleased my Mum. I remember her saying around 1960 when I'd been playing bass for about six months, 'Do you really like playing bass?' 'Yes'. I said. That's all she said. In her way of wanting to make sure that I was doing what I wanted to do. But I knew she was thinking I had more in me and the medium of four strings of the bass guitar was not enough. She was right. She always was.

Dave was up for it and in November 1972 Chas & Dave were born. My wife Joan was really pleased about the idea. So was Dave's wife Sue. Joan and Sue became close friends and are to this day. So now, first and foremost in my mind was to earn some money to pay the rent and feed the kids. I had two at the time. Juliet who was five and Katie who was one. A friend put us in touch with an agent who booked solo acts or duos for the Trueman pub circuit in and around London.

We were away! The pubs we particularly liked we began to do once a week. Like the Charcoal Burner, Colliers Row, and the Prince of Wales, Gravesend. We used to take my Mum regularly to the Prince of Wales, along with Alfie. Alfie was unique. Mum looked after Alfie. Alfie had his own versions of what things were in the world. He didn't know it, but they were better than the real thing. Names, for instance. Robert Redford was 'Robert Rag Bag'. Billy Joe Spears was 'Billy Goat Spears'. An antique was an 'ol teek' and an amplifier was an 'umptyfier'.

Dave still calls amps umptyfiers today. Roadies look at him with a mixed look of, 'Is this something I should know about, or is he having a laugh?' The thing is Dave has been using the term for so long, he don't know he's using it, so roadies are none the wiser. Alfie had a great way with lyrics too. He used to get up and sing with my Mum up the pub. The Beatles 'Obla Di' was one of his favourites. Only his version went: 'Happy as a racca in the market place, Molly hits the children with her hand...Obla Di, Obla Da, luggoles on.' Lovely stuff.

He died about ten years ago.

About five years ago me and Joan finally got a proper marble engraved cross made for Mum's grave. The original wooden cross was falling apart but the grave had been well tended I could see. I hadn't been there since the funeral, but my sister Jean had. She'd planted flowers, and recently too. There was fresh garden centre compost for me and Joan to make use of, earthing up new daffodil bulbs. A favourite of Mum's. I spoke to my sister after about the new cross and she was pleased about it. I told her we made good use of the potting compost.

'What potting compost?' She said.

'The compost in that dish.' I said.

'They were Alfie's ashes!' She said.

I didn't tell Joan. She'll find out when she reads this book!

Mum got on well with the governor and the missus at the Prince of Wales, Tom and Ann and she used to play in between me and Dave's sets. It was at one of these gigs that I heard my Mum playing a melody that wasn't familiar but really caught my ear.

She told me it was the verse to 'Sunshine of Your Smile'. I'd only heard the chorus before and wasn't too enamoured with it. But bearing in mind I'd only ever heard it sung by pissed blokes outside the pub at chucking out time that ain't surprising. It ended up becoming one of my favourite old songs. I suggested it to Mike Berry when I produced him in 1980. It made the top ten.

So we did pub gigs in the evenings and a few club gigs here and there and we began to get a bit of a name around London. The rent was getting paid and the kids were getting fed. Great! That left the days free for this new venture. Songwriting. I had written one or two things before with The Outlaws and Heads, Hands & Feet but this was a journey to discover the real me and as Dave was coming along too, the real us.

The place of writing was to be my front room when we got together. Me, Joan and the kids were living in a little bungalow in Broxbourne, Hertfordshire at the time. Dave would turn up say around 2pm and we would chuck ideas about until we both agreed we had something. The hardest part and the most important was making the natural 'me' accent come out when I sang. I had for so long sung in American. Then I began to discover simple tricks. Obvious now. I'd write a couple of lines and before I attempted to sing, I spoke 'em. Out loud. Then put the natural spoken phrasing with a melody. Eureka! That's it. The way forward! Now we know where the goal is all we've got to do is keep putting the balls in the net. Easier said than done I know, but a plan of action had been found.

'One Fing 'n' Anuvver' was the first breakthrough for our style which was to become known as 'Rockney'. A good start was made on the lyrics but when the melody was added it didn't sound real. Before Dave came round next day I revised the words and tried the 'Speak 'em out Loud' method. It worked! I knew I had something. I couldn't wait for Dave to come round. He bore out what I'd hoped for. He liked it.

'Rockney' was born.

'Rockney' was born but the child was at least three years old before it was given a name. Dave remembers when. It was on a train Dave says, on the way back from Newcastle. We were on tour with 10 cc (1976; I'll tell you more about that later). I came out with this word to describe our music purely because it needed one. 'Rockney'.

'One Fing 'n' Anuvver' was the first real 'Rockney' song we wrote, but the first song we ever wrote was 'Better get your Shoes on'. Around 1973 we were doing some sessions in London with Teresa Brewer. She liked it and recorded it. The sessions dough-wise were very handy rent payers. I'd done sessions all my life from the Joe Meek days. Now me and Dave were officially a duo, any sessions I got called up for, I rowed Dave in. I'd say I was not the bass player any more, Dave was. I now play piano or guitar. In most cases, in fact all as I remember it, we'd both get booked. The Teresa Brewer sessions came about through Steve Rowlands. Steve was an American and had done a bit of acting in his time. He was Tele Savalas' sidekick in *The Battle of the Bulge*. Steve produced the London Sessions for Jerry Lee Lewis which I played on. Then he got a commission to produce Teresa Brewer and wanted me in on it. I was happy to oblige as long as Dave was rowed in. I got double session money on the Jerry Lee dates so I got Dave in on the same. Teresa Brewer had hits in the '50s with songs like 'Put another Nickel in'. She was married to Bob Thiele who financed the sessions. Found out later it was Bob Thiele who got Buddy Holly on record. Alongside Norman Petty he produced 'Rave on'. Didn't know at the time. We'd've kissed his feet and wouldn't have fucked about so much. No, we didn't really fuck about. Bob Thiele ran 'Flying Dutchman' records in New York. He wanted an album from me and Dave. So we did one. Bob wanted to call us 'Oily Rags', so that's what we became for this album. It was me and Dave's rhyming slang for 'fags'. Cigarettes, not homosexuals. 'Got an oily boy?' would be a popular request from either one of us in our fag smoking days. Anyway, Bob Thiele liked it and the album came out. But like all that went before, after the big smiles and dancing there was not a lot of money. Record companyies are all the same. They still try to get away with it but tried it on especially in the early days. They figured they were doing the artist a favour by getting his voice heard on radio stations. And most artists didn't care anyway as long as they had enough money for a pint. I know I didn't. Someone said to me recently in an interview, 'What business advice would you give to a young person going into the business?' I couldn't think of any! It's not easy. If you start off saying you're not signing this and not signing that or let lawyers battle it out for you (done it!), you end up with a big bill and a potential fuck all at the end of it. So yes, get a lawyer to check it out, but ask him what it's gonna cost and make sure whatever contract it is, management, recording or publishing, you don't sign forever. Maximum five years. After that you get the option if you want it to continue. That way you can't get completely fucked. Only slightly. Or almost completely. Good business advice eh? Well it's the best I can do. Now where was I? Oh yeah. Talking session work. Bob Thiele.

He was a big jazz producer in New York. He got us doing sessions with people like Elvin Jones and Oliver Nelson. Though we didn't meet Oliver Nelson we did an album with him. He overdubbed his bit in New York. Nat Hentoff, the noted American jazz critic, did the liner notes on the album. We still didn't get any money out of the record company, but we didn't sign anything so we were only very slightly fucked. In fact barely interfered with really.

Other noted rent paying sessions were with Derek Lawrence. I'd been doing sessions for Del since the '60s. Del rang me up one day for a bass playing session. (Del by the way, produced the early Deep Purple albums and when they hit big in America, Del deservedly copped a bit of dough that financed his record company, Retreat Records. Me and Dave's first record label as 'Chas & Dave'. (But more about that in a minute.)

'Del, I don't play bass anymore.'

'What?'

'I play piano and guitar. Dave plays bass. We're a duo now.'

'Well get both of your arses down here I want some recording done!' Great! Dave was rowed in. The basic session band for Derek after me and Dave had teamed up was me, piano and/or guitar, Dave bass, Big Jim Sullivan, arranger and guitarist and Ian Wallace, drums. Big Jim Sullivan was Britain's first real guitarist. We had some good electric guitar players but not many of 'em could Rock 'n' Roll like the Americans. In fact hardly any. But Jim could. He was mentor to people that followed like Ritchie Blackmore (Jim gave him guitar lessons), Jimmy Page (he was second guitar to Big Jim on many '60s recording sessions), and a hero to many younger musicians, including me.

The first time that I met and played with Jim was on a TV show that Jack Good was producing. Jack made the great early English Rock 'n' Roll TV shows like *Oh Boy* and *Boy Meets Girl*, and produced *The Beatles* TV shows (at their request) in America later on. Anyway, my gig came about this way.

I was doing a session playing bass at Joe Meek's and Charles Blackwell was the arranger. I had just turned seventeen. I twigged that Charles Blackwell was impressed with what I was doing. At the end of the session he came over and said there was a new TV show coming up that Jack Good was producing and would I fancy being the bass player in the band? Of course I would and the next minute I was at rehearsals. Everybody was there. The whole band. Forty-piece. Tony Meehan on drums. Just recently left The Shadows. Well respected. The Vernons Girls. Full TV crew and no, I don't believe it! That's Jim Sullivan on guitar!

I had turned up about forty-five minutes late but there didn't seem to be much happening so I wandered over to Jack Good. I remember he had the most filthiest shirt on you'd ever seen. The grime round the top of the white collar was not grubby, it was black. That ain't important really but I'd never experienced similar before with famous people. I quietly went up to Jack Good, not wishing to interrupt, but thought I should get official leave from the boss. 'Is it okay?' I said, 'to go and get a cup of tea, 'til you need me?' He absolutely exploded! In front of the whole lot of 'em. '*YOU WANT A CUP OF TEA? YOU TURN UP HERE AN HOUR LATE AND YOU WANT A FUCKING CUP OF TEA?*' I changed my mind. I went back and sat by my bass amp with my bass on my knee at the ready. (Some fifteen years later, around 1976, Jack Good predicted in a national newspaper Chas & Dave were going to be the next big thing. He used to come and see us on East End gigs. I never mentioned the much earlier meeting. I thought not much point.)

Jack Good's new show was to be called *Your Big Chance*. The idea being that potential performers sent in audition tapes which Jack Good listened to and chose the best ten. Then he got Charles Blackwell to do an exact arrangement working from the tape. Then those people were contacted saying thank you for the tape which was still being considered and in the meantime Jack Good is doing another show and as a thank you for your effort will send a car to pick you up. Then on the big night, unbeknown to them, the arrangement to their song all ready to go, Jack Good would announce, 'Is there a Freddy Brown in here tonight?' Lone voice from the audience pipes up. 'Can you come up to the stage please?' Now onto what actually happened on the night. Freddy Brown wanders up bewildered. 'Did you send a tape in to a TV company?' 'Yeh.' 'Well this forty-piece band you see before you have rehearsed an arrangement of your song from your tape. There's the microphone. Take it away Freddy!' Freddy did. The song was 'Yes Sir that's my Baby'. He intro'd it on the tape as, 'one, two...free four five', and all in. Charles Blackwell intro'd it the same at rehearsals, as per tape. But Freddy didn't. He'd forgotten how he'd done it on the tape. He didn't do it anything at all like it was on the tape. And who can blame him? I rarely do a song the same twice. I might add an extra piano solo, or go into the bridge again, or not, or whatever. After the 'one, two...free four five', which Charles Blackwell had to do hoping there was nobody out there who knew him from Music College, Freddy went for it.

He spun all around the stage while we desperately looked at each other wondering what the fuck was going to happen with this thing. Jim sort of pulled it together with a couple of great Rock 'n' Roll solos but Freddy wasn't stopping. I don't think he knew how to. It was Charles Blackwell raising and jabbing that conductor's arm that brought us all to a halt. All except Freddy, who continued round the stage in shadow boxing style until Jack Good jumped in like a 'second', flung his arms round him, calming him, while beckoning the crowd to show their appreciation.

The rest of the show didn't work either. The magic of the whole thing was supposed to be the spontaneity and in an ideal world it would have worked, but it ain't an ideal world. Next up was a young lady. She sung the whole song facing the band instead of the audience. None of it ever went out on air.

So yes, Big Jim Sullivan along with me and Dave and Ian Wallace (who was with King Crimson and went on to join Bob Dylan) were the Derek Lawrence session men of the '70s. One of the batch of sessions was an album with Labi Siffre. I remember Derek wanted to call the album, *A Dose of the Siffre*. Labi laughed. But I think Derek was serious. Labi did a good version of a song me and Dave wrote on this album, 'Old Time Song'. He also did a track he entitled 'I Got The'. It was a last minute filler track. Jim did one of his quirky funky arrangements of it which we all followed and thought no more about.

Many years later the riff we played popped up on a worldwide hit by Eminem. 'My Name Is'. Where he got the album from I don't know, but he liked the riff, sampled it and the rest is history. (I fuckin' hate that phrase, let me redo it.) He liked the riff, sampled it and how's y'father. (Much better.)

Big Jim wasn't only the session band leader, Jim was also in partnership with Derek. They ran Retreat Records which was a subsidiary of EMI. Derek and Jim wanted to produce an album with me and Dave for their label but I had definite ideas that I didn't fancy arguing out with a producer like, 'It's a big world out there. Do you think this singing in your own accent is a good thing?' They would get to Dave. 'Talk to Charlie. Try to get him to change his mind.' Dave would pass on the message and knowing me ol' pal I knew it was a case of, 'Well that's what they've asked me to do, so I've done it.'

But in the end, Derek and Jim said OK. You can have your head. Go in the studio and record your album.

What a great feeling!

Chapter 20

First Record Deal

Retreat Records was run by Derek and Jim from an office in De Lane Lea Studios, Wembley. Derek Lawrence also had a publishing company. Me and Dave found out later that this was no big deal. Anybody can start a publishing company. Which me and Dave did as soon as. The main reason for doing so is to ensure that we got paid. We publish it so the money comes straight to us. Also 100 per cent of it and not something like 50 per cent because half goes to the publisher. Who does fuck all. We've leased our publishing out a couple of times in the past when we needed extra cash for income tax or what have you and they promise you how they are going to work and get you covers and songs in films etc etc. But they don't. They are just a collection agency, which has its advantages, but they bullshit.

Except our New York Publisher, Stanley Mills. He is a descendant of the most famous American publishers in the last century, Mills Music. Stanley works a song he has on his books.

He has good old fashioned qualities like when publishers did work on the songs they had. He got our songs recorded by Tom Jones, Bobby Vinton, Queen Ida, (Zydeco, New Orleans music) and others. Not one other publisher we've been with has ever got us anything. Thanks Stanley! (and Judy.) See you soon.

Oh yeah...Derek... Until we wised up and formed our own publishing company here in Britain, we signed our new songs as we wrote them, to Derek. We'd go up to De Lane Lea for a session with another couple of songs in our pockets. Derek would say, 'Okay boys, the contracts already drawn up for the publishing of your new songs.' (Don't it sound great, we thought, us, having songs published!)

At this point a funny story comes to mind. This particular time we had arrived at De Lane Lea for a session. Couple of songs in pocket but mainly a demo record I wanted to play. Derek was in the bar.

'Go down to my office,' he said, 'There's a record player at the back. And you can meet my new secretary, Godzilla.'

I managed a wry smile, Derek Lawrence humour. Down to his office we went.

There behind his desk was a lovely girl. She really was. But she was big. She wasn't out of proportion big. She was well in proportion all over, but big! Now I'll pause here for a moment if I may. It could be classed as a 'What happened next?' moment. Let me give you a brief rundown. On Dave.

Now Dave always had this thing, which is nice, of making a point of remembering first names of new people we met and addressing them as such immediately. A friendly thing. In general I would have to ask twice what their name was. So, usually, if anybody was to get their name wrong after being introduced, it would be me. Dave knew this. At times could be almost cocky about it.

First Record Deal

So there was this great big girl behind the desk. I've smiled at her. 'I want to use the record player. Okay?' I was itching to hear this demo. 'Certainly,' she said. The record player was behind her on the window sill. As I'm studying the controls to find out how it works I heard Dave say the following (truly not believing my ears!) and in saying it he was making a double point to me. One, that I rudely didn't introduce myself and two, that I wouldn't have remembered her name anyway. 'Well then,' Dave's thinking, 'Just let me show him how to be a gentleman!'

'Pleased to meet you. I'm Dave. You're Godzilla aren't you?'

Dave! I don't believe it! My head was well into hearing that demo. But I stopped rigid in my tracks! An earthquake wouldn't have had the same effect! I looked at Dave. He was in front of her desk facing her. I was behind her facing him. Shaking my head and mouthing the word, 'NO!' But Dave was in one of his defiantly cocky moods. He knew I was looking at him but he wouldn't look at me. 'Charlie don't know. I do. I remember Derek telling us her name. He don't. Now, how can I remember it? Okay. When you die and go to heaven, God is going to look like Cilla Black.' (Dave does this. Actually I do too. When I want) 'God...Cilla! That's how I'll remember it.' And remember it he did! I'm shaking my head at him wildly but he's determined. 'Charlie's such a dope,' his expression says, 'Why don't he listen?'

'Pardon?' She said.

'I said I'm pleased to meet you Godzilla, my name's Dave.'

'I'm not Godzilla if you don't mind! My name's Cathy!'

For the first time Dave took on a look of, 'I think I'm not on safe ground any more.' He gave me a 'what now?' look.

'Cathy,' I said, 'I'm Chas by the way. Any idea how this record player works?'

169

'Try plugging it in Chas!' said Cathy.

Smiling our goodbyes we left the office ten minutes later. Outside I said to Dave, 'What on earth were you thinking about? Calling her Godzilla?'

'Well Derek said that was her name!'

Then it dawned on me.

'Dave. You don't know who Godzilla is do ya?'

'Well it's just a name ain't it? A Spanish sounding name.'

'It's an enormous monster in a horror film!'

Everybody in the world knew but Dave. Now everybody in the world knows. And Dave.

On 21 March 1974 my son Nicholas was born. So all was good in 1974. I've now got a son and two daughters and me and Dave were about to record our first self-penned album. What a buzz!

As I said 'One Fing 'n' Anuvver' was the first real 'Rockney' song and this became the title of the album. 'Gertcha' was probably the next. It was called 'Woorcha' on the album. We couldn't decide whether it should be Gertcha, Ertcha or Woortcha. But when that single came out we reckoned the most common usage of the 'word' was Gertcha. So that it became. But more on the single later.

We rented a cottage in Wales to write the bulk of the songs for the album. This idea of renting a cottage to write worked well for us. We did it for most albums. It was especially good in the later years when we had become 'famous'. We were doing loads of TV, radio, recordings, gigs, photo sessions, interviews. And a lot of these all in one day, every day! I remember thinking at the time 'How we gonna write in among all this?' But then we'd hire a cottage for a couple of weeks and it was heaven! All we had to do was write songs and go down the pub in the evening. No TV. No radio. No interviews. No photo sessions. I remember writing some lyrics to a song Dave started that summed it up.

One o' them days when I ain't gonna worry 'bout no one.

They can do as they like, and I'll do as I please.

Today I ain't gonna be part of that rat race.

I'm gonna please myself and do just what suits me.

We had a pretty good plan of survival on these writing vacations. We lived on stew which we both loved. I made the first one on arrival, say beef and vegetables and what was left went in the fridge. The next day it was topped up with maybe rabbit, or a bacon joint, more vegetables and so on. This was done daily so after two weeks you had a lovely mixture of the fortnight's daily repast. If you try it, don't try to keep cooking continually like they were supposed to have done in the old days, it begins to take on the flavour of mud. (We tried it.) When you've had your evening meal, let it get cold (in the fridge) and add more fresh veg and meat next day. Apparently this is where the saying 'Pot Luck' came from. 'What's for supper Ma?' 'Well the stew's been on the go for a few days now, so take pot luck.' Could be true. Wonder what would happen if you kept it going for years. You could be eating something that your Great-grandfather grew, or feasting on a now banned substance. In the way that although seatbelts have to be worn by law, I don't have to have them in my old 1943 Willys Jeep because of the age of it. What the fuck am I on about? Time to get back to where I was.

On the *One Fing 'n' Anuvver* album we used two studios. Advision in Gosfield street, W1 and De Lane Lea, Wembley. If one wasn't available then we'd book the other one and so on. It worked well, there were good engineers at both. With Dave's encouragement I went straight in the deep end with brass and string arrangements on this album. Before then I'd done a bit of brass arranging before with Cliff Bennett & The Rebel Rousers but had never done strings. I suggested to Dave that we get a proper arranger but he said no and that I should do it because the 'feeling' would be better. He was right. I set to work to learn how to 'score' music. Jim Sullivan gave me some tips on this, I got some books out of the library and away I went. I was pretty pleased with the result. In my experience before that when an outside arranger was brought in, a nice professional arrangement was provided, but it mainly showed off the talents of the arranger and that ain't how it is supposed to be. I do all the brass and string arrangements to this day and I always make sure that whatever I write is bringing out the flavour of the song/track. Making the warmer bits warmer, the exciting bits more so, and lifting any dull spots with a riff or an apt musical passage. A good arrangement cannot salvage a bad track but it can enhance it, and if it's a good track, enhance it tremendously. I love gigging, songwriting and recording. Arranging is another very exciting thing for me to do. Thanks Dave, for having faith in the early days that I could do it.

In the summer of 1974 the album was finished. It was released in 1975. Time to plug. Time for the people to hear what Chas & Dave have done. Chas & Dave's best mate Terry Adams played a big part in this, and indeed a big part in many things throughout our careers. His name will crop up many times from now on. Charlie Gillett in those days had a great Sunday morning radio show on Radio London, with well good guests like Professor Longhair, Carl Perkins and the like. Terry was and is a London cabby. 'Give me a copy of the LP and I'll drop It round to Charlie Gillett. He'll love it.'

Terry didn't just take it to the radio station, he knew where Charlie Gillett lived so he took it round his house. Charlie began to play it. Although he admitted he wasn't too sure on first hearing, it got hold of him enough to warrant a second listen. He began to play it more and we grew on him. He invited us into the studio one Sunday morning and we played a live session. As I said, it was a great radio show. For musicians and punters alike. Charlie would interview real players and performers and plug the bands gigs in and around London. People began to pay more attention to us. They'd come up and say, 'Great! We came down because we heard you on Charlie Gillett.' So a big thank you to Terry Adams and Charlie Gillett for playing an important part in getting us off the ground.

I remember saying something to Dave about then, and certain dawnings are magical. We were going into the West End for something or other. I remember exactly where we were. When something special happens you always do. We were driving along Albany Street. It hit me! 'Ain't it great!' I said, 'We are not just two blokes who want to make a record anymore. We're becoming a known duo.' Or an 'item' as they say today. (Although I always think of Paul and Heather when I hear that phrase. He was the first one I ever heard use it.) 'People are talking about "Chas & Dave". We're on our way!'

We were getting busier and more popular and we were enjoying it. It was around this time, I think the end of 1974, that I got a call from Albert Lee. He was now living in LA. He wanted me and Dave to go over to LA and do an album with him. Dough was negotiated and off we went for a couple of weeks. We did get some recording done, which appeared on an album he had out called *Hiding,* but we spent most of the time at the Palomino club or in the local honky tonks rocking and picking. We had a great time! I think our album *One Fing 'n' Anuvver* was released not long after we got back.

One Fing 'n' Anuvver didn't do no great shakes but it done a lot to establish this new 'item', Chas & Dave. The pub and club gigs were ticking over while we continued to write songs. Then, in 1976 we got offered a UK tour with 10 cc. By the way, this is when Mick Burt our drummer officially joined Chas & Dave. People often say why ain't it Chas, Dave & Mick? Well now you know. Mick's the new boy. Chas & Dave were established round the pubs and clubs for close on four years! Can't change the name now. Well, can yer? Anyway we're still trying him out.

In the middle of that tour we did a live radio interview for Swansea radio. Now the set up was this. We were to do it from Cardiff, and so to get a better voice sound, they set up two live microphones in a local AA office. Their questions we would be able to hear through telephones, but our answers they would hear through the microphones set up before us. So the interview commenced.

'We've got Chas & Dave on the line, currently on tour with 10 cc. How are you boys?' Chas & Dave: 'Fine, fine. Lovely, lovely.' DJ: 'And how's the tour going?' Now at this point both mine and Dave's telephones spit and crackle and we hear just dialling tones like you've been cut off or the caller's put the phone down, and because of the unusualness of the set up the live mike was completely forgotten about. When a phone cuts off and you can't hear them you naturally presume they can't hear you. But they could. Live!

'Fuckin' hell. It's gone dead!' I say to Dave. (We found out later that the DJ thought we were referring to the tour!) Then Dave's gone, 'What a cunt, Charlie. It started off so good.' Referring to the telephone interview and not the tour as the DJ thought. Unaware this was happening I've rung the radio station. 'Hello, this is Chas of Chas & Dave here. We've just been doing an interview here and...' At this point I got cut off again but this time with, 'Yes! And don't we know it! All hell's broken loose here! I don't know who you two think you are. Trying to cause a sensation!' With a shudder I realised they'd heard everything we'd said! 'But we'd forgotten the mikes were still on!' I reasoned. 'Some story! We ain't falling for that one!'

Next day, the DJ from Swansea drove to Cardiff to interview us in our hotel. I knew by his face he still didn't believe it was a genuine accident. This happened about a year before the Sex Pistols swore on the Bill Grundy show. Did we spark something off? But no. How could they ever have thought that Chas & Dave would resort to swearing? Bunch of cunts.

There was one or two wild hotel parties on that tour. I remember one instance wandering along the hotel corridor at two in the morning feeling happy, beer in one hand and cigar in the other, when coming towards me at a high speed was Dave being pushed on a trolley playing the banjo. I moved aside to let 'em pass. They did, then stopped and the trolley pusher knocked on a hotel room door. A man opened it. 'Sir! Room service, at your service. One banjo player, as ordered! Where do you want him wheeled to?' 'Piss off!' So they did, but four doors away repeated the whole thing over again. Apparently, it was said, that the trolley pusher and Dave continued this until breakfast time. I was proud of him.

Tour finished and back to the pubs and clubs. But that was alright. It would give us time to write for our next album. But Derek Lawrence's Retreat Records were beginning to wind down and would soon be winding up. Funny contradictory terms ain't they? Retreat Records were fucked. Who do we turn to?

We'd got to know Bob Mercer at EMI when he was looking after their subsidiary companies. Retreat Records being one of them. He would come down to the studio now and then. He liked what me and Dave were up to. Then he got promoted and at an EMI party he said to me if Derek goes under, come and see him. He'll give us a deal. So we did and so he did.

Great! We were now signed direct to EMI. We got a couple of grand advance. Dave spent his on a Gibson banjo and I spent mine on a Martin guitar and a Park Lines site hut that would go at the end of my garden for a music room. Like a couple of navvies me and Dave dug the trench to lay the electric cable and sawed great chunks of chipboard that would sandwich polystyrene on the walls and ceiling to soundproof it.

We didn't do a bad job at all. I bought an old stove to put in it and there was a compost heap outside the door where we could piss. I was into growing my own vegetables and still am. Natural piss helps the compost rot down nicely.

So all in all we had a nice little deal going on down there. Tea could be made and songs produced. Maybe after dark a Guinness or two. Bulldog Guinness was the bizzo. It had sediment. It matured in the bottle. Don't know if you can still get it but a bottle of it was like a day down Southend with Grandad. Life was good. In fact it was great. 1977. Great family. Joan and the kids. Kid 1: Juliet, 9. Kid 2: Kate, 5. Kid 3: Nicholas (Nik.) We lived in a nice little bungalow in Broxbourne and now I had my own music room at the end of the garden. The garden was about two hundred and fifty feet long and overlooked waste land and a fishing pit so we could make a reasonable amount of noise without complaint. Writing was a pleasure and now could be carried out at any time of the day or night.

We set to work and by the beginning of 1977 we'd written enough for a new album; but the money began to dry up. One option to get some money was to sell our publishing on our songs. We thought you had to sell or not in those days. We didn't know anything about leasing. Anyway, we hadn't had any hits so who's gonna lay out a lot of dough? One publisher was interested and said he would give us £2000 advance in exchange for 50 per cent of our publishing for life. We decided to go for it and arranged a meeting in a West End pub to clinch the deal. We were so skint and so naive.

But something happened. Or didn't happen that I'm so glad about to this day.

He didn't turn up.

I rang him up. He had forgotten about the appointment and was doing some work on his studio. It immediately felt to me like a last-minute reprieve. Dave was disappointed and I think he thought I was making the best of it when I said, 'There's a reason for this. It's for the best.' I just knew it was. I had a think and said, 'Let's jump on the tube and go and see John Darnley at EMI. John Darnley was the A&R man at EMI who was put in charge to look after us. John was a good nut. We told him of our plight.

'I think Bob Mercer thinks enough of you to help you out.' He said and called him immediately. John was right. Bob advanced us the extra dough we needed and we kept full control of our publishing. We would have given away a whole lot of money. And still be giving it away today. Thank you John and Bob.

The publisher, so we're told, still wakes up to this day in the midde of the night shouting, 'Rabbit, rabbit, rabbit, rabbit' until he's exhausted and goes back to sleep again. John Darnley wanted us to have a producer for the new album. Okay, we said, who? He came up with Tony Ashton. Now I'd known Tony on and off for a few years. I first met him at Joe Meek's, (see 'Chas Before Dave', the first half of this book, to find out about Joe Meek) when I was eighteen in 1962. Joe Meek had bought a new Lowry organ and said to us Outlaws, 'I've got a new young organist coming down from Blackpool to audition for me. Be nice to him.' He knew we were prone to fuck about. Doing numerous sessions in a day for pretty Joe Meek protégés proned us to fuck about. And if there isn't such a word as 'proned', well there is now. Tony introduced himself in a polite quiet way and sat down at the organ. Yes, we were nice to him. He could play. Never saw him at Joe Meek's after that though.

He had a hit some years after with Ashton, Gardner and Dyke, 'Resurrection Shuffle'. I'd done sessions with him. He was on the Jerry Lee London sessions with me in 1972. He did a piano duet with Jerry Lee on one song and Jerry Lee was impressed and paid him a compliment. Rare for Jerry Lee. I have been paid compliments by Jerry Lee which I list and treasure. I mention this because Jerry Lee is my hero and mentor. As described earlier I first saw him in 1958 when I was a fourteen-year-old kid playing guitar in a Skiffle group. It was then I knew I had to become a piano player. But it proved to be a lot harder than Skiffle guitar. Then, in 1963, I went on tour playing bass for him in Britain and Germany. (I know I've wandered from the plot, but I'm talking about Jerry Lee! Let me get it off my chest. I'll remember where I was. Don't worry.) That's when I really began to learn piano. Watching him every night. If any bits I couldn't quite see how he'd 'done it', I'd ask him. He'd show me once. My eagle eye would take note and I'd try it out on a piano as soon as I spotted one.

In 1967 I got a phone call from my Jerry Lee pal Terry Adams. Jerry Lee was coming over to England to do a TV show for Jack Good. (Yes, the same!) Terry had got talking to Jack Good. Jack Good had booked the studio with the big band, singers, dancers and everything for a week's rehearsal before the show. But Jerry Lee said he couldn't (or wouldn't) make the rehearsal. I think Jerry Lee was getting in a couple of days before but still Jack Good was panicking a bit. Terry said to Jack, 'I know someone who knows Jerry Lee inside out. He plays the piano and sings just like him. You could book him to rehearse with the band and everyone else on the show and he could clue Jerry Lee in as to what's happening when he arrives.' Jack Good said, 'Get the boy down here quick!'

Terry came round to see me. I was living at Cockfosters at the time in a flat above a shop with my wife Joan and our first born, Juliet, who was about six months old. The gig came in very handy. The Rebel Rousers had just split from Cliff Bennett and there wasn't a lot of work around. I can't remember the exact fee but I know the daily dough from the TV company was good. So I've gone to audition for Jack Good. (Now I'd forgotten all about this. Terry mentioned it a few months ago. I asked him what size shoes he took and could he lend me a pair as mine had holes in the bottom and the audition might require me to put my foot up on the piano! This sounds about right for me at the time. Don't know how I got around this. I take size eleven. Knowing Terry better now I think he takes about a size nine. I'll consult Terry and get back to you on this one. I'm seeing him Saturday down the 100 Club.)

Well, audition passed, I now held the proud position of Jerry Lee Lewis's understudy for the week. The first one I had to do, I think was something like 'Good Golly Miss Molly'. The big band played an instrumental in B flat then, bang! Straight in vocally. But this was to be a tone up, in C with no instrumental run in. Now I could do it by 'thinking' up a tone while the instrumental was going on and I did it but I said to Terry after, 'I think Jerry Lee's gonna have trouble with that. He'll need an instrumental run in to give him the key.' Terry told me to tell the bandleader. The bandleader just looked at me and smiled as if to say, 'Hang on sonny, how come you know what Jerry Lee can and can't do? 'Let's just wait until Jerry Lee arrives shall we?' He said, 'I'm sure he'll sort it out.' Jerry Lee did.

'Ah jess cain't come in like that! I need an instrumental run in! You jess wait for me while I play a piano chord and when I got the key we'll get this whole deal off the ground and rockin'!' There was more respect in the bandleader's eye for me after that.

I rehearsed for about three or four days and Jerry Lee arrived for I think the last two days rehearsal. At the end of the first day Jack Good came over to me and said, 'Chas! Can I ask you to do me a big favour?'(By the way, he did remember me from that show some five years ago. Couldn't remember giving me a bollocking but remembered me as a good bass player. Okay by me.)

'Chas, there's a song I want Jerry Lee to do but he says he hasn't got time to learn it. Would you take it home tonight, learn it and play it to Jerry Lee tomorrow? You see, when he sees you can do it, he'll do it. He won't let no whippersnapper youngster beat him at his own game. If he don't do it, you can do it on the show.' I had no aspirations of being a solo performer at the time, but yes, I was up for it. So off I went home with the recording of the song and learned it. It was a song by Sheb Wooley. This is how it went.

A group of liberal thinkers, bathless unwashed stinkers, got together for a love in near our town.

There were rows and rows of hippies, some yippies and some gippies. At the day trippers, wine sippers, society spurners, card burners, liberal thinkers love in near our town.

One super hippie fella, his hair was long and yella, and a ringlet from his left ear dangled down.

On his arm he had a real hip chick, wearing psychedelic lipstick. (At the day trippers, etc.)

Long haired, head banded hippies, and flower wearing yippies. Togetherness was visible all around.

But I tell you what the worst is, there were fellas carrying purses! (At the day trippers, etc.)

Next day we gathered in a room with a piano. Jack Good, Jerry Lee, one or two Jerry Lee fans and me.

'Chas has got something to play you Jerry Lee. He went home and learnt that song last night. He'll show you how it goes. Come up to the piano Chas.' I did. Surprisingly not nervous at all. I went through it from start to finish without a hitch.

There are around today some who witnessed what my hero said next. 'Well Mr Good, all I can say is, what do you need me for?' Can't remember what was said next, but in next to no time Jerry Lee was on the piano playing the song. With a wink at me, he stuck some cheeky extra chords in. The show never went on air because of a TV strike but I done alright out of it and enjoyed every minute.

We did a one-off live show with him before he went back home, at Kempton Park. Me on bass, Micky Burt on drums and Kenny Lovelace on guitar. Kenny had just joined Jerry Lee and it was his first trip to England, I found out later. Kenny has become a good friend of mine and has been with Jerry Lee over forty years now. He still remembers that first gig we all did together. Jerry Lee had a current hit in the States at the time, 'What made Milwaukee famous'. He wanted to do it that day at Kempton Park. Kenny asked me if I had heard it. I hadn't, but I said put me in view of Jerry Lee's left hand and I won't miss a note. I didn't. Kenny remembers it to this day. 'You said you wouldn't miss a note and you didn't Chas!' It was a great gig. Shame it didn't get recorded. Micky Burt played superb and Jerry Lee said he was the best drummer he'd ever worked with.

The next time I worked with Jerry Lee was on the *London Sessions* album in 1972. Loads of early '70s and late '60s superstars and some not so super at the time were on it. The highlight for me was when Jerry Lee was running through 'Bad Moon Rising'. I was positioned just behind him in sight of his left hand as usual. I was, without realising it, singing along in harmony. 'Get the killer a microphone!' said Jerry Lee and I sang harmony with him on the record.

Just one more Jerry Lee bit for the moment. He quotes me as his all-time favourite bass player. How do I know? His guitar player Kenny Lovelace told me. That's good enough for me.

Now where was I? You've forgotten ain't ya? No not me. You. I ain't! It is 1977 and me and Dave are about to go into the studio to record the *Rockney* album with Tony Ashton as the producer, who played on the Jerry Lee *London Sessions*.

Chapter 21

Second Record Deal

Tony Ashton was a lovely man and was one of the great piss artists of the music world. Catch him sober, or half sober, or half pissed. (The last two phrases mean the same don't they? Or do they? Do you consider your glass half empty or half full? I think I've got it. The first one says, 'I'm going home after this one.' – and the second one says, 'I'll have another drink after this.') And Tony had some good production ideas but you had to grab 'em quick before the 'This glass is half full, and I've had enough' time and he was ready to go home and leave it. Me and Dave would rock 'til dawn in the studio whether we were on booze or coffee or both.

Tony would turn up dressed differently each night. One night he'd turn up as a city gent. The next night a follower of flower power. The next night like someone out of Dickens. I don't think anyone ever mentioned it. It was Tony's normal way of going about.

Mark Dearnley was the engineer on that album. He was

great. He got a great sound on the fart noise on strumming. Early sort of 'chorus' effect. 'Great!' said Tony. 'A real "pan" job!' Mark got other good sounds as well.

We recorded that album at Roundhouse studios, Chalk Farm Road. It was finished in 1977. We gave it to EMI and waited to hear. And waited. And waited. In the meantime we got back pubbing and clubbing it and enjoying ourselves.

EMI I knew were not sure what to do with it. It was nothing like anything they'd had to deal with before. They couldn't pigeonhole it. But people were beginning to talk favourably about Chas & Dave. If there was a deciding factor that swayed them to the side of, 'Yes, we want to release this album', I think it was this.

When John Darnley was first commissioned by EMI to be the A&R man for Chas & Dave he said he wanted to come to see us play live. We'd just begun to do a regular gig at the Essex Arms, Canning Town, Thursday nights. John came down to see us on the second Thursday we did it. We all had a good time but I don't think there was a dozen people in there. The next time he came down was about six weeks later. In the meantime we'd been getting plugs by Charlie Gillett on Radio London and good feedback was building up in general.

John Darnley arrived at the Essex Arms but couldn't get in the door. The place was packed. There were bands there and all kinds of musicians. Albert Lee came down with Don Everly of the Everly Brothers. My Mum played piano in the interval. Don Everly came up to me after and said, 'There's a song I heard tonight that's bugging me. I really liked it. I think I've heard it before but I can't think where.' I thought, great! He liked what we done! I rattled off some songs from our set to try to find out which one he was talking about. 'No,' he said, 'It wasn't in your set. It was one your Mum played. She sung it too.' He thought we were okay but my Mum was the star! The song turned out to be, 'Just a Little Loving'. I found out Eddie Arnold had a hit with it in the late forties.

So anyway, there was John Darnley, staring through the window of the pub. Couldn't get in. Place was packed and rocking. Albert Lee was on stage with us at the time. Now in the space of six weeks the Essex Arms had gone from an audience of a dozen polite punters to a heaving mass of rockers. And all on our own steam. My guess was he was thinking, 'If they can do this on their own, with our help they can do this all round the country.' Then went back to the office next day and told them so. Because on the following Monday I got a phone call saying, 'We love your album and want to release it as soon as possible.' Well done John. So the *Rockney* album was released and it started getting plays.

Peter Clayton, mainly a jazz critic, played a couple of tracks on his Sunday show and commented on it very favourably. We were chuffed with this. We were both fans of Peter Clayton. Then Simon Bates on Radio One picked up on 'Strummin'. He said, on air, if Chas & Dave put this out as a single, he would make it his record of the week. This gives you an idea of the mixed market we'd made for ourselves. It suited us but confused a lot of the people in the business that like to pigeonhole you as soon as possible.

So 'Strummin' was released and we got our first *Top of the Pops*. On 11 November 1978 'Strummin' peaked at number 52 in the national charts and our feet were planted in the novelty slot. This will be easy to shake off. We've got too many good songs. But would it? Or would it even matter?

Chapter 22

Bob England and 'Gertcha!'

It was a couple of months before 'Strummin' charted that we signed a management deal with Bob England. He was managing Darts at the time and they were getting hits. Terry Adams spotted him. He promoted the Jerry Lee Lewis tour in 1977. Terry said Jerry Lee was impressed with him. Terry knew we were looking for management and suggested him to us. It sounded like a good idea to us so Terry went round to Bob's office and got him to come and see us at the 100 Club in Oxford Street. We clicked and signed a five-year deal.

Now Bob was a bit like Del boy. Had a bit more taste than Del Boy, but not much. He even had similar movements and facial expressions. His game was, if there was money to be made out of a project, then that was all that mattered. For instance, someone might call the office and say, 'I want Chas & Dave dressed as Pearly Kings strolling down the Old Kent road singing the Lambeth Walk and I'll guarantee news coverage plus £5000.' He'd say 'Got a good one boys! This one's good profile'

'How good?' we'd say. 'Well, £5000 good and TV coverage. All you've got to do is…' Here we go. 'But Bob, we don't wanna do it. It ain't what we're all about.' 'So what then? All of a sudden you're ashamed of your roots? You're Londoners. Pearly Kings are London. This is a real Bums on Seats project and you're getting paid for it! £5000! I'm your manager. I'm getting you good paid work plus publicity and you're turning it down?'

And so we'd battle through. But he was a grafter. Dave would get humpy and talk to me. 'Why does he keep putting forward these crappy ideas to us?' My philosophy was sooner have to keep turning down stuff, than have a manager like we had briefly before, Bill Hurly who managed Smokey, who came up with not much at all. Sooner be on the phone turning down work for whatever reason than being on the phone saying, 'Have you got any?' As I said, Bob was a grafter, and usually sooner rather than later, he'd come up with something we were happy with.

In early 1979 Courage brewers put out a TV advert using 'Gertcha' to plug their Courage Best. It was a good ad. A man from the BMP advertising agency, Dave Trott, had seen us playing 'Gertcha'(or 'Woortcha') at the Oxford Arms in the East End. As I said earlier we changed it later to 'Gertcha' because we decided it was the more common usage of the word. He said he would like to use it for a Courage beer ad. We gave him our manager's number and thought no more about it, like you do. But this proved to be one of the few true promises. We were told about the style of the ad and as the ad came about because of the song and not the other way round, we knew it would reflect 'us'. The verse and meaning for the ad was acceptable. Sort of 'Gertcha!', you wimpy little bastard, drinking a girl's drink. Have a pint of beer. In real life it don't matter, but in the song writing world it's great playing a part or writing about somebody else's experience as though it were yourself. There are a lot of blokes that will say, 'Don't bring that poofy little git along with his gin and tonics, how we gonna pull anything with him around?' That is the beauty of song writing. You can be what or whoever you want to be and you don't have to necessarily agree with the sentiments of the person you are portraying. 'Gertcha' in fact was a good proportion of how Dave's Dad would have used the word. Dave just wrote 'em down and I added a few of my Grandad's. Then we picked out the best and left out the rest.

'Gertcha' was a word all my uncles and aunts used 'over Hackney', as I'd say. Same as Dave's Dad, uncles and aunts in and around Ponders End and Enfield. It was a very common word in those days. It was a polite way of saying, 'Get out of it you little bastard!' or 'Fuck off!' It was the first word that come to mind if you opened up your front door and a dog was having a shit on your step. 'Get out of it you little bastard!' became squeezed in and chopped to make one short frightening shout. 'Gertcha!' 'Get out of it you!' 'Get out you!' 'Gertyou!' And so…'*Gertcha*!' That said, the foot swung out towards the dog's arse. Well wasteful though. The dog was ten houses away. Good word that. We wrote the song originally to make Jim Sullivan laugh as we'd all been using the word for a giggle in the studio some weeks before. He remembered his relatives using it. It became a real 'Rockney' 'in' word and the perfect title for a Chas & Dave song. All we had to do was write it. So we did. The album recording,'Woortcha!', was slow and funky, but when we went into the studio to do the TV ad, it had to be sped up some to fit the gist into the allotted twenty-eight and a half seconds of advertising time. It's amazing how precise you can get when you have to. After three or four takes we got it to exactly twenty-eight and a half seconds. The big bonus was it was all the better for it. It had energy and was more Rock 'n' Roll.

The ad began to get popular. People loved it. Then Bob England turned up at a gig one night and said EMI wanted to put it out as a single. The album version. The slow 'Woortcha'. Dave wasn't too bothered but I said, 'That can't go out! It's the 'ad' version people like! It's much better. We've got to re-record it!' 'There's no time,'said Bob, 'They want it out immediately.' 'Then we'll record it immediately!' I said. 'It will have to be tomorrow,' said Bob. 'Okay. tomorrow!' 'Where?' 'Anywhere!'

Next day Bob rang and said he'd booked us in Portland Studios W1 at 3pm that day. And so we met for the first time Andy Miller who was to engineer many albums for us after this initial session and it was Chas & Dave's first visit to the studio that was to be our recording home for the next few years. Until the end of its life as a studio anyway, at the end of the '80s. It had been a studio since the '50s and possibly the '40s. I recorded there when it was IBC in the '60s with The Outlaws and others. Glyn Johns was engineering. An alright bloke. He liked me anyway.

So in we went at 3 o'clock. When we told Andy what we were going to do he was knocked out. He said it would be a hit even if we recorded it live on a cassette. So with a big buzz we started. Before pub time not only had we put a great 'Gertcha' track down, but we finished writing a song that Dave had started, 'The Banging in the Head'. Then we put down that track too and went out the back way for the first time to the Devonshire Arms in Devonshire Mews for a deserved pint. (This pub was going to figure high in our session breaks in the next few years!)

After not long we were back in the studio vocalising. In no time we had finished and mixed 'em both. The best way to record. There's nothing like it when you're buzzing. Everything just flows and it comes straight back off that record everytime you play it. We left a 7½ i.p.s. quarter-inch tape of the finished mixes for Bob to get picked up and listen to next day. I wrote on it, 'We done it! Here's to Top of the Pops!' I rang him as soon as I got up. Sue England answered, his sister. She worked at the office. A lovely girl. 'Has Bob heard the tape Sue?' 'Heard it? He's been dancing round the office for the last two hours making "whooping" noises only stopping to play the tape all over again! I'll see if I can calm him enough to come to the phone!' Then: (Bob) 'Charlie it's fantastic! Fuckin' hell! Fuckin' hell!'

It seemed more and more that we were heading for our first real hit!

It was released around the beginning of May 1979. It started getting plays. Chas & Dave phone calls were becoming more and more regular in the office. Only this time it was them calling Bob and not Bob calling them. As the record snuck up the charts, more and more stuff was coming in. Interviews, radio spots, TV spots. All stuff we'd been doing but could've done more of. Now there wasn't enough time in the day to do a fraction of what we were being offered. Overnight it seemed, it was all happening.

I remember likening it to pushing a car up a hill. Little by little, bit by bit you were getting there. Slow maybe, but you were getting there. Then you reach the top of the hill and your car, (your career) now takes on a life of its own. It begins to run away down the other side of the hill and you've got to really fight to keep it under control.

Then it was *Top of the Pops* time with 'Gertcha'. We did it once with 'Strummin' but we were about to do a few with 'Gertcha'. We always insisted that we played live on TV recordings. The TV people didn't really want you to and most bands didn't want to either. Neither had the confidence. The bands didn't have the confidence to play and the TV people didn't have the confidence to balance a good sound. The current thinking was that bands spent a month in the studio doing one track, consequently no one in the TV world could mix an instant good sound because they never got the chance to try as no bands did it. They were frightened to. But we wanted to play live and when we insisted they shit themselves and said they hadn't got enough mikes etc. So with some persuasion from our management, who could see a potential hit record taking a dive, I was talked into by those around me into using a backing track. But I made sure the vocals had to be live. So we did our first 'Gertcha!' on *Top of the Pops*.

Now this next proviso might have been the reason why they let us do the vocals live. We were told just before the recording that we mustn't say the word 'Cowson.' Yes, someone had spotted this old fashioned swear word that we were trying to bring back in fashion. Who spotted it for fuck sake? Turned out to be the producer's Mum. She heard it on the radio and rang him up. 'Make 'em cut it out son, there's a good boy.' So we weren't allowed to say 'Cowson' on the recording. So what do we say instead? 'Give me some alternatives,' said the producer. 'Okay, how about 'Gertcha wanker' 'No!' 'Gertcha shit bag?' 'No!' 'Gertcha git face?' 'No!' 'Why can't we just say 'Cowson' like the record?' 'Because you can't!' So we decided on leaving it blank where the word 'Cowson' should be. We rehearsed it and it worked reasonably. 'That's fine. I'm sure my mother won't be offended by that. Break for lunch everybody, back at 2 o'clock!' They didn't need us for the afternoon rehearsal so it was back in the evening for the real thing.

Our turn came. Nice lively crowd. Way we went, 'Now

there's a word that I don't understand...' Crowd responding well, get to the chorus, 'Gertcha Cowson...' 'Cut!Cut! Chas & Dave! I told you no Cowson!' 'Sorry!' I said. 'I completely forgot!' I had too. 'Go again! Roll cameras. Chas & Dave. Cue!' 'Now there's a word that I don't understand...' Crowd responding well, get to the chorus, 'Gertcha Cowson...' 'Cut!' Oh fuck it! I've done it again! 'Chas, I know you're doing it on purpose hoping I won't notice it but it won't wash!' I wasn't doing it on purpose! I'd been so used to singing it like that on stage and what with the excitement of the show, 'I'm not doing it on purpose! Honestly! It just...' 'One more "Cowson" and you're off the show!'

They never believe us do they? They didn't on that Swansea radio show that time did they?

Well we finally did it. Not a 'Cowson' in sight. I nearly did it once though. I bit my lip and my eyes did roll but both my lips were tight. I saw it on telly the other day on *Top of the Pops 2*. It was quite effective. A real producer's Mum-pleaser.

'Gertcha' charted in May 1979 and peaked at number 20. (Good ol' *Guinness Book of Hit Singles*, thanks!) As well as *Top of the Pops* we did quite a bit of other TV on it and 'Gertcha' got us well established. We supported Eric Clapton on tour that year and Led Zeppelin at Knebworth.

It was at Knebworth with the Led Zeps that 'The Bollocks Song' was born. Well, at least the title. We did it two weeks running. The first week, us, we found it hard to get the crowd's full attention. Fair enough some might say, that's normal for a support act. They were here to see the Led Zeps. Any distraction would turn their heads elsewhere. Their heads were turned elsewhere. While we were on stage, a fire broke out at the back of the field. A good portion of 'em turned to look at the fire. A smattering of applause from the ones who didn't at the end of our set was appreciated, but on the whole I was not happy. We hadn't disgraced ourselves, it was a normal 'only the support act, to be took not a lot of notice of, and they're only there to kill time before the act we've come to see are on.'

But that wasn't good enough for me. When we found out a couple of days later that we were going to be back the next week for another go, I thought, 'Great! Another chance! We need an attention grabber.' Now, a swearword always commands attention. 'Listen here you cunts!' Would swivel heads but then what? No, that ain't no good. So let's work on the swearword. How about 'Bollocks'? Perfect. Not an aggressive word but still taboo enough (in 1979) to offend quite a few people. Lovely. Sex Pistols helped out here. Next move, full attention grabber, get 'em all too shout it out. How? (My brain really did work all this out like this. It was worth it.) Now I drew on a Bob Dylan interview I heard on the radio some years before when he said one-word titles of songs were a good idea and also thinking of the title first can also be a good idea. That in fact sparked off the idea of 'Gertcha'. We had the one-word title first. 'Bollocks' was a perfect one-word title. It was week number two at Knebworth. When we were a couple of numbers into the set I announced to the crowd that I needed their help. They were actually paying pretty good attention this time. We had quite a few of them but not most of them. This got most of 'em. I said, 'We're working on a follow up to 'Gertcha'. It's another one-word title. We're gonna record it live and we're gonna have audience participation where everybody shouts the title. We're gonna test it out on you. After a count of three, all shout it out, ONE, TWO...Sorry! I forgot to tell you. The song is called, "BOLLOCKS!"...ONE, TWO, THREE!'...'BOLLOCKS!' the crowd hollered back. It was good! 'One more, ONE, TWO, THREE!' And the ones who didn't shout first time suddenly wondered why they didn't then, 'BOLLOCKS!' Even better! 'One more time?' 'YEAH!' 'ONE, TWO, THREE'…'BOLLOCKS!' It was bollockmania.

Follow that Led Zeppos!

The 'Bollocks Song' aside, what did me and Dave think the next single should be? We reckoned 'The Sideboard Song'. It had to be. Me and Dave had a big buzz for it. I would say we had more fun writing this song than any other. We wrote it in the summer of 1978 in a cottage we rented for the purpose in a little village called Ashington in West Sussex. We started to write 'Rabbit' in that cottage too. We virtually finished 'Wallop' in that cottage too. That was inspired by Uncle (cousin, but I'd always known him as 'Uncle') Charlie, a spitfire pilot in the war. He was telling me and Dave one time about a fracas he'd had outside his house the week before. 'These cheeky little cunts started coming at me. One's took a swing. I've grabbed hold of him. Pop! He's gawn down. Another one's swung out. I've caught hold of his arm and let him have it. Pop! He's gawn down. The other one legged it.' 'What were they doing Charlie?' Picturing serious thugs. 'Fucking about with the lights on my lorry. Bleeding kids!' So of course we had to write a song about it! Just changed the 'Pop' to 'Wallop.' It fitted the rhythm better.

Going away to the country to write when it became close to 'new album' time was perfect for us. Dave always said the same thing, (tho' he won't realise it, until he reads this!) 'Every time we go away to write, I don't wanna go. But then when it's time to go home I don't wanna go home either!'

The night we wrote the 'Sideboard Song' we'd come back from the pub with a few bottles of Guinness. I drank a couple of bottles and dozed off in a chair. Waking up, I said to Dave, who was looking at his writing book, 'Got anything happening

Dave?' 'Dunno really, might be the start of something. Sort of a Cajunny feel.' I had a look at his words. 'Skinny little belly now it's sticking out the front.' Well, what rhymes with front? Yes. Conjures up quite a good line actually. Makes sense but can't have that. Well I liked the metre but the words needed sorting out. Then from out of nowhere I went. 'I don't care, I don't care, got my beer in the sideboard here!' Dave jumped out of his chair and was dancing round the front room like a nutter! I got up and joined him. 'I don't care, I don't care, I don't care if he comes round here, Got my beer in the sideboard here, let mother sort it out if he comes round here!' We chanted almost simultaneously. 'Hang on!' says Dave, 'Hang on. I've got some more ideas on it!' 'So have I!' I said. 'We'll go in different rooms!' We did. We came back with identical ideas! The 'crossover' bit where Dave does one bit and I sing another but it all fits. Fuck me! We went wild! The whole song was finished in no time. We put it on tape and played it 'til the dawn came up. Even went to bed and put it on to 'continuous' play.

The 'Sideboard Song' came out but didn't do as good as we'd hoped chart-wise. The highest it got was number 55 in September 1979. But it goes to show that chart positions have little to do with longevity. It's top of the list today. When we play it live, punters dance around like nutters like me and Dave did when we wrote it in that cottage in West Sussex thirty years ago!

Around that time we went on tour with Lindisfarne. They had a Newcastle Brown image like we acquired a Courage Best image. It could be a pain at times. They had the same problems as us. They'd arrive at a gig, as we would, around three or four in the afternoon, the promoter would say, 'I know what you like boys, it's all laid on. In fact they're already poured out!' There would be all the pints lined up when all you really wanted at that time of day was a cup of tea.

But after sundown, beer feelings beckon and suddenly it all seems to be such a good idea. Many a hotel has refused us return bookings. But it will always be. Some people like live music at two o'clock in the morning and some don't.

Lindisfarne were master songwriters. Their songs were like classical folk songs. Alan Hull once said, and I was inclined to agree with him in general: 'You've got the best musicians down south but we've got the best writers in the north.'

I love writing but mastering a musical passage (there again, one that I've written), whether it be on guitar or piano, gives me the finest buzz. I don't really know what I've just said, but it's the sort of thing that if I said it on an interview, the interviewer would nod in agreement.

We toured in the Lindisfarne tour bus and at the time one of them had a real ale guide. Around lunch time, certain days, on the way to the next gig, the bus driver would be guided towards real ale. From directions in the guide book, he'd squeeze the bus round country roads, tractor tracks and bike lanes to reach some quaint old inn with an original one arm bandit and a barrel of real ale ready to go. So what I said earlier about only wanting tea in the afternoon was partly bollocks.

That reminds me. We continued the audience participation that we began on the Led Zeppo's gig on this tour. 'BOLLOCKS' was proving to be a winner. In fact all our act was sprinkled with a few swearwords here and there. Nothing aggressive. All in fun. We did get the odd complaint though. At Newcastle City Hall a woman walked out at the beginning of our set. We let slip one or two expletives and she was off to see the manager. She found Mike Elliot (a great Geordie) who was compere/comedian on the show. He related all this to us later. He said he had hell's work calming her down. She'd 'never been so disgusted in all her life, the Newcastle City Hall should be ashamed of itself!' and she was going to report it to the local paper. Mike turned on his full Geordie charm and it done the trick.

'Madam, believe me, they are lovely fellas. Please go back and see the rest of their show because you are missing some lovely songs.'

She finally gave in and allowed herself to be led back to the auditorium. Mike opened the door for her and at the exact moment she re-entered, the whole of Newcastle City Hall shouted, 'BOLLOCKS!' Chas & Dave were in 'audience participation' mode. That's what I call timing.

The Lindisfarne tour was over at the end of '79 and a great time had by everybody. Now the '80s were here.

Around the spring of 1980, our recording contract with EMI was to expire and was up for renewal. Bob England, our manager, negotiated a new deal which we were all happy with. We'd had a couple of singles out that didn't chart, but now we had 'Rabbit' in the can. Then Courage Best clamoured for it and an ad was filmed. Another mini video for our single. Free plugging. In those days thirty seconds on prime time viewing cost advertisers around £10,000. It's probably ten or more times than that now. These ads got our songs across to people with minimal lyric change, they were shot around our song, and we got paid for it. We had that good feeling of, 'It's hit time again!' But things were about to get held up. EMI, (since the negotiation of our contract) had been taken over by Thorn Electronics, who had different plans for a lot of the music acts they had acquired.

Our manager got a letter from them saying they know we'd been offered a new deal by EMI but disregard it. This is the deal that is now being offered. It was crap. Bob said it was an insult. So we turned it down and went to PRT. They shuffled about, made unpositive grunts and in the end, faded away.

This was to be another occasion that at the time seemed a

major disaster, but most certainly wasn't. Although we didn't know it at the time, it was to prove invaluable. To this day me & Dave own 90 per cent of our own recordings. (EMI have the other 10 per cent.) If we had signed to any of these companies, they would have owned everything with me and Dave just on a royalty percentage. But this is the norm. Everybody from The Beatles downwards signed to record companies. That's what you did. It was the only way to get a record out. Unless you had your own Record Company. *UNLESS YOU HAD YOUR OWN RECORD COMPANY!* Bob came up with the suggestion.

Bob had and was having success with the British 'do wop' band Darts. He had money coming in and needed to spend some before the tax man got it. He said he'd always fancied having a record company and he felt the timing was right. Why don't us three become 'Rockney Records'? And so we did.

Bob grafted to get the company properly up and running before we released anything, which was going to be 'Rabbit'. In the meantime there was plenty to do for me and Dave. In between gigs we were ready to record songs we had written. But there was no real pressure as we already had the next single in the can. Then I responded to a call I got from Mike Berry to produce three or four tracks for him. He was after getting a single out of it.

Mike wanted me purely as a producer. This would be a nice thing to do while the wheels on Rockney Records were beginning to turn. Mike had three or four songs which were OK, but I was convinced that 'Sunshine of your Smile' was a hit song and I wanted him to do it. After I heard my Mum play that verse at that pub in Gravesend a few years back I got her to show me the chords and I began to play it here and there. People began to comment favourably without being asked 'What do you think of this?' It's then that you begin to know that you're right. The first time it happened was in Los Angeles when we were staying at Joe Cocker's house getting songs together for Albert Lee's album. I was sitting at the piano one afternoon and I began playing it. Pete Gavin, who I was in Heads Hands & Feet with, said, 'That's a nice song Charlie. Where did that come from?' I told him. It impressed me and got me thinking more about the song's commercial potential. Pete Gavin. An off the wall bloke. Great drummer. Not the sort of bloke I would have thought to pick up on this song. But he did.

Albert Lee did record it in LA but it didn't go no farther. Me and Dave started doing it in the act. A sort of reggae style version. It got requests. When I played it to Mike he wasn't enamoured with it. But my enthusiasm got him humming. I began working on an arrangement of it while me and Dave were on the road. Acoustic Martin guitar became the intro, a 2/4 , 4/4 timing piece I worked out. I played all instruments on it apart from drums. I didn't play strings but I arranged the part. It was four violins and two cellos (or 'celli' as Jim Sullivan taught me). As somebody remarked later, 'It was a very commercial "pit orchestra" sound.' I didn't say to myself, 'I want a pit orchestra sound,' but yes, that sound must have been at the back of my head because of my Mum taking me as a young kid in the '50s to the Hackney Empire and the Finsbury Park Empire to see acts like Joseph Lock, Arthur English, Rose Murphy and Peter Sellers. The pit orchestra was there to play 'em on and off, and during if they wanted, as Joseph Lock the Welsh tenor did. The string section was small in those theatres for economy reasons and every player had to *play*. No hiding behind anybody like some have been known to do in big orchestras. I like the sound better. It is really 'up front'. On Mike Berry's session I put the track down singing the lead line. Just me and drums. After overdubs, my voice was replaced with

Mike Berry's. A couple of careful mixes and it was finished. It was a hit. It made the top ten in August 1980.

Meanwhile, back at Rockney Records, Bob was bubbling under. Rockney Records was ready for its first release. 'Rabbit!'

As I said, 'Rabbit' began to come into existence the same week the 'Sideboard Song' did, in that cottage in Ashington, in the summer of '78. Because of the 'Sideboard Song' being the one to go with at the time, 'Rabbit' was put in the pending department like songs do get properly put. Now 'Rabbit' was about to come out and become an 'in your shops now!' record.

So fill in the gaps Chas. How did it get from an idea to the finished recording? Let's start in that cottage in 1978. Dave had some words about someone who talked a lot and was known as a 'Jaw me Dead'. Not terribly awe inspiring but he had a start of something. That's how we did it. Anything goes until something takes shape. Right, rather than 'Jaw me dead' which sounds like an old girl you'd sooner not meet on the street, how about the most beautiful and sexy girl you would love to meet on the street, but she don't ever stop talking. Or rabbiting. Yes that's it! 'Rabbit!' What a good title! This could be an English version of that American Rock 'n' Roll song, 'You talk too much!' So we chucked words back and forth 'til we felt we were getting there. Or getting near to there. I remember coming up with the line, 'You got more rabbit than Sainsbury's' and discarding it as I said it. But Dave liked it. So did a lot of other people since.

I'm still not mad on it, but it's passable. That was our unwritten rule on a line, a word or phrase. Both love it? It's in. One loves it, one thinks it's passable. It's in. One loves it, one thinks it's crap. It's out. Two passables? Will do for the present until something else comes up. So, song finished and arranged, it was now ready for the recording studio.

Dave had come up with a nice bass riff for the intro and in between chorus and verse throughout. We settled on a laid back Rock 'n' Roll feel.[4]

True to our style, track finished, over the pub for a beer (Devonshire Arms out back in the Mews), then back for vocals and mix time. As Andy Miller was balancing the mix, Dave began to mouth eight to the bar 'rabbits' on the fade out.

'Great idea!' I said.

'No good,' said Dave.' It's impossible to do 'em that fast.' But he'd started me off and I wasn't letting go. In my head it sounded so good. There's got to be a way.

'Wait, wait...what if you do four rabbits to the bar on the '*on*' beat, and I do four rabbits to the bar on the '*off*' beat. Let's go down into the studio and try it. Hold the mix Andy!'

We ran downstairs into the studio and Andy fired up the mike. After about five or six goes we got it near something worth having a listen to. We heard the playback and a couple of times we got it dead right. It was so effective that I said to Dave it can't be just used on the fade. It would be such a waste. It's got to be a major part of the song. So it was used right on the intro, after chorus's and on the fade. Then we mixed it.

Then we all looked at each other with big grins on our faces. We knew we had created another hit! It was played continually

---

4 Today, (2008). Just got back an hour ago from a gig in Coolham, West Sussex. Big Jim Sullivan lives there now. Me, Dave and Mick done a gig in his village hall. Jim got up and played and our old talented mate Jackie Lynton got up and sang. It was a great night. We are going to make it a yearly event. Coincidence:We were just five miles away from Ashington where we wrote the 'Sideboard Song' and began 'Rabbit'. Me and Dave drove down to find the cottage we'd hired over thirty years ago. It had changed a bit but we found it.

all the way home in the band wagon, like we always did after the night's recordings, on the journey home.

That version became the album version. We re-recorded it a couple of weeks later for a Courage beer promotion. Then we decided that this version was perfect for the single. It was shorter by one verse and had a more 'live' feel.

Just before 'Rabbit' was released we went on tour with Eric Clapton. Around May 1980. It was in Eric's drinking days. And he sure was drinking. He's straight now and he's here because he is. Large vodkas for breakfast can seem like a fun way to start the day, but at the end of the day, a good way of putting it, you realise they ain't. Dave used to laugh at Eric when we'd stop at a motorway cafe and Eric would order a big sausage and chips dinner and then say, 'I'll beat that Burtie!' (Micky Burt. Who *could* eat.) But poor Eric at the time knew he should be eating but only wanted to drink. But he's alright now. Albert Lee was on that tour. In Eric's band. Albert would join in with me and Dave at the end of our set. He was my pal from days of old and became a pal of Dave's. We played together years ago. But Eric got a bit upset. 'How comes you don't invite me up? It's always Albert all the time.' Of course we loved Eric's playing as well as Albert's but obviously thought it would take the edge off his show if he came on stage beforehand. 'I don't care about that, I wanna come on with you.' So from then on both Albert and Eric joined us at the end of our set.

Not long after that tour, 'Rabbit' was released and great! It started to creep into the charts. But it also gained some controversiality (don't know if that's a word, but it is now) that we didn't expect. As it began to rise up the charts it began to rise up the snouts of a few feminists. Letters in newspapers began to appear.

'Chas & Dave's song is exactly what the typical male attitude is today. They want their women to be quiet. Totally uninterested in what she has to say!'

Eh? We're only having a laugh! There ain't no serious message in this one darling! It's an out and out comic Rock 'n' Roll Rockney song! Our wives think it's great! Me and Dave felt it could be an English version of a song Lieber & Stoller might have written for the Coasters years ago.

Then as it continued to rise we got a call from Radio One. They wanted us to do our whole show live from The London University. The date was fixed. But the day before the recording, a worried BBC producer rang our office. They'd had phone calls from a feminist group saying that if the Chas & Dave concert went ahead, they were going to disrupt it in a big way. 'So for safety's sake, can the boys record the whole thing in the afternoon, so in case of major disruption while going out live, we can switch to the tape?' Of course. But over-reaction I would say.

Not thinking a lot more about it we arrived at the university early afternoon ready for soundcheck and pre-recording. Round the corner came two or three girls and a bloke. He stopped in his tracks. '*THERE THEY ARE, THE SEXIST BASTARDS!*' he said, hustling the girls away like we were a couple of big bad wolves about to eat 'em all up. I began to wonder. I know I'm not a newspaper man. I don't read 'em. But is this feminist thing bigger than I thought? But no. You don't have to read newspapers to know what's going on. In fact it's dead opposite. You form your own opinions when you don't read papers. I always think that there's a whole lotta truth in the old joke where the kid says, 'Isn't it funny daddy that there's just enough news everyday to fill up a newspaper!' I always picture the editor saying, 'Come on you lot, we've got blank pages to fill up here! We need seventy pages today! Can't you think of anything?

A publicity photo from the 80s. Dave hates this picture!

Top: Dave and I performed a Chas & Dave medley at the Children's Royalty Variety Performance in 1982. We were honoured to meet HRH Princess Margaret, and had a good rabbit with her, our classiest fan, during dinner that night.

Bottom: Some ladies, however, were less impressed. Feminists demonstrating outside the London University where Dave and I were scheduled to do a live show for Radio 1. 'Rabbit' had caused some controversy, but it all helped to push it up the charts.

Scenes from recording sessions at the Portland Studios, Portland Place. 'Gertcha!' was the first track Chas & Dave recorded there, in 1979. Our last one was 'Snooker Loopy' in 1986. (*Centre*) Mike Berry and me. (*Bottom*) Andy Miller (engineer), and snoozing Mick Burt.

Immortalised in print: cartoons from *Mirabelle* magazine and the *Daily Express*, early 1980s.

I grew up within the sound of fans cheering on Spurs at White Hart Lane, so it's been an honour to write and record for the team. © *Mirrorpix*

Top: Chas and J.I. I spent a week in Nashville recording this album with J.I. Allison, legendary drummer with Buddy Holly and The Crickets. (*Right*) The original photo which was reversed and then enhanced with an old car in the background.

Bottom: I've been lucky to go to some fantastic places on tour, including (*right*) New York (not that you can tell with all the cloud in the background) and (*above*) on the plane to Australia. I wrote 'Snake Eyes Burt' after seeing this picture of Mick on that plane.

Top: Joan and me with J.I. and Joanie at the Allison ranch in Nashville, 2007.

Bottom left: Kate and me in the Wonder Pub. Note Harry Garner 'bump' between her arms listening to the piano.

Bottom right: Me, Dave and kids in my 1943 Willys Jeep; and rock 'n' rolling in Belgium. (*Left to right*) Mick Burt, Darren Juniper, promoter and me, 2007.

My lovely family and Dave and Sue's godchildren.

Top left: My eldest daughter Juliet with her daughter Charlie and her husband Chris at Glastonbury 2007.

Top right: Daughter Kate with husband Paul Garner.

Above left: My son Nik and Mym.

Above right: Harry Albert Bob Garner, mine and Joan's grandson, to whom this book is dedicated.

Bob England and 'Gertcha!'

We've filled up nearly sixty. Just ten to go. Now come on!' 'How about another slant on the Princess Diana saga?' 'No you dozy bastard. That's well milked for the moment. Anyway we've got that booked for a month's time. Now come one you dozy gits!' 'How about the feminists? They stirred up trouble in America. Why not here?' 'Lovely! Now you're cooking on gas! Geoffrey! Go through the waste paper basket and retrieve them Chas & Dave "Don't like Rabbit" letters.'

So in case of major disruption, we recorded the whole live show in the afternoon. We went over to the pub for a break before the show. There were young women outside the pub and gig with placards that read, 'CHAS & DAVE ARE SEXISTS' and 'WOMEN UNITE AGAINST CHAS & DAVE'. But one of them gave me a comely smile. I was confused. Was this part of the plan?

So the concert went up and we gertcha'd straight into it. It was going a storm. 700 students bopping. We gave our future biggest record its first hearing at that concert. 'Ain't no Pleasin' You.' It went good. But it was looming. 'Rabbit' time. Almost here. Shall I announce it? Or go straight in. 'Straight in' announces itself. After a count of four the next thing you hear is a Whole Lotta 'Rabbits' Goin' On...So...'Straight in boys! One, Two, Three, Four! 'RABBIT, RABBIT, RABBIT, RABBIT!'

If there was ever any truth that crowd reaction could actually raise the roof then it would have happened that night. The BBC have got it on tape somewhere. I heard it myself on the tape recording when I got home. It was like England scoring the winning goal for the second time in the history of the World Cup! We found out later that about a dozen feminists had their own protest in one of the classrooms and that was that. 'Rabbit' continued to creep up the charts.

The Saturday following, it got an even better plug. On

Tiswas. The best Saturday morning kids show ever. Well everybody watched it. Viewers organised their own pie fights at home in sync with *Tiswas* similar action on the telly.

We were regulars on the show and we loved it and the people on it. John Gorman, Chris Tarrant, Sally James, Lenny Henry. They'd book everybody (all the guests) into the Holiday Inn next to Central TV Birmingham so that everybody could have a nice sleep before getting up to do the show. But celebs don't often get the chance to really socialise with each other. They are just passing gigs in the night. Don't even meet in the Blue Boar no more. (Popular band meeting place on way back from gigs in the '60s. Watford Gap Services on the M1.)

So at the Holiday Inn Friday nights before morning *Tiswas*, all famous musicians and celebrities all shook hands, all smiled, all cuddled each other and all got pissed. Non-celeb 'respectable' regular guests would complain about the drunken singing that accompanied their cornflakes in the morning, but we never actually got banned from the hotel. So I couldn't have been that loud.

This particular Saturday morning we were to do two spots. Some sort of pie chucking sketch early and then 'Rabbit' as a finisher while they rolled the credits. What a good plug! But as the morning progressed it began to slip away. John Gorman came over when there was about an hour to go and said the show was running over and they might have to cut the song. But. They are going to going to cut seconds here and there so with any luck we may be able to do a minute of the song. I knew they were genuine. So genuine in fact by the time they had around fifteen minutes to go, Chris Tarrant came over & said, 'Boys! We've overdone it! It's gone the other way! We've cut out too much! Can you do a ten-minute version of "Rabbit"?'

But of course! And so we did. Closing the show with it.

Absolute mayhem. John Gorman, Chris Tarrant and Lenny Henry pogoing about in rabbit suits. Cannon & Ball doing some sort of crazy conga. Sally James attacking me with a stuffed rabbit. The whole studio. Wild! All the while I kept looking at the producer for a signal that we could stop because it had gone off air, but no! 'Keep going!' He motioned, 'We're still on air!' So I carried on. 'Rabbit, rabbit, rabbit, rabbit, ya won't stop talking!' Finally we went off air. Everybody collapsed in a heap. Laughing.

As soon as I could I got to a payphone to ring my wife. It was absolute chaos in there although we enjoyed it. But how did it come across on telly? You never know at the time. We enjoyed it but I wanted Joan to give me an honest opinion. She did.

'It was absolutely fantastic my darling! So bloody good!'

If I could have yodelled, which I can't, I would have so yodelled.

In those days the new chart came out on Tuesdays. Bob England, our manager rang me at noon the following Tuesday. 'Charlie! "Rabbit" has gone up twenty places!' Them was good ol' *Tiswas* days!

'Rabbit' charted on 29 November 1980. It got to number eight. By the way, somebody checked with Sainsbury's recently to see if they sold rabbit. Yes they did. Tinned. In cat food!

Chapter 23

How do we Follow 'Rabbit'?

1981 was on us and a new single was needed to follow 'Rabbit.' Now we had already recorded 'Ain't no Pleasin' You' and had been doing it on stage. It was getting some reaction. People were coming up and saying, 'I love that Oh Darlin' one. Can we get it in the shops?' We told Bob, our manager. Me and Dave knew this should be the next single. We both loved it and it was getting natural reaction from the punters. 'Let's see what the record plugger thinks.' said Bob.

The record plugger said, '"Ain't no Pleasin' You" is a lovely song boys but it ain't a hit.' The record plugger was Alan James, gawd bless him. I'm not gonna undermine his cred, he'd been right a few times, but not this time. We loved him, and still do with all our hearts but he was doing his research from his plugger's office like record companies do, while me and Dave were getting reaction directly from the people and always will. It's what we do. The best way to test a likely hit.

I've never thought, 'Would the punters like this one?' when a song is being written. It's always been, 'I like it. Dave likes it. That's good enough.' Then maybe five new songs are put into the act and if after a couple of months a great reaction is happening on three of them and not so great on two of them, then the two get dropped. Simple. But people in offices can't do this. But then they should respect those that do. And they didn't. And don't. (But it didn't matter in the end.) 'Turn that Noise Down' was to be the next single. Bob said it was getting better response than 'Ain't no Pleasin' You' when he was plugging it over the phone.

'But of course it will!' I said. A song has to be *heard*! You can describe 'Turn that Noise Down' over the phone and it sounds fun. 'It's about a young kid who keeps playing his records too loud and his Mum and Dad get the hump about it.' 'Great! What's the other one about?' 'Well it's about a bloke who's fed up with his missus and ends up leaving her.' 'That won't be a hit. Chas & Dave write funny songs.'

I remember saying all this to Bob. 'I know it's easier to sell "Turn that Noise Down" over the phone than "No Pleasin' You" but once the people hear "No Pleasin" there will be no contest.' But it got pushed out of the way for the moment, to rear its lovely head later on.

'Turn that Noise Down' came out as a single. We liked it but it done nothing. Was now the time for 'No Pleasin'? Not quite yet. To begin with Tottenham Hotspur's footballing skills were beginning to make their mark once again on English Football. It looked like they were up for winning the FA Cup. Now me and Dave were and are Spurs fans. I was born, not within the sound of Bow Bells, but I would say within the sound of the Spurs crowd. North Middlesex Hospital, Edmonton. But I love Spurs in a gentle way. If they win? Lovely. If they lose? Never mind chums. And I don't hate the Arsenal. But that don't mean

I like 'em. Like the fat kid who sat next to you at school who had bad breath and was always farting. You didn't hate him but you'd hardly buy a season ticket to go and see him every Saturday. It's the same with the Arsenal. So there you are. No point. End of. Bob England was a passionate Spurs fan and hated the Arsenal as much as he loved the Spurs. Colin Smythe who was Bob's right hand man at the office was Arsenal. Colin used to tour manage us. He'd smilingly relate the latest Spurs/Arsenal /Bob/Colin office banter on gig journeys.

(Colin sadly died in a helicopter crash when he was working for Eric Clapton in the early '90s. Stevie Ray Vaughan died in the same crash.)

Bob had decided that as Spurs were on a roll, they should have a song. He didn't go for me because my Spurs knowledge was out of date. My Spurs song would've been about Ted Ditchburn, goalkeeper. Alf Ramsey, left back, and so on. It was now Ossie Ardiles, Ricky Villa. I'd heard of 'em but didn't know much about 'em 'cos I stopped going up the Spurs when I started playing guitar. 1956. I remember seeing Danny Blanchflower's first game for Spurs around the first time I heard Lonnie Donegan. Both masters in their own arts. But for me it was then that music took over and football went out the window. I didn't even go to see the double team in the '60s parade from Edmonton Town Hall to Tottenham Town Hall. My Mum went down to see 'em at the end of the road. she said, 'Are you coming?' Then of course seeing me holding my guitar knew where I was happiest.

So Bob didn't go for me, he went for Dave with this Spurs song. I kept out of it. Dave would tell me Colin would ring him and say, 'Have you done this Spurs song yet for Christ sake? Bob is driving me mad!' Finally Dave wrote it and did a demo. Played it to me. I wasn't sure about the 'Knees have gone all trembly' bit but Bob said (too late to change it) the Spurs players love it! It was called 'Ossie's Dream'.

I didn't think it would amount to much. What a fool I was! It even featured on the clever and funny *Alas Smith & Jones* series on one of their 'head-to-head banter' scenes not long after. 'Ossie's going to Wembley, his knees have gone all trembly. They don't write songs like that no more. Thank Gawd!' As I write this, 26th February 2008, Spurs won a cup at Wembley yesterday and I was told the song everybody was singing was, 'Spurs are on their way to Wembley'. Over a quarter of a century later!

Some things don't change. I didn't watch it. I was playing my guitar.

So we got the whole Spurs squad into Portland Studios to record the song the day after they won the semi-final. They'd been listening to the demo in the team bus for the last couple of weeks so they had a good idea of how it went. We particularly wanted to feature Ossie Ardiles saying, 'In de cup for Tottingham!' But when he came to do it he said, 'In de cup for Tottenham!' We said, 'No! You must say Tottingham!' 'But I can say Tottenham now!' 'But we want you to say Tottingham!' 'Okay!' He did it admirably! They sang their hearts out on the B-side too, 'Glory, Glory Tottenham Hotspur'. Then left to go nightclubbing (I'm only guessing!) leaving me and Dave to mix it.

We started the recording on a Tuesday and we finished mixing A-side and B-side in the early hours of Wednesday morning. The quarter-inch mix arrived on Bob's desk first thing Wednesday morning. In fact it didn't. Bob had already arranged this. It went straight to the pressing plant. He had already rung round a week before in case of. He said most pressing plants said they can't do it that quick. How about a week later? No good. The selling period is limited. It may be only from now up until the Cup Final. Just over a couple of weeks if they lose. (Can't believe it. Did Bob, over the phone, actually say, 'If they lose?!') But it was amazing, Bob said, how many came back to him saying they could manage a few thousand when they knew the genuine absolute urgency of the situation. He farmed it out and got the job done to his satisfaction.

On the Thursday there were records pressed ready to be sold. My wife Joan and Bob's wife Natasha were recruited, dressed in Spurs gear, to personally get the records to the shops around north London. They both did a fantastic job. They offloaded hundreds of boxfuls on the Thursday and the rest in the days following.

Now I reckon a 'record' was set here with this record. It was recorded on the Tuesday and the following Thursday there were people who had bought it commercially from a record shop, playing it at home in their houses. From studio to shop, to listening to it at home in forty-eight hours. On 7-inch vinyl single. Can't see that being beat. Bob was good at that.

We done the ol' *Top of the Pops* thing which the Spurs players absolutely loved. I think it was better than the Cup Final for them. It ended up getting to number 5 in May of 1981. Of course they won the Cup Final after a replay with Ricky Villa's historic goal. We played live on the open-topped bus with them on the Sunday from Edmonton to Tottenham, pounding out 'Spurs are on their way to Wembley' all the way.

So was 'Ain't no Pleasin' You' to be the next single? No. It was still getting sidetracked.

The next single was never meant to be a single as far as I was concerned, and it's the only Chas & Dave single I still wish never was. Looking back, I was beginning to lose some battles and it was telling. I was on top of most things but not all.

I didn't want this out as a single. This track was done as a B-side piss take of what was overtaking the charts at the time. The endless medleys of pop songs that were given the tag, 'Stars on 45'. ('45' meaning the 45 rpm record that you bought as a single.) I thought of the idea while having a drink in my local pub. Why not call one, 'Stars *over* 45' and pick three or four of the corniest old tunes you could think of? 'When I'm Cleaning Windows', 'Any Old Iron', 'The Laughing Policeman' etc. What a great thing for a B-side. Chas & Dave taking the piss out of the pop charts of the day. It had to be done in a 100 per cent professional manner. Which we did do. But too good.

The joke was too well hidden and the music business pluggers and media men our manager played it to said that this, as a single, would put Chas & Dave back in the charts. Bob, 'Del Boy', England saw £ signs in multiple. The whole point of it being a piss take B-side was quickly disappearing out the window.

But I didn't keep my head while all around were losing theirs. (Though they didn't think this to be the case.) I should have stood firm. But I didn't. I was outnumbered. But that's no excuse. I still should have stopped it. A dozy video was done in which I looked dozy doing dozy things and Dave looked dozy doing dozy things.

I was hoping the record would quickly fade away but it didn't. It started selling and then it was *Top of the Pops* time. Bob England and his then wife, Natasha, set the stall out. It was a pretty duff affair. Well naff laughing policeman and corny knees-uppers.

Don't tolerate it at any cost if it comes on the telly. I shall deny it thrice before sunrise. It peaked at number 21 on 12 December 1981, then thankfully faded away to make way for our next release. A song to become a personal ambition fulfilled.

At last. 'Ain't no Pleasin' You'.

Chapter 24

No Pleasin' You

'**A**in't no pleasin' You' came into the world initially while me and Dave were away writing in a cottage in Ashton around 1980. The 'Sideboard Song' cottage in Ashington wouldn't let us back in. They said we'd burnt a hole in the carpet and left it in a mess. We didn't. But there you are. Once someone's got it in for you, that's it.

But even so, we thought we were going back there. Bob booked us in and said he'd received no objection. I thought it strange but thought fuck it. But I just had this feeling, though. Our roadie, 'Tubs', was to deliver the piano on the day we were to arrive. He did. Well almost. He got it out on the pavement and knocked on the door. The woman took one look at the piano and said, 'Oh no! It's *them*! They're not coming in here!'

On a chance call to the office at a phone box in Guildford on our journey there, (no mobiles then) we were told turn round and head north to Peterborough. Another cottage had been acquired that was owned by Tony Brainsby, a well known journalist. He understood the likes of us. The cottage was in Ashton near Oundle. We went on to write quite a few songs in this cottage. We were in the middle of writing a song one evening. I think it was 'London Girls'. From out of nowhere a tune came to my head. I felt it had something. I said to Dave I just want to put it down quickly on cassette and we can carry on doing what we're doing. So I did. Great. It was safely on cassette to deal with later. We carried on writing. Eventually for the forthcoming album, (which was to be called *Mustn't Grumble*, though the song of the same name wasn't on it as we had yet to write it!) we had a tot up and reckoned we needed to write one more song. The obvious song to write would be 'Mustn't Grumble'(you're thinking) as the album was called that. But it wasn't obvious at that moment as we hadn't yet thought of a title for the album. That would come later after we'd finished recording. Got it? Anyway, what we needed now was one more song. I remembered the ballad style tune I'd hummed and strummed a few bars of at the cottage a few weeks back. I dug out the cassette and played it. Yes, it had something. Dave thought so too. We began working on it. In the meantime we began recording in the studio the finished songs we had. And in the betweentime of the meantime we got together to get a start on some lyrics for this ballad. The first idea I had was based on an old song I heard as a kid, 'A man came home from work one night, and found his house without a light'. He finds his wife dead. She's committed suicide. Then the story unfolds. I suggested to Dave that we could use this as a basis but leave out the doomy death bit. He comes home from work. House is without a light. But he knows why. She's left him. The utter loneliness of him coming home from work to an empty cold house and thinking how it used to be. So a lyric got started. 'Put the key into the old front door, like I've done so many times before…But this time…it don't feel the same.'

No Pleasin' You

Nightly in the studio Terry would be there. We'd play him bits of what we were doing. 'You've got to finish that "But this time" song. It's gonna be a winner!' Me and Dave continued writing and lyrics were progressing. An end result was in view even though there was a way to go. Now at this point you can judge if the 'way to go' is the right way. You've had the inspiration. Now it's simply perspiration. Graft. But. You've got to get a buzz out of what ain't finished. My mind began to drift away from the plot. I began to feel better. New, simpler lyrics were dawning. Thick and fast they came. Inspiration was now working alongside of perspiration and the two worked well. Before I knew it the lyrics were finished. For the verses anyway. It just needed Dave's approval. 'Dave, I've got some lyrics here. Really they seem quite ordinary. But they've got something about them. What do you think about this? "I built my life around you, did what I thought was right, But you never cared about me, now I've seen the light, Oh Darlin' there ain't no pleasin' you." Then the rest apart from the bridge.' 'I like it!' said Dave.

And we felt we were on a winner.

Now it needed the bridge. Within the next few days I played around with a chord sequence. I didn't want obvious chord changes but at the same time I wanted it to be melodic and flow. I finally came up with a tune and a chord pattern I liked and I put some words to it. I played it to Dave and he liked it. We now had a full song! Ready to record.

The idea for the tempo, though it be a Fats Domino style feel, came after hearing John Lennon's 'Starting Over.' This was a hit just before we recorded 'No Pleasin'. I mentioned the idea for the tempo to Dave but only mentioned Fats Domino. I knew he wouldn't object to any Fats Domino-related idea.

So that's how we did it. The day of the recording was magic. We put the track down early in the evening. Over the pub, brought a few beers back and then the vocals. I went down into the studio while Dave, Terry, Andy Miller (Engineer) and Mick were listening in the box. After the run through I asked Dave what it was sounding like. 'Chas, it's fantastic. Just do it like you're doing and we've got it!'

We finished it and listened to the multitrack about twenty or thirty times before we went home. We just loved it. In a week's time we were coming in to mix it. *But.* Before we went home – and I'm so glad I did it – I said, 'Do a rough mix of this Andy, on 15 ips tape. Just for reference.' Knowing from experience that coming in to do the 'proper mix' can and does create unforeseen problems. Problems that you don't even know are there until you listen to the final mix and you realize you've unknowingly mixed all the bollocks out of it. What happens is on the rough mix you sling all the faders up , quick balance, quick equalization, sit back and enjoy. Then you go home full of joy thinking when you come back to mix the real one it's going to be even better. But it ain't necessarily so if you ain't careful. You've got to know when to stop or fussiness begins to creep in. And once it does it's hard to stop it. You begin the 'real' mix. OK, bring up each individual track and E Q (add bass or top, or take away) to your liking. Great. Bring all the tracks in one by one. Sounding good. Now. And here comes the danger. Anything that is wrong with the mix should be heard on the first run through. OK. Voice jumps out a bit on the first line of the bridge. Make a mark with the chinagraph pencil to pull fader down at that point. Overdub guitar needs to come up on solo. Make another mark. Great. Roll it. Fine, but forgot to bring the guitar solo up. One more. Done it. Let's have a listen. Listen again. Twice. It's great. (Here comes danger.) But ain't the bass a bit loud? Yes of course. Why didn't we all spot that before? Okay, one more. That's the one…Ain't it?…Yes, but the last note of the guitar solo seems to jump out a bit. Yes, you're right. One more. Then from then on it's spot anything that jumps out. Snare drum a bit loud on intro, bass is great but needs to come up in last bar of bridge, vocals are great but dip 'em a bit on last line of last verse. The worst of it is that everybody agrees. Because everybody's ears work the same when only listening for things that might annoy. And so my dears, you end up with a finished product that does not irk in any way at all, but also does not excite in any way at all. You've cleverly knocked all the bollocks out of it. Been there, done it.

So we go in to do the 'real'mix of 'No Pleasin' a few days later. Usual procedure. Drums first. Then bass. Then piano, then the rest of any overdubs bit by bit. After about two hours we'd completed the mix and it sounded good. We all looked at each other and nodded our approval. But we weren't buzzing like we were the other night. Now was this natural? Did it really sound as good, if not better, but had we simply heard it too many times and needed to rest it and listen in a week's time? A pretty reasonable assumption. How would we ever know?

Well we can now travel back in time and listen to the exact sound we were enthralled with a week ago.

'Andy, put on that 15 ips rough mix we did last week.' The boys had forgotten about it. Now we all felt we'd improved on that, including me, but we were about to find out. Andy rolled the tape...Drums were a bit loud...Intro a bit shaky...But it gave off some magic that the new mix lacked. Or was that just me? It did sound better. To me anyway. But I ain't gonna dictate. I'm gonna look round and clock faces. I did. One by one everybody's face was saying yes. This is the real mix! Don't know why. It had certain technical levels wrong. Andy said the reverb he put on the drum beat after, 'That's what I'm Gonna', was one sided. But all this didn't matter.

The answer to the whole mystery is that this mix was mixed from the heart. The new mix was mixed from the head. There

Ladies and Gentlemen, I rest my case. Mixing to this day is still not a cut and dried affair but at least I've discovered for myself why a rough mix can be better than a planned mix. It used to be a complete mystery. All we did was edit a different drum intro from another take onto it. But when Andy played it back it had a really odd number of beats. He'd edited in the wrong place. But we left it because we liked it.

It's funny but I never knew where I'd got the idea for the lyrics from until some months later. Everything comes from somewhere and this was planted in the back of my head unbeknownst to me waiting to come out.

It was my brother Dave's situation with his missus. They were on the verge of splitting up and they ended up doing so. He lived at the time round the corner to me and we would meet down the pub. I remember him saying one night near to the split, 'You know what? I was putting up some curtains tonight. She watched me doing it and then when I'd finished she said I hadn't put 'em up straight! I said, "There ain't no fuckin' pleasin' you is there?" And I come down the pub.' Now I didn't think at the time, 'That's a good idea for a song!' but it sure turned out to be. Now my brother saying 'There ain't no Fuckin' Pleasin' You' (5/4 timing?) reminds me of that old musician's joke about a drunk in a club who wants to get up and sing with the band, 'Life is just a Bowl of Cherries' in 5/4 timing. If you want to know the joke it's at the bottom of the page. If not, read on. Or both.[5]

---

5 A drunk in a club goes up to the band and says, 'I wanna sing a song.' It's coming towards the end of the night so the bandleader says, 'What do you want to sing?' 'I wanna sing "Life is Just a Bowl of Cherries' in 5/4 time!"' 'But the song ain't in 5/4, it's in 4/4!' 'I wanna sing it in 5/4!' insists the drunk. The bandleader lets him get up. The drunk settles himself on the mike and away he goes. 'Life is Just a Fuckin' Bowl of Cherries.'

No Pleasin' You

Another nice and significant 'Ain't no Pleasin' You' memory happened a couple of days after that initial magic rough mix day. I was playing the mix back at home on the Revox tape recorder. It had just finished and there was a knock on the door. It was my mate Reggy Hawkins. Schoolmate and rhythm guitarist in The Outlaws. 'See what you think of this Reg.' I said. 'Me and Dave have just recorded it.' 'It's great !' said Reg. 'I've already heard it. You're really *singing*. Put it on again!' 'When did you hear it?' I said. 'About four minutes ago!' said Reg. It was playing as I walked up to your house. It was too good to interrupt. I stood outside listening!'

Me and Dave were in no doubt that this should be our next single. But the general feeling from the record company and song plugger was still, 'Lovely song boys, but not a hit.' (The song plugger by the way was the man in black, Alan James. You got this one a bit wrong, Jamesy!) My wife Joan absolutely loved it. I had written 'Wish I Could Write a Love Song' for her but this was the one she really liked. We did it on an obscure TV show just after we recorded it and Joan recorded it on video. I arrived home one evening at a time Joan wouldn't have guessed and found her watching it.

'What's happening with this song? It's got to be a single,' she said. She was so right. But it was getting knocked back right left and centre so what next? We'd been doing it on stage and getting great reaction. We need to do it more on TV. And TV that had big viewing figures. Easier said than done. But! There was one coming up. I think it was called *The Comedians*. Quickfire comics of the day delivered quick wit and we were to do a couple of songs in among. It had been going for a while and was getting good viewing figures. So we did 'The Sideboard Song' which was familiar and I said to Dave, 'Lets do "Ain't no Pleasin' You"' which wasn't familiar and I expected objections

from the producer like, 'Can't you do "Rabbit", or "Gertcha"?'
But it wasn't objected to. We got it done.

And 'Job Done' it really was! The day after that recording
was shown the office got a call after call asking where they
could get this 'Oh Darlin' song. Bob rang me and said they were
going with it for the next single. The phone calls had finally
convinced him.

At last! All I wanted to do now before it went out was
arrange a string part for it. The icing on the cake. I did this
while we were on the road. I finished it in the Sandpiper Hotel,
Manchester, where we've had many a party night. I overdubbed
the strings straight to the original rough mix. Eight violins and
two celli. I love arranging for strings. Such a wonderful feeling
hearing those professional string players playing all those notes
you thought of while sitting on your own, alone in your music
room in the early hours of the morning. You think of a sound
in your head that fills you with immense pleasure, then it can be
brought to life and recorded to be shared again with everybody.
Forever. This is real heaven to me.

Two mixes of the string overdubs were left to be decided
upon later. We chose it on the actual cut. (The cut to the acetate
that the final vinyl disc is made from.) It was released at the
beginning of 1982 and in Bob's words, 'it had its own legs'. It
seemed to just walk up the charts. Everybody loved it. From the
Kenny Everett Show, *Top of the Pops*, *Jim'll Fix it*, we done 'em
all. Each TV spot knocked it up the charts a bit more. It reached
number 2 in March of that year.

But it was number 1 in the *Melody Maker* chart. Always was
a good music paper.

Something that I've often thought of since, that I really would
have been knocked out with at the time, if it had happened, but
so glad now that it didn't. I was going to ask Eric Clapton to

play guitar on 'Ain't no Pleasin' You'. I know he would have done it because he liked the song and he liked me and Dave. But something was stopping me and I'm glad that 'something' did. A lot of people today would be saying, 'Well, it is a good song, but it only got where it did because Eric was playing on it.' And how would we be able to prove different? We would never have known.

The B-side of 'No Pleasin' was 'Give it some Stick Mick'. I've got the single on my jukebox now and both of them are good jukebox records. They've both got 'Get 'em out the bar!' intros. By that I mean (and I got this term from Terry Adams), a big percentage of punters at gigs while the support band is on, spend their time at the bar. A 'creep up on you' intro is great when you're the star and you already have their attention but the support band needs an 'all in' eight to the bar piano riff 'bang' so those in the bar go, 'What the fuck was that? Let's get in there quick and have some!' (Not a bad title that. 'Get 'em out the Bar!' Could be written, recorded and in the charts before this book comes out.)

The excitement on 'Give it some Stick' was the result of pure pent-up energy that at last was able to burst out. I'll tell you how. It was a cold November night in Portland Studios, Portland Place and we were ready for a bit of Chas & Dave Rock 'n' Roll to warm us up before we went to the pub. But on playing the piano there was an annoying buzzing sound. It was pretty quiet but loud enough. So after investigation under the piano lid, (a nice Bechstein Grand by the way, my favourite make – they're a bit more Rock 'n' Roll in general than Steinways), and no clue to the buzzing to be found, it was suggested that we abandon the session.

No thank you very much, I'm here to Rock 'n' Roll and Rock 'n' Roll I will. So I began to dismantle the piano and finally found the culprit. A tiny glass bead from a necklace or something was sitting on the soundboard. As the soundboard vibrated to the sound of the strings, so the bead did its mini-dance. But such a big rattle from such a tiny thing! Bead removed, the feeling of 'Let's Go!' was in the air. And so we did.

'Oi Mick! What? Give it some stick!' Away we went!

When 'No Pleasin' began to chart in Britain, we were in America playing at the Lone Star Cafe, New York. We were going down well and were getting some serious interest here. The plan was to spend some time in America to get our music known. The American time was booked some months before the release of 'No Pleasin' was decided upon. But news from England of it beginning to climb the charts in a determined way prompted a change of plan. We were needed back home. TV shows at that moment in time could not function properly without Chas & Dave and 'Ain't no Pleasin' You' on the bill. What else could we do? OK, I'm exaggerating. But not much. So we went home to plug the song to number 1. (In the *Melody Maker* Chart. The sensible paper.)

Now is fate really fate? Or do you make your own fate. Like I believe you make your own luck. The plan was to spend some time in America and make our mark but circumstances called us back home. If 'Ain't no Pleasin' You' hadn't charted at that time in our career, would we have 'Cracked America' as they say? But I'm a strong believer in building the apartments and not laying the paths 'til you see where the people walk. This has nothing at all to do with cracking America. But it makes so much sense.

The next release was 'Margate'. This song, unlike the others, was a Courage advert first and then a song. All the others were Chas & Dave songs first and then Courage ads. But to confuse you all the more, 'Margate' although not being initially a Chas & Dave song, was born of a Chas & Dave song.

The ad agency after 'Gertcha!' and 'Rabbit' and 'Sideboard Song' became big Courage beer selling ads, clamoured for anything else we'd got recorded. They liked 'Massage Parlour'. One we'd recorded a while back for EMI. Their idea was use the 'Massage Parlour' tune and have the lyrics about a day trip to Margate. Good idea. But it ended there. They thought they had, but they hadn't got any further than the idea. So I, with Dave overseeing, rewrote the idea. We recorded it, they put the pictures to it and the ad began to get shown on television. It was another popular ad. So we decided to write full Chas & Dave lyrics to 'Margate' and record it.

We put it out as a single in July 1982. It only got to number 46. But it's funny about chart positions; on live shows today it's as big as 'No Pleasin'', 'Gertcha', 'Rabbit' or any of our other higher chart entries. Beauty is in the ear of the Billy. (An affectionate word me and Dave use for punters. Billies. Billy Bunters.)

Courage ended up using eight of our songs for their ads. 'Gertcha', 'Margate', 'Sideboard Song', 'I'm in Trouble', 'Wallop', 'That's What I Like', 'Rabbit' and, I know there's another one. I'll think of it in a minute... 'Miserable Saturday Night'! It became 'What a Lovely Saturday Night', with the word lovely used in a sarcastic way. It's what it should have been in the first place. The title would have been more appealing.

The next single we put out was 'Wish I Could Write a Love Song'. We had high hopes for it. But we had been spoilt by 'No Pleasin''. Accept nothing less than a number 1 (*Melody Maker*) or number 2 if it's the *Top of the Pops* chart. But although it's a big requested song to this day, it didn't even make the top fifty. But 1982 was a good year for us and we finished it with a television Christmas special for LWT with Albert Lee, Jim Davidson and Eric Clapton among others guesting on it. In the early summer of 1983 Eric Clapton decided to get married to Pattie Boyd and invited me and Dave.

The reception was held at his house and a big marquee set up with a stage equipped with amps and instruments for anybody who fancied playing. All his music pals were there. Paul McCartney, George Harrison, Ringo Starr, Ginger Baker, The Rolling Stones. We had been recording with Lonnie Donegan and he sort of gate crashed but I don't think Eric minded. Eric was a big Lonnie fan. As the day progressed some of the guests' kids began to get up on the stage and bang about on the instruments. Time for a bit of gentle parental discipline to quieten the kids' racket. I think it might have been Ringo who got up first and then Paul. Just jamming. Ray Cooper was doodling on the electric piano. I walked over to Ray and asked if I could take over. He smilingly obliged and I got up.

It needed some positive livening so I went into some Rock 'n' Roll. I think it was something like 'Roll over Beethoven.' Then George Harrison felt the 'call' and was up on stage plugging in his guitar.

We were rocking! Paul, George, Ringo and Chas!

First and only time the remaining Beatles played together since they split. After 'Beethoven' finished I started singing to Paul to prompt him, 'Joe Joe was a man etc.' boogying on the piano at the same time. A good Rock 'n' Roll Beatles song. He joined in and took over. 'Get back! Get back! Get back to where you once belonged!'

I do love doing that. Setting a boogie beat on the piano and watching people's faces light up and join in. Paul said to me after. 'You must be older than you look to play Rock 'n' Roll like that.'

Paul to this day is a Chas & Dave fan and so was Linda. We met many times on various occasions. TV shows or sessions I did for him. I always make sure I get a copy of our latest album to him and he always replies with a constructive opinion which I never divulge publicly.

He is probably my most admired English music person. Like me, music is his life. I mentioned in my earlier book about the Outlaws being better 'players' than the Beatles but Paul chooses fabulous notes on the bass. He was and is an exception.

Paul McCartney, who *was* the Beatles, changed the whole of America's attitude to British music. Albeit good in their own way, Led Zeppelin, Deep Purple and other British bands who cracked America would not have even had the opportunity if it hadn't have been for Paul McCartney and The Beatles. Eric Clapton's wedding was great. Ringo's ex wife Maureen (she's dead now), took pictures that evening of me and The Beatles. She spoke to Joan and was going to send copies. But later said she was told she mustn't. So there's a good chance there are photos around somewhere of Chas and The Beatles. Probably come to light when I'm dead. But that's going to be a while. I'm banking on quite a bit of me moving about ahead.

John Peel died halfway through his book and his wife finished it. Well I'm past the halfway mark and I ain't dying yet. (I've come back to do this section. I'm actually, in reality further on in the book. Up to about 1993. Well past the halfway mark.) In any case, though I love my wife dearly I don't want her finishing this book. The first thing she'll do is go through it and cross out all the swearwords. Fuck that.

Don't worry about it. We're now well into 1983 and ' No Pleasin' was beginning to sell well in other countries, Australia and New Zealand in particular. At home we'd been offered our own TV series following the Eric Clapton Christmas Special.

Chapter 25

Knees up Down Under

The TV series was to be called *Chas & Dave's Knees up*. Could've been a better title but I always think that as long as the content is there, it don't matter what it's called at the end of the day. We got some good guests on it. Clarence Frogman Henry was one. One of the masters in our eyes. He'd already recorded 'No Pleasin' on an album. He sung it great but the production was a bit iffy. So we had to get him in the studio. He was more than willing. We booked PRT Studios, Marble Arch. (A favourite of ours.) The song we had for him was 'That ol' Piano'.

Me and Dave's version was in the key of A. Not a good Rock 'n' Roll piano key. I chose it because the range is pretty wide in that song so a key had to be picked so that high vocal notes in the bridge and lower notes in the verses could be managed with ease.

Clarence began the session trying to do the intro like I'd done it on our record. I was in the producer's chair. Andy Miller engineer. Dave on bass. Mick on drums. A good producer should only interrupt when he feels it's going in the wrong direction. It was. I interrupted. 'Clarence!' I said over the talk back. 'How would you approach it if it was your song?' He immediately went into a rolling New Orleans riff. We one and all shouted our approval!

'Okay studio. We're on our way to a hit record! If it ain't a hit it won't be our fault!'

Georgie Fame, a mate of mine from the early days, was in the next door studio. He heard me and Dave were in and came in to see us. He was mad on New Orleans music like me and Dave were. He could not believe his eyes and ears when he walked in. 'There's me! Next door! My one aim is to get something down on tape that might sound a bit like New Orleans. Then I come next door and it's the real thing! Right here!'

The record came out. It didn't sell many but we were proud of it. Clarence said his son loved it. 'If he likes it then I know I've got a good record!' Records don't have to get in the charts for them to be successful in your heart. We also recorded on that session, 'I miss ya Gel'. He did a good version. It never came out. We should think about that.

At the end of 1983, me and Dave (and Bob) went to Australia for a promotional ten days. 'No Pleasin'' was doing well there. We did some TV mainly on the Don Lane show and made our mark. We went back to tour in the spring of 1984. It was a twilight period for me. My Mum had not long died. She died in the January of that year. But now I was touring Australia with my wife Joan, daughter Juliet, daughter Kate and son Nicholas. It couldn't have been better in helping me to adjust.

Back home I was halfway through *Chas before Dave* (the first half of this book.) You can see that 'My Mum is' became 'My Mum was' around the halfway mark. I stopped writing it for a while and only continued when Joan encouraged me to do so. Then she got Bob on the ball to get it published. Joan is a great motivator. My mate Terry is also. They are both Leos and I think astrology is a load of old rubbish. So what do you think about that?

As the '80s progressed it got a bit madder on the road. We were earning more money in the wake of the big hits but some things were beginning to get out of hand. Everything was getting bigger and louder and it seemed like we were not in control of our own money. We weren't in fact. We were advised to be more money-headed. But we were musicians. It is almost unheard of for truly creative musicians to have business heads. Also truly creative people are usually trusting people. Not believing that as soon as their back is turned, there are those that thieve. While me and Dave's noses were into songs, gigs and recording studios there were other noses and claws that were pleased we were so much into our art. Then they could safely and without interruption grab large portions of the generous amounts of money we were accruing. It's hard to track 'em down. But they craftily track you down. They seek out musicians that are earning loads of money. It ain't like taking candy from a baby, it's far, far easier. A baby will cry. Musicians don't. Give 'em a beer, or a line of coke, or whatever pleases 'em and you can take what you want.

But that's life and I'm here to tell the tale. I ain't like some people who think that life is just something you do when you can't get to sleep. It's part of the game. Like Jesus. Before him nothing was made that was made.

We've had our share of coke freak roadies. Roadies were always coming and going. Me and Dave never knew who they were apart from the one or two regulars. On one tour a new roadie was going around finding out if anybody had any coke. He was a real case. A couple of days into the tour our regular lighting man, Pete Kiederling, came over to me and said, 'Did that new bloke come over to you on a coke mission?' 'As a matter of fact he did, why?' 'Well he's sorted now.' 'What do you mean?' 'He kept on at me,' said Pete, 'So yesterday I stopped at a sweet shop in the gig town and got some of them kids "flying saucer" sherbert sweets, emptied the sherbert out of them (he didn't see this bit!) and chopped out with me credit card (he watched this bit), two nice lines of white powder on a record cover, in one of the dressing rooms. "There you are my son!" I said. He was there with a rolled up fiver like a shot. Straight up the snout! Ten minutes later I was setting up the lights on stage. He came strolling by. Looked at me with thumbs up and a wink. "Fucking good gear!" he said.'

An afterthought. I wonder if Pete had hit on something? Rolling a joint of coconut tobacco, or a tab of jelly babies, comes to mind. Who knows? Mother, bring me cheese, with a deep sigh of glee. I love grannies who play the banjo.

Around the mid-'80s we began to get louder, and louder, and LOUDER. Our sound bloke's attitude was, 'We've got the gear! Let's use it!' Dumb cunt. It's a frightening thing that you are at the mercy of the soundman out front. But you most certainly are. You can be playing the best set you've ever played and he, out front, can completely fuck you up. And he has done. If Terry Adams is there he is our 'ears' out front. I straightway ask him what the sound was like.

We've got a good soundman now. Steve Norris. He tailors the sound to the venue. Common sense you say. Yes you're right but power prevails with most of 'em. 'We've got the gear! Let's use it!' They are so fucking annoying! We had a tour manager and soundman that would, in the early days (we're in a tiny night club) demand that half the tables were removed to make way for the PA system! So the half that were left were deafened. The half that couldn't get in stayed home and probably heard us better from there. Then as gigs continued more monitors were added. Then more was wanted in the monitors.

In among songwriting and TV shows and recording and interviews I knew that time must be took out to get this sound thing sorted once and for all. Then came the day. At last.

We were setting up in the afternoon for a gig at the Fairfield Halls, Croydon. We had complaints about the sound the last time we were here. Soundman was doing his dumb soundcheck. Getting Mick to bang on one tom tom for twenty minutes and then another tom tom for twenty minutes and so on. This venue is naturally very echoey. Amplification has to be used carefully. I've gone out front to listen.

There's Soundman okaying it. 'That's good Mick. Now snare drum.' BANG! Snare drum shakes the roof. Now I know that this is the level Soundman will stick to. Once that fader is up, there ain't no coming down, so everything else must rise above the drum sound.

'Play the full kit Mick!' Mick does. It is a tremendously loud and powerful sound. On its own just about headbanger bearable. 'Okay,' says Soundman, 'That's the drum level set. Now for the bass, piano & vocals.' Hang on!' says Mick, 'I need more drums in my monitors.' Now Mick's got a six foot by six foot bank of monitors. 'Okay!' says Soundman, 'Tom toms first. Tell me when you're happy!' 'Boomp, boomp, boomp, BOOMP, BOOMP, BOOMP!'...'I'm happy!' shouts Mick.

But I wasn't! The building was shaking. Major milestone in the Chas & Dave sound policy is about to begin.

'Soundman!' I said, 'Take all the drums out of the PA and the monitors.' 'What?' 'You heard, just do it.' So he done it. 'Mick!' I said, 'Why do you need all the drums in those monitors?' 'Because I can't hear 'em once I've got the bass, piano and vocals in 'em!'

'Okay. Let's start from scratch. No amplification Soundman. Play the drums Mick.' Mick played. They sounded fantastic out front. Just acoustic. Using the natural ambience of the theatre. 'Can you hear all the drums Mick?' 'Of course!' 'Dave, can you jump on the piano and play a bit of boogie alongside Mick?' Dave can do this. He did. I got Soundman to turn it up just enough so that Mick could hear it comfortably. Still no drums in PA or in monitor. In that naturally echoey theatre it was sounding good already. Dave did some vocal. Mick was given just enough in his monitor once more.

The end result was a sound balance of piano, bass and vocals around a completely acoustic drum sound. Possibly a soupçon of bass drum. Everybody getting just enough of what they wanted in the monitors. That night me and Dave's 'ears out front', Terry Adams, said it was the best sound he'd ever heard at the Fairfield Halls. The secret was simply, need to hear more of a particular instrument? Don't ask for it to be turned up. Ask for the rest to be turned down. This is what we practise today.

Still on the 'sound' subject, if ever the occasion arises, and it does on rare ones, where we have to use a soundman who ain't familiar with our stuff I just say, 'In all the years we've been on the road we've never had complaints that you can't hear the drums. We've never had complaints you can't hear the bass. We have had complaints you can't hear the words. We have had complaints you can't hear the piano. The soundman says, 'understand you perfectly'.

You build the apartments and note where the people walk before you put in the paths. Somebody once said this. I think it was me a few chapters back. Now I've said it twice. Once you know the answer it is so simple. Like the Eastern Mystic squatting in the souk. He could put out his hand, lift up his camel's bollocks and tell you the time. How did he do that?

Eastern magic? No. By lifting up his bollocks, he could just about see the town clock in the square.

Around the middle of the '80s I met Johnny Speight. Both me and Dave were fans of his. The Alf Garnett character Johnny came up with was pure genius. The shows don't get repeated today because of the 'political correctness' thing. It's a shame.

Johnny's writing ridiculed the Alf Garnett characters of the world, but at the same time managed to drag great original humour from it. Johnny was like me. A night bird. We'd talk 'til two or three in the morning on the phone. I'm not a great phone rabbiter. But I could with John. Well, I let John do most of the talking, which I enjoyed.

The original Alf Garnett series, *Till Death do us Part* in the '60s had continued over to the '70s but when I met John it was no more. Then a clever, but simple rethink of the title put it back on its feet again. (I said something about titles don't matter earlier didn't I? Take no notice.) It became *In Sickness and in Health*. Now Alf and his wife Elsie were older and slower it was a perfect way for the series to continue. A signature tune was needed. Roger Race who produced it rang me up and asked if we could do it. What? Write a song for one of my heroes, Johnny Speight? Not likely!

We wrote and recorded 'In Sickness and in Health' for the series and also an extended version for the single. The single didn't do much chartwise but we still do it in the act now and then. It's often requested. Johnny paid me a great compliment when he read my book, 'Chas before Dave.'(First half of this book.) He said, 'You write to ex*press, not im*press.'

He was writing a new Alf Garnett series at the time and asked me if he could use the 'Gene Vincent and the dog shit' bit with the kids playing the same trick on Alf. (The bit that Gene Vincent told me him and his mates used to do as kids. Find a fresh bit of dog shit. Put it on someone's doorstep. Put some newspaper over the top of it, set light to it, knock at the door and run away. The bloke would come out, see no one but the burning newspaper, stamp it out, only to go back in treading dog shit all around the house.) I was only too pleased to let Johnny use it. But it wasn't to be. I think Johnny wrote the episodes but they never got took up. Johnny died in the latter part of the '90s.

We had written a musical together with John but it got so fucked up and mishandled by me and Dave's management at the time, and John's management (not his family) being very awkward after his death, that the 'big headache' was better off being dropped and life got on with. We've still got the songs though.

Meanwhile, back in 1985, me and Dave have gone and bought a pub. Seemed a great idea at the time. We really went for it in a big way. Bob was in on it. It was the Old Pegasus in Green Lanes, North London. Courage Brewery got it all refurbished. Fred and Chris Cooke who ran the best pie and mash shop in London were friends of ours and they supplied the pub with their pie, mash and eels. (Shut up. I'm feeling hungry.) We had a free jukebox and had live music most nights.

We had some great nights down there. One night in December of 1985, Bob said that Australia (we hadn't long been back from our second tour) wanted us to do a live televised spot from our pub. We more or less went straight from a sell out week at the London Palladium with Alf Garnett (things were happening!) to the pub.

We got there and I met the director. 'What do you want us to do?' I said. He seemed a bit vague. 'Well, when we go live just say something like, "Here we are in London enjoying the rain".' 'So then what?' 'Well that's really all you need to say.' 'But...?.' But he was gone. Into the crowd.

The band had soundchecked and was ready to go. We had the whole sax section. Sid Philips (old mate from the Rebel Rousers who got the fish hook in his ear – remember?), tenor sax, Nick Payne, tenor sax, Tony Hall, tenor sax, and Nick Pentelowe, baritone sax.

These four probably made the best Rock 'n' Roll sax section in Britain. Probably in the world at the time. Four piece Rock 'n' Roll sax sections were a thing of the past then. Even Little Richard wasn't using one.

So we were ready to go at the drop of a hat, live to Australia. But the director was oh so vague. I spotted Dave in the crowd. 'Have you spoke to the director?' I said. Dave said he had. 'So do you know what's going on? Is it live to the Don Lane Show? Or Aussie breakfast telly? Or what?' 'Don't know,' said Dave. '*He* don't seem to know!'

Okay! I thought, time to take the reins. Work out a bit of banter ourselves. Keep it simple but positive. When we go live we'll just say something like, 'Hello to all our new fans in Australia. We had a great time on the tour and we'll be back next year! Merry Christmas from Chas & Dave!' Then I'll count straight in the number. Short and sweet and positive. Dave was happy with this so I went to find the director. I found him and told him what we were going to say. 'Alright.' He said, hardly listening. 'Do you want a drink?' he said. I said I'll have a beer and we went to the bar.

Then he began to 'Billie' me. This is me and Dave's term for a tiresome punter (Billy Bunter) that continually asks you questions not knowing when to stop. 'I bet you're really pleased with yourselves topping the bill at the London Palladium for the week?' 'Well, yes, we are.' 'I bet you've met lots of famous people'...Fuck me. Where did they find this wanker? Then Bob England intervened and said I should get on stage as we were going live to Aussie any minute now. So ready to go, on cue, short introduction as planned and straight into some Rock 'n' Roll. And we were rocking along lovely.

Then some weirdo with a ginger beard and a mac and flat cap walks across the front of the stage carrying something and decides to come up onto the stage. Okay, these things happen, I'll deal with it, just keep playing boys. But they didn't to my annoyance. They stopped. I'll bollock 'em later.

Then the ginger-bearded weirdo removed his hat and his beard and revealed himself.

Eamonn Andrews. *This is Your Life.*

It turned out the director was only an extra put up for the part so all was forgiven. They had coaches waiting outside to take all the pub punters to the Royalty Theatre in the Strand where they filmed the episode. I went in a limo with Eamonn who was well excited. I don't know how Dave got there. I'll have to ask him! Of course there was a big party afterwards! Eamonn sent us a nice personal letter after it had been on TV saying how much his folks at home enjoyed it and how he reckoned it was one of the best he'd ever done. It went out on New Year's Eve, 1985.

Chapter 26

Bob Bails Out

In 1986, being interested in astronomy, I was looking forward to the appearance of Halley's Comet. It only comes round once every seventy-six years so most people only get one chance in a lifetime to see it. In fact there can't be anybody alive today who has seen it twice. The one before before 1986 was 1910 so if, say anybody, saw it as a five-year-old in 1910, they would have to be one hundred and three today to be able to say they've seen it twice. Not much chance.

Reading up about it, the 1910 visit was quite spectacular. The tail spreading halfway across the sky for some six or seven days. Before I'd ever seen a comet I thought they behaved like a gigantic fireworks day rocket but going about as fast as you see an aeroplane moving high in the sky. But they don't. They look quite still. But the position changes nightly. Also the tail always points towards the sun even if it's travelling towards the sun. Fascinating ain't it? Watch it! It can take over. I really got into it in the late '60s and began getting books and drawing up

charts. I had to stop. Music was beginning to take a back seat.
Not that it would've for long. Well it didn't. I made sure of that.
But it was becoming a sort of addiction. So I had to cut down
on it. Also there are stars out there that you are looking at now
that are already burnt out. Years before you were born. But
they're so far away that...OK! That's enough!

But I said to Dave that we must write a song about Halley's
Comet. We won't get another chance. So we did. We put it out
as a single. My daughter Juliet with her artistic talent and
experience did a great job on the cover. We got to meet Patrick
Moore and had some pictures done with him. I had a hundred
and three questions I wanted to ask him but couldn't think of
one! I've met him a few times since and I've managed a few.
Along with Jerry Lee, Little Richard, Paul McCartney, Mozart
and Chopin, he is one of my all-time heroes. The single didn't
do much but I was pleased with it and there's no reason why it
shouldn't be re-released next time round in the year 2062.

Then the next single to come out in 1986 was 'Snooker Loopy!'

So how did that come about? Well, listen here. Once upon a
time there were five snooker players and a manager. The
manager heard that there were a couple of likely lads that had
the knack of coaxing musical notes out of successful sports
people and providing them with hit records. Can they do this
with snooker players? Only one way to find out. So he gets on
the dog and bone to the man who looks after the likely lads. It
comes at the right time. There is no pressing project and the
lads are up for it.

Me and Dave got together after I had spoken to Barry Hearn
who managed Steve Davis, Tony Meo, Terry Griffiths, Denis
Taylor and Willie Thorn. I asked Barry to give me a run down
on each of their personalities so as to provide fuel to fire up the
song. I wanted each one to have their own verse. We had

positive ideas for Steve Davis. (The famous final with Denis Taylor in 1985.) Also Willie Thorn. That was Dave's department. He likes a 'Bald Head' song. We also had a rough outline of a 'Denis Taylor's unusual glasses' verse. As for Tony Meo, Barry informed me that Tony cried if he lost, and cried if he won, so that was taken note of. And Terry Griffiths was so particular about his barnet that he carried about with him a special bag full of combs and hairbrushes.

Armed with all of that we set about composing a song. I'd already thought of the title which Dave liked. 'Snooker Loopy'. Now it needed their personalities put in the verses, a chorus that begins and ends with 'Snooker Loopy' and a tempo and a tune for the whole thing.

Let's go for nailing the chorus first, tempo and tune-wise. A Rock 'n' Roll tempo was tried first which we are extremely good at. Only the best in the world at the present time. So we give it the Little Richard approach. It was very danceable but we decided it wasn't right for them five snooker players.

Then a very positive image came to me. Snow White and the Seven Dwarves.

Barry Hearn being Snow White. Waiting for the fruits of the workers to be brought home. 'High ho, high ho, and off to work we go.' I could then see the seven dwarves going into, 'Snooker loopy nuts are we, me and him and them and me.'

Great! I'd cracked it. Dave liked it and we're away. The verses we wrote between us, Dave giving it 100 per cent on the 'Bald Head' verse and after some three or four hours the whole thing was finished. Actually I remember Dave completing the 'Bald Head' verse as we got to Swiss Cottage on the way to the recording session. It was exactly there that he got the 'walk it/chalk it' rhyme happening.

'Snooker Loopy' in 1986 was the last session we ever did at

35 Portland Place, which began for Chas & Dave with 'Gertcha!' in 1979. It got sold off for offices. Many happy, party, boozy (but always in control) times were had there. 'No Pleasin' You', 'Rabbit' and most albums all happened in that studio. I have memories of great feelings waiting outside the studio and looking down the length of the road at all the street lights at three o'clock in the morning while the roadie brings the band wagon to take us home and thinking about what we'd just recorded. I tell you there ain't a feeling in this business like it. Knowing you've just recorded something that you know people are going to be singing forever more.

I knew 'Snooker Loopy' was going to be a hit when I asked my son Nik, who was twelve at the time if any of the kids at school had heard it. 'Heard it?'he said, 'They've all been singing it in the playground!' 'Snooker Loopy' done alright for itself. It got to number 6 in May 1986.

1987 was a real mixed year of happenings. A mixture of good and bad.

I'll start at 1/ Bad. Summer season at Margate. First ever Summer Season. I think Bob booked the Margate Summer season for convenience sake. It's done with. Ain't gotta be on the phone with this gig or the other. Chas & Dave are sorted for the summer of '87.

Dave didn't seem to mind but to me it was a taste of how it feels when old people are put in comfortable homes. Nothing to complain about but not a buzz anywhere. You go past the same lampost everyday at the same time everyday, you do everything you do everyday at the same time everyday. It was boredom apart from the all-night piss ups down at the Mad Chef's Bistro in Broadstairs. We met him by chance a few months before on a fish and chip shop search. We found no fish and chip shop but found his seafood restaurant. The Mad Chef was one of those predictably unpredictable people. We'd all go down to his restaurant most nights after the gig. Managers, roadies and all. Make him put the Mills Brothers on the music system and basically proceed to have a pissed-up knees up.

He loved our wild parties but he didn't enjoy regular restaurant hours with the ordinary punters. 'Why not?' We'd say. 'Cos I fucking hate *people*!' He'd say, banging on the table to make his point.

One night he said to his wife, 'I'm not going to open tomorrow, I'm not in the mood to face the cunts!' 'But we've got bookings!' said his wife. 'We've got to!' With that he's gone round the restaurant and smashed every plate in the house. 'Now we can't open,' he patiently explained, 'because we've got no fucking plates.'

The Mad Chef made the season bearable but when it finished we went back to the road and it was heaven. Never again no summer seasons.

2/ Good. TV Special. We did a TV special that year that Denis Kirkland produced. Another well quirky likeable character. The Mad Chef and D.K. never ever met but that would have been really interesting. Too late now. They're both dead. They were both like nobody else you'd ever met. Completely different to each other but both gave me the feeling that I wanted to be in their company.

Denis Kirkland produced most of the Benny Hill shows. He could have been a top star actor if he had wanted. He could turn instantly into any character. And would be that character. The danger was that when he did it I would be instantly there playing opposite. The first time Joan met him we were in the players lounge at the Spurs about to film 'No Pleasin' on the pitch. Bar is full of people. Denis goes into acting mode and I follow suit.

'Okay Mr. Hodges,' Denis says loudly, 'empty that glass pretty damn quick and put out the cigar. It's time for work.' Den has decided his character today is a loud drunk desperately trying to pull himself together. 'When I'm good and ready, Mr. Piss Head,' I've gone. We're now deep into acting mode.

'Mr. Piss Head? Mr. P…Mr. Prod. Stroke. Dir. if you don't mind, Mr. Rockney Tiny Weasel. Now get your arse in gear and show me you know more than two fucking chords on the piano.'

'How you gonna know? Can't count past two can ya?'

And so we'd continue. Fuckin' about. Me and Den enjoying it immensely. I couldn't wait to ask Joan later what she thought of him.

'Well I didn't like the way he spoke to you!' she said. But we were…I mentioned this to Den later. 'We really must stop doing that!' he said.

The TV special had its moments. Playing 'No Pleasin' on the back of a truck going round the West End and by clever editing finishing it on the Spurs pitch. As I write this Denis Kirkland has not long died. His family got in touch and said his dying wish was for me and Dave to play 'No Pleasin' You' at his funeral, which we did. His coffin was carried out of the church to the crematorium accompanied by Jerry Lee Lewis's 'Great Balls of Fire.' Den always liked to make an impressive exit.

In this business I'm in, live gigs are at the top of my list and always will be. I love 'em even more as years go on. Writing and recording come next. They are marvellous, creative and fulfilling mediums that provide you with a musical piece of a part of your life that can be played back from now until the end of time.

TV shows are the most boring. They get you to turn up at 10am. You run through for five minutes. Then they don't want to see you until 3pm, for another five-minute run through. But you can't leave the building in case they change the plan. At eight o'clock you do the three-minute show and you hang about 'til ten for a 'clear'. (In those days, a check to make sure everything went down on tape OK. Or a Chinese poof as Ronnie Barker used to say.)

But a TV show with Denis Kirkland producing was something to be looked forward to. Thames TV took us to New York with Benny Hill and others for a 'Salute to Thames'. I had a great time because of Den Kirkland. We found a few music clubs. He was great company.

Benny Hill was an OK chap. Very quiet, but a likeable person. When Benny died in 1992 we went to his memorial service in a church on Trafalgar Square. Our friend Terry Adams chauffeured us there. It was a well attended affair. Max Bygraves, Bob Todd, Freddy Starr and others of that ilk were dotted about. We sat where we could. Terry found a seat up front. Dave up the back. I found a seat right in the middle. Centre of attraction. But that's alright. But it so happened that the person I'd came to sit next to was a grimy wiry tramp (come in from the cold) with a well stubbly beard and a battered pork pie hat. Sidelong glances towards my direction began to happen. Now I don't look at people's eyes in public places anymore. It's obviously easier for me. I get less hassle. But Terry was. He told me later. He said you could read the people's faces. They're looking round at me and thinking, 'There's ol' Chas. He don't look too bad. But look at the fucking state of Dave! He's let himself go, ain't he?'

3/ Bad. Spurs losing FA Cup. Spurs versus Coventry. Typical case of we thought we'd won it before we'd even played the game. Especially when we scored first in the first two minutes. A marquee was set up with a stage in the middle of the White Hart Lane pitch for us to play after. We made plans beforehand where to meet and where to park after. It's gonna be manic, we all said. Didn't even enter our heads that we might lose. I think the team felt the same too and that's exactly why we did lose. Getting to the ground after was easy. The streets were empty. We drove right into the ground no bother.

Pleaty came into the tent crying. But sorrows soon got drowned in booze and plenty of Chas & Dave music. It was broad daylight when we all left. By then most people had forgotten the score and thought we'd won.

The song we'd done for 'em that year was, 'Hot Shot Tottenham'. But the absolute gem was Nico Clausen on the B-side. We'd written him a line where he's singing to Ossie, 'Are you gonna play a blinder?' And Ossie replies, 'I do my best for Tottingham, mate!' We coached Nico as to how to deliver his line when he got to it and his Cockney/Belgian deliverance was an absolute classic. The whole Spurs squad fell on their backs like the Martians in the Cadburys Smash advert. Ossie just about got his line out.

4 / Good. *Flying* album released. The album got released and we put out the 'Diddlum Song' as a single. We did it as part of a Chas & Dave medley on the Children's Royal Variety Show for Princess Margaret. We met her after and she said to me, 'Your new song had me jumping up and down in my seat!' We then all filed into the big hall for dinner.

Me and Dave sat about six tables away from where Princess Margaret was sitting. Me and Dave were in need of a beer and as the waiters were pretty busy running around serving the starters, we decided to go to the bar and serve ourselves. Having done so we were about to go back to our seats when Princess Margaret looked up and summoned us to her table.

The two people sitting on her right and left hand were politely reseated and me and Dave were seated each side of her. She began by saying how much she loved our show and how she loved old London songs. Then how one of her Grandma Queen Mary's favourites was, 'Knocked 'em in the Old Kent Road'. Time flew by. We talked about music and old songs. When she was ready to go she gracefully stood up and the whole room got to their feet. Something like a hundred people stood up immediately. This is obviously what you do when in the presence of Royalty. I was impressed and more than impressed with the beautiful Princess Margaret.

The *Flying* album unfortunately was handled (or mishandled) by a crumbling record label, PRT. I sort of got an idea something was amiss the day after that Royal Variety performance of the 'Diddlum Song' was shown on National TV. I rang the record company.

'How many orders came in today for the new single after last night's showing?' I said.

'Hang on, I'll check,' said a girl from the company. 'Here it is...nine.'

'9,000? Not bad!' I said. 'Good start.'

'No, nine.'

'900?'

'No. We've had an order for nine records,' she said.

Something's wrong! The viewing figures on this show was something like twenty million. And they got orders for nine records? It had Princess Margaret jumping up and down in her seat. There's gotta be more than nine people out of twenty million at home doing the same?

'No,' said the record company. 'You ain't gonna crack it with this one Chas & Dave.'

No we ain't. Not with you lot. Bunch of washouts.

The company crumbled soon after but we got the rights to our recordings back. Thanks to the help of John Morton. Me knowing not a lot about record company business and having no manager (see the next paragraph), I was at a loss as to the next move and anything above banjo put Dave into a sea of confusion. But John dictated over the phone to me some letters to write, which I did and it helped tremendously. Thanks John.

5/ Bad. Bob England quits. Bob quit managing us at the end of summer 1987. His company, Towerbell, earlier that year had gone under owing a lot of people money. When he quit he owed us £8,000. He forwent his commission on gigs he'd already booked to pay that back. I don't know how much he owed other people on his company's bankruptcy but as Peter Sellers would say in his role as 'Mr Iron', 'That's not my concern, is it?'

Bob did not owe Chas & Dave a penny when he went under. He announced his departure to us when we were just finishing the Margate Summer Season. (Did we really do a 'put out to graze' ol' chaps summer season in 1987? At least it finally got made up for at Glastonbury nearly twenty years later!)

Bob was feeling the pinch. He didn't say as much but although he was back in business, people were frightened to do business with him because of what had gone on before. A top City lawyer said to me some years ago that's one thing that entertainers and musicians have in their favour above other self-employed professional people. They don't lose work through going bankrupt. If a builder, or a showbiz manager, or an accountant goes bankrupt, they are going to find it hard to get back on their feet. And harder to get back where they were. People will be rightfully wary of doing business with them and will shy away. But with musicians and entertainers it's different. If somebody is advertised to be appearing in your home town and you like what the person does, you'll pay your money at the door. Don't matter whether he's been bankrupt or not. And a lot of 'em have been.

Bob Bails Out

It's lovely being a musician. Always knew it would be. My Mum said to Joan my wife – and I'll only mention sex once in this book – when me and Joan were courting (okay, laugh, that's what we called it):

'You do know that musicians like sex a lot.'

Joan to this day don't know if it was meant as a warning or an assurance. But it seemed like a warning.

Now I've only just thought about that, my Mum saying that. Now what did she know? My Dad was a lorry driver. He did sing, but didn't play anything. Second husband, Larry, worked down the rolling mills, Enfield. Music? None evident. Third husband, John, from Aughnacloy, Ireland. Muscial prowess? None.

Now I do remember when I was about ten years old, around 1953, Mum saying that the electric guitar player from the Billy Ternant band used to come into the pub regularly to see her play. I'd heard of Billy Ternant but I hadn't heard of an electric guitar. Nor had Mum. 'I suppose it's just got a flex attached,' said Mum, 'and you plug it in the light socket.' What a marvellous idea! It's just the sort of thing I would have tried to rig up if I could have laid my hands on anything that resembled the right components. Good job I couldn't. I've had a few electric shocks in my time. Experimenting. Earth wires on gas pipes. Bang! Shock! Everything fused. It gives you an instant funny taste in your mouth. Like freshly baked wire wool. Just cooled down but only just. Then just as you are tasting this Nan calls up the stairs, 'What are you bloody well up to now!'

But Billy Ternant's guitar player. Mum was unattached to anybody at the time. I wonder if she was thinking of marriage? Just the fact that she mentioned him to me more than once in a 'sounding out' manner makes me think. He sounded alright to me. Then I wonder if she found out he was just after one thing and dropped him? Hence her 'musicians are highly sexed' theory. Who knows?

But one thing is for sure, if anybody around today is related to Billy Ternant's guitar player, then it could have been Billy Cotton's guitar player. Or Billy May's? Or Billy Butlin's? I'm not getting involved.

Towards the end of '87 we got asked by Bill Wyman and Ringo Starr to go to Atlanta, Georgia, along with Jerry Lee Lewis to open a restaurant called 'Sticky Fingers'. It sounded good after the boring Margate Summer Season so we said yes.

Jerry Lee was out of it. Not of this planet. He was in among a crowd when we got to the restaurant. I went over and spoke to him. When he saw me he sparked into life. He hadn't expected to see me there. 'Hey! It's Chas!' he said to a new wife. 'He sang "Bad Moon Rising" with me on the *London Sessions* album!'

Me and Dave went on and done ourselves proud. Jerry Lee was on next. In his dressing room he seemed a little more together. Bill Wyman and Ringo were to back him.

'Shall I come on and play bass?' I said to Jerry Lee. 'You know I know your stuff better than Bill does.'

'I know you do Chas. There ain't nobody better. But the deal was for Bill and Ringo to back me. I guess I can't back out now.'

So that's what happened. Jerry Lee came on looking out of it. Bill and Ringo came on looking frightened and some sort of set was performed.

I say no more.

We discovered we had a day off next day and most of the following prior to the last performance before going home. Then a nice coincidence occurred. It just so happened that Terry Adams and his wife Hazel were holidaying in a similar part of the States at that time and with a bit of juggling it was fixed that we could all meet the next day at a place we'd all wanted to go to all our lives. The Sun Studios in Memphis.

We arrived At Terry's hotel in Memphis early on the day. I rang his room from the reception. I put a handkerchief over the phone & shouted.

'Tel!' I hollered.

'Chas!' said Tel. It worked. He had disappointment in his voice. 'What's happened? Where are you?'

I gave it two seconds, then, 'Downstairs! Come on, hurry up! We're booked in to record at Sun Studios and we've just got time to go round Elvis's gaff after.' Terry's cheer had barely faded before he appeared downstairs ready to go.

We got an hour booked in the studio and went to work. The engineer wanted to put a track down and then vocals separate etc. But we wanted to take home a souvenir of how it used to be done. In fact how we still do it. The whole thing live. The best way. We have been known to do tracks first and vocals later but that's only when lyrics have yet to be finalised. But here in Memphis we picked two tracks we were well familiar with stagewise. 'No Pleasin' You' and 'Bangin' in Your Head'.

We put these recordings on the B-side of 'The Diddlum Song' later. We went round Elvis's gaff before we flew back to Atlanta. The first thing I noticed was that his swimming pool wasn't as big as the one I had back in England at the time. The house isn't that big either. Or his kitchen. It's funny ain't it, but I pictured that everything Elvis had has gotta be bigger than anything I'd ever seen.

But that made me warm to the man. He could have had whatever he wanted far bigger than anybody else's but he loved to retain that homeliness. In his heart he loved the real ordinary things in life. Shame those around him didn't respect that.

We finished 1987 by releasing a Christmas Carol album with the Cambridge Heath Salvation Army Band. It was slightly expedient but not really. Bob wanted a Christmas album out. Now you know we ain't had time with all the things we've been doing this year to get an album together as well, don't ya? You've just been reading about it. But Bob didn't. But you don't stop learning do ya? Knowing what I know now, it would have alleviated the boredom of the Margate Summer Season to have planned an original Christmas album in those daytimes. But as I said, the Christmas Carol album was not completely a substitute for what should have been. It was something that I thought should be put down as part of the Chas & Dave library sooner or later anyway. Honest!

I love Christmas Carols and felt we should do an LP of one. People can play this during Christmas dinner and then out with the Knees up Jamboree Bags when the dinner's gone down.

1988 began with Bob starting a new life in Antigua running a restaurant and us with a new agency. International Artists.

Chapter 27

I'm a Grandad!

We were happy with the new agency. It was run by Laurie Mansfield and we were looked after mainly by Bob Voice. Both okay chaps. Mandy Ward worked there for us too and worked very well.

The next couple of years were spent pleasantly gigging and then in 1991 Spurs once more got into the Cup Final. They beat, of all teams, the Arsenal in the semi-final, and Chas & Dave were called upon for another song.

Our Spurs song history was, idea-wise: 'Ossie's Dream' (Dave wrote 90 per cent of the song) 'Tottenham, Tottenham' (My idea for the theme based on 'Let's twist again like we did last Summer/We're gonna do it like we did last year). Plus 'Hot Shot Tottenham' (Dave's basic idea, which we finished together). I'd started and finished many of our own songs on my own but never a Spurs song. But I had a positive idea for this one. Me and Dave met in my music room.

'I've got the title and most of the new Spurs song written Dave,' I said.

'Good! What's it called?'

'The Arsenal!'

'Yes, I know! We beat the Arsenal in the semi. No one's gonna forget Gazza's magnificent free kick, but what's this song? What's it called?'

'I told ya! *The Arsenal*! "We're off to Wembley 'cos we beat the Arsenal!" That's the full title.'

'We can't have that!'

'Why not?'

'Because. Well because it mentions Arsenal.'

'Exactly! And the fact that we beat 'em in the semi-final and that's why we're going to Wembley! Because we beat the Arsenal!'

'Well. Yeah. I'm beginning to see it.'

So we recorded it and were well pleased. But when the Arsenal Club found out about it they were none too pleased. They sent us a copy of the patent saying that the 'Arsenal' was their name and we were not allowed to put the record out. But we found out all this was bollocks so it came out. Anyway it was only a laugh. And we carried on laughing to victory in the final!

In the early '90s we continued the odd trips abroad to Germany, The Middle East and other faraway places with strange sounding names.

'Rabbit' got in the German disco chart and a couple of German bands covered Chas & Dave songs. 'Gertcha' was translated into 'Urphie!' in German! 'Sideboard Song' got covered by another band but I can't remember what they called it. 'No Pleasin' came out by us with me singing in German. I was a bit familiar in German from my Hamburg days with Jerry Lee and Gene Vincent.

I remember me, Dave and Mick going to Baden-Baden to do a TV show. I think it was there we met Doug Sahm. ('She's

About a Mover'.) We were fans of his and he absolutely raved over 'Rabbit'. We were thrilled about that!

Baden-Baden was a lovely town. Sort of like a large pretty village. We stayed in a nice classy, but non yuppy-type hotel. Lovely people who spoke little English. But when them lovely German beers were pumped out in the evening bars so the smiles and chatter got pumped out between us. We made friends with this dear little old lady and her husband. They loved and were proud of their beer and in the few German words I knew I told them how much we liked their beer too. Then they just kept saying to us, as they raised their glasses, the German toast, 'Prost!' And we delightfully kept saying it back.

Then I felt the timing was right for a slightly different slant on the enjoyable but sparse banter. It wouldn't have felt right two hours ago but it was right now. Life is knowing when to keep life afloat.

'Prost!' I said to the little old lady and her husband.

'Prost!' They said, raising their glasses

'In England!' I said. 'Yah? Verstehen?'

'Yah!' They cheerfully understood.

'In England, nicht "Prost!" We say "Fuckemall!"'

'*Fuckemall*!' The lovely little old lady and her husband shouted cheerfully. Raising their glasses.

No more 'Prost!' for the rest of the night. 'Fuckemall!' was the word.

The next day I went for a walk in the town. Lovely spring afternoon. It really was a lovely town. Across the street I spotted the little old lady and her husband merrily ambling along. They spotted me and with a wave and a happy grin shouted across the street, '*Fuckemall*!' Feeling it quite safe to answer in similar way, I did.

I've known Joe Brown a good few years now. In fact I knew him before I knew Dave. I first met Joe when I was playing bass in The Stormers who became The Outlaws back in 1961. We were backing Danny Rivers on tour and Joe became guest lead guitarist on some of the gigs. Chas & Dave and Joe were big fans of Lonnie Donegan and we all came together to do me and Dave's twentieth anniversary gig at The London Palladium in 1992.

(By the way, Bob England had got bored with the sun and sand in Antigua and by invitation and to his joy, had now come back home to manage us once more.) Long serving Chas & Dave supporting comic and pal Freddy Stuart was on the bill too and another act who goes back to The Outlaws days with me and who Dave was also a big fan of, Screaming Lord Sutch.

Sutch really never got the credit he deserved. It was him who nurtured the likes of Ritchie Blackmore and others. He put the wildness in 'em and turned 'em loose. They went forth and took over America. He was so full of life. But little did any of us know he harboured a deep depression. He hanged himself at his home in 1999.

Bob, the cunt, kept saying we shouldn't have him on it. I don't think he felt he was London Palladium material but he fucking well was. He deserved it.

We decided on a tour with Joe Brown after this. It worked well. We all enjoyed it and had a really good time. But I remember arriving at one of the gigs to be greeted by an atmosphere you could cut with a knife. You know how I try to not use too many clichés but 'cut with a knife' really fits. Mick had gone on his own and had arrived before us. He was in the dressing room with his drumsticks doing paradiddles all over the chairs like he does. He stopped when me and Dave arrived and looked up with a quiet grin on his face. 'You won't believe what's gone on.' He said without moving his lips, retaining the quiet grin. 'Well!...'

Then come the story.

Joe had arrived to see great big lettering outside saying who was on. And who did it say was on?

'CHAS AND DAVE.' That's all.

Joe quite rightfully asked the manager why it didn't also say, 'JOE BROWN'.

'Well,' said the manager,'Unfortunately, there was nothing to be done about it. You see, when my assistant, who puts the lettering up outside, got to your name, he found he'd run out of "N"s.'

'Run out of fuckin' "N"s!' exploded Joe.

'Yes. He only had one. They get stolen from outside you see. But I don't know why they stole "N"s. "E"s are usually mostly stolen. The kids like to hang the "E"s round their necks. It's to do with them Ecstasy pills they get on.'

'RUN OUT OF FUCKIN' "N"s!' exploded Joe once more. 'Why couldn't he have put, "CHAS DAVE JOE BROWN" or even, "CHAS AND DAVE JOE BROW". "Joe Brow" would have been better than fuck all! At least they would have known somebody else was on the show with them!'

'Yes, I suppose you have a point.'

'Of course I've got a fuckin' point!'

Joe was wild! He needed to shout at someone so he done what he usually done. He rung up his manager John Taylor and shouted at him. Fuckin' right an' all. Well you pay him good money Joe don't ya?

On another gig somewhere, just before we were going on, Joe's come running into my dressing room laughing his bollocks off.

'Your mate Peacock fuckin' kills me!' he said.

'What's he done now?' I said. He could hardly tell me for laughing.

'He's come back from the pub looking worried about how strong the beer was down there and how he didn't realise it was that strong and now he's got to go on stage and play the banjo. Then, with that, he's opened up a tin of Boddingtons and almost downed it in one. I asked him what was he doing? "Trying to fuckin' water it down. Boddingtons ain't so strong. That should do it".' That's my pal!

1994 was a special year. On 15 September me and Joan's first grandchild was born to my eldest daughter Juliet and her partner Chris Cumpson. They named her Charlie. More about Charlie the musician later in this book.

1995 was the 50th anniversary of the end of World War Two. I was a war baby and wartime songs had always been a big part of family get-togethers. I said to Bob England that I thought me and Dave should do a special commemorative album. Now this had particular appeal to me. A great heartfelt reason to do it. Which always comes first, like 'Halleys Comet'. But this one had commercial appeal which I knew 'Halleys Comet' didn't. It meant something to me and it meant record sales to Bob. Dave was well up for it too.

Most wartime songs me and Dave already knew from family get-togethers but Bob came up with his proviso, 'Got to be over an hour and got to be over fifty songs.' (Proper 'Del Boy' terms!) Okay. I think this can be done. But I need to do some research.

I said to Bob that I wanted a list of every popular song that was released in Britain between 1939 and 1945. Then after going through them in various hotel rooms while on the road I picked out the best, then gave the list to Dave for his approval. There were a few I'd never heard of that I liked and so did

Dave. 'Even Hitler had a Mother' was one. I just liked the title so we had to make it fit.

This happens in life now and then. Certain things you see and you like and you know you're gonna make 'em fit. I remember seeing an old cast iron back for an inglenook fireplace years ago that I really liked. I didn't know if it was too big or not. The man who sold it said I can bring it back if it don't. But he said, 'I bet you don't. I can tell. You'll make it fit.' I knew what he meant. I knew when I first spotted it and I did make it fit.

Whatever it may be, if you really wish it to be part of your life, then you'll make it fit. Even if you have to build everything else around it. We had great fun recording the wartime album at Geoff Calvert's studio in Widford and it got in the charts. I think it got to number three but check in the discography at the back if you want to find out exactly.

In complete contrast to the wartime songs we were doing in that year of 1995, we got news of surprise cover versions of two or our songs. 'That's what I like' and 'London Girls.' By whom? Tori Amos, no less. They were superb. We've yet to meet her. I'm dying to find out how she came by them. I'd love to do one of her songs. Pick me out one and let me know, Tori.

Chapter 29

Troublesome Roadies Number 1 and Number 2

Every now and then, in the '90s mainly, we'd take a trip to the Middle East. United Arab Emirates. Bahrain, Doha, Qatar. We first went in the '80s as a stepping stone to Australia and got the taste for it. The Arab souks (markets) are the most colourful markets you have ever seen. The orange and red and green and yellow fabrics arrayed on the stalls can only be described as mouthwatering. Put all these colours with ice and a piece of lime in a cocktail glass and you'll choose it everytime. The colours of the market are as mouthwatering to the eye as the spices sold at it are to the nose. Don't walk through there hungry! It'll be like being locked up and celibate for a year and then having to walk through a harem.

I bought some myrrh in a souk with a little brass myrrh burning lamp. Myrrh is like a piece of resin. I got it going at home. You set the lamp alight and it gently cooks the piece of myrrh placed above it. A lovely smell. That wise man knew what he was doing with his plan to mask the donkey shit.

The gigs are good there. Mostly Brits clubs. We get well looked after. The roadies love it. After they've set up for the first night they don't have much else to do for the rest of the week except eat, drink and go swimming. Booze is allowed at Brits' apartments so parties are set up.

One sunny afternoon on one of the Middle East trips, we were all sitting round the pool. The band and the roadies alike. It was beginning to get pretty hot. I was thinking about having one more dip and going inside to the cool down when Mark, one of our young roadies, came over to me.

'Chas! Something's going wrong with Nipper!' he said. 'I asked him if he wanted a hamburger and he didn't answer. Then I looked at him and he started talking but sort of gobbling and gabbling. And he's acting weird. It's freakin' me out man! Look. He's up there on that sun bed.'

I've looked up there. There was Nipper sitting up on his sun bed, his head semi-jerking from left to right as if surveying his surroundings, but really quickly. His head was close on a blur. Then it stopped. Then started. Like a sped-up film that kept having the pause button pushed sporadically.

'Quick man!' said Mark. 'We've got to do something!'

I'd never seen anything like it. Me and Mark run to the end of the pool where Nipper was. Dave looked across from the other side of the pool. He sussed something was up. I motioned him to follow us. He come running. Us three arrived at Nipper's side simultaneously.

'Nipper!' I said, 'What the fuck's the matter?'

We knew it couldn't be drugs. This was Middle East. Dabble and death penalty.

Nipper was now sitting up motionless on his sunbed staring at a forty-five degree angle into the sky in front of him. He didn't answer. We looked to where he was looking. Nothing.

We looked at each other. Nothing. So what do we do now? Nipper suddenly got off the sunbed and started walking. Not knowing what else to do, we followed him. In a line.

He walked round the outside of the pool where the plants are. Gobbing in each one as he went. 'Nipper!'I said. But that's all I said. Because I didn't know what to say after that. We continued following him round the hotel grounds two or three times, him still gobbing in plants as he went, when I decided it was time to take the lead.

'Follow me!' I said as I run to the front. I knew where the hotel manager's office was. We've got to get Nipper to a doctor. Thankfully Nipper conformed. We all arrived at the manager's office, still in a line, a couple of minutes later. Thankfully again, through the glass door, we could see that the manager was there. Behind his desk.

In we've gone. As me and Dave try to explain to the manager, who didn't speak much English, that we need to get Nipper to a hospital, Nipper glides round the office and finds a big electric fan, stands with his back to it, raises his arms, grins, glassy eyed at all of us and says, 'I coovy down!'

It was the first time Nipper spoke.

'What the fuck did he say?' said Dave.

'I coovy down!?' I said. Me and Dave just looked at each other.

Then Dave said, 'Nipper!' Nipper still in 'coovy down' pose. 'Nipper! What do you know? What do you remember?'Dave looked at me, worried, then back to Nipper. 'What is my wife's name?' said Dave, '*Who is our drummer*?' Dave was getting desperate and testing Nipper to the hilt. Nipper's ginger balding head and bright red face looked towards me and Dave but not *at* us, *beyond* us. Over our shoulders. We eagerly awaited his answer.

'One Hunden Fezzunts,' he said.

'Fuckinell!' said Dave, looking at me for the next move.

'Let's get him to the hospital!' I said.

Me and Dave took him in a cab to the hospital. On the way he began to come round. Bit by bit he began to remember what Dave's wife's name was, and who our drummer was. We got him checked out and were told he'd simply 'boiled up' in the Middle Eastern sun. A 'ginger baldy head' was just asking for it.

Troublesome Roadie Story Number Two

In 1996 we got booked into a club in Hong Kong for a week. This sounded like an interesting gig. Never been there before. The first thing that sprung to mind was the fact that you can get tailor-made silk suits for fifty quid there. Eric Clapton had one. He wore it on the tour we did with him. Right. We were there for a week. That's the first thing I'll do. Get measured for a suit. Should be time enough. So I did. Yes sir. Can be done. How much? £750. Oh well, forget it. I'll get one when I go home. Well, Eric was pissed when he told me it was only £50. Might have known.

Now anybody who says that Hong Kong is the finest place on Earth, I wanna know what bit they went to. The finest people, yes they were, but it is a strange ol' place. It starts off with the plane landing, (I think it's changed now) in between skyscrapers each side of you so you think you are crashing, not landing. But you are reassured by calm stewardesses.

The hotel was lovely. We ordered the recommended Chinese dish in the restaurant. This ain't the 'Slow Boat' in north London. This has got to be good. The verdict was that it tasted like minced scrubber's drawers in cat piss.

The market place was full of stalls with fat frogs and toads jumping all over the place. Nifty stallholders cleverly caught these frogs and toads in mid-air with one hand and chopped off their heads with the cleaver they had in the other. Then they put 'em in paper bags and sold 'em to little old ladies who were shopping for their husband's tea. I likened it to my Nan buying a herring bloater in the market for my Grandad's tea and the Chinese nan buying a bag of fresh headless frog and toads for a Chinese Grandad's tea. My granddad when he'd finished, would lean back, fart, and do the football pools. I bet there was a similar after tea ritual with the Chinaman. So you've got the gist. The band are in Hong Kong and all things considered are having a good time. Shows are going well. But this is supposed to be another roadie story ain't it? Okay, here it comes.

We had a roadie named Ted who had a drink problem we found out. We didn't know for a while because he was fighting it hard, gawd bless him. His name actually wasn't Ted. I've changed it to help him. I think he's off the booze now and if he read this story under the heading of his real name, it might put him straight back on it. See what a good bloke I am B...! Oops! I nearly said his name!

The Hong Kong gig finished successfully and on the day of departure we decided on a time to all meet in the hotel lobby for cabs to the airport. Earlier on in the day Ted was being a bit unreasonably troublesome. (I now know why.) We were going back to do a one-off show at the Dominion, Tottenham Court Road. We were using strings and I said to Ted to get mini sony mikes that clip on the bridge. They work well. We've tried 'em.

Ted went into one. That ain't the way to mike stage violins. He knows a better way. Better mikes and everything. I said to Ted you may or may not be right, but it is for one night only. I know this works. I've tried it, so it's the safe thing to do. If we were there for a week we would have time to try your idea out. But we ain't. (I know now he was getting the shits about it because it was a big gig and was slugging on some booze as a nerve calmer.)

So it was the day of departure. We met in the lobby. Mick was there first. Always is. Then me and Dave. Cab ordered for the airport and we waited for Ted. Five minutes. Ten minutes. I asked the reception to give his room a ring. No answer.

'I'll go up and give him a knock,' said Dave. Dave's come back. 'He must be well asleep, I've been banging the fuck out of his door.' He got a spare key from reception. Dave's come down ten minutes later.

'He's laid across his bed! Pissed! I can't move him,' said Dave, 'All he keeps slurring is "Oh boys I'm sorry! Oh boys I'm sorry!" He's cleaned out the mini-bar!'

We've both run upstairs. There's Ted, laid out. Surrounded by little miniature booze bottles. Empty. Whisky, vodka, rum, gin, brandy. Ted's mixed himself a cocktail and a half. 'OH BOYS I'M SORRY! I'M S...!

'Oh, for fuck sake!' I said. Ted continued weeping and a wailing.'Shut up Ted!' OK. Time to take control. No time now for bollockings. They can come later.

'Now, Ted, just do what you're told. We have to get to the airport and on that plane!'

We got him into the cab but he would keep sprawling all over me and Dave saying, 'Oh boys I'm sorry! Oh boys...'

'For fuck sake shut UP Ted! We need to get through security and on that plane. Keep quiet and we can do it!'

We got to the airport and queued for security. Me and Dave supporting him either side. Every now and then Ted breaking into the sprawling and wailing.

'Ted you dozy little bastard. If you don't shut up they ain't gonna let us on!'

Then a security woman has spotted us. Fuck! OK. Keep cool. We're stood either side of Ted holding him up. He virtually passes out in between bouts of, 'I'm sorry boys! I'm sorry!'

She comes over. Ted is only upright because me and Dave hold him up. But he is quiet. His eyes are closed.

'Is that man drunk?' she asks. I think quick.

'No.' I said, 'He's our roadie and he's a workaholic. He's had no sleep for two days. Just had half a lager while we were waiting and he's gone straight to sleep! We'll look after him.'

It worked! She had a slight look of suspicion in her eye but we looked no trouble so she waved us on. Great. We were through security. A couple more wailing and sprawling bouts, then he would pass out again. Which thankfully he did as we arrived at the gate to get on the plane.

We queued up again. Just ten minutes to go before we were on. There were two people in front of us. We were about to get on next. Then Ted came round and started up again. Not with as much vigour, but don't forget he'd done ten uncalled-for encores. He was feeling the strain. He slobbered into his apologies once again. 'Oh boys, I'm sorry!' 'Ted! For ffff...!' But it was enough. The game was up. An airport official came over and asked us to leave the queue and come with them.

Ted you fucking little wanker! We were almost on!

Me and Dave tried everything to get them to let Ted on the plane but that was it. We can go but he can't. Me, Dave and Mick had to get on this plane. We had the Dominion, Tottenham Court Road gig as soon as we were back in England. I concocted a story to the airport official that Ted had a health problem, namely epilepsy, so could he be taken to a hospital and put on a plane the next day? We were assured this would be done.

On arrival at Heathrow Airport his poor wife was there to meet him and we had to tell her what had happened. She was very upset but didn't seem that surprised. It was Ted's first drunken stupor bout for us, but it obviously wasn't hers. We told her they were taking him to a hospital and putting him on a plane the next day. In fact he was probably boarding at this very moment. The Dominion gig went well. We used the Sony mikes on the strings. Lovely! So all was well.

Except that Ted had not arrived at Heathrow yet. He should have been on the next plane. But he wasn't. Or the next one. Or the next one.

The office finally found out his whereabouts. The airport officials didn't take him to a hospital at all. We never found out the full story. All we know is that they put him back in the Hong Kong hotel where he had cleaned out the original mini-bar. So he got straight back on the piss and cleaned out another one. Two days later he was still there. On continual room service. 'This is Ted with the Chas & Dave party. Can you send up another mini-bar please?' Or slurs to that effect.

In the end his brother had to fly out to Hong Kong to bring him back. His brother, from a distance, was told he looked like Dave. Which I suppose he did. Sort of. In a funny way. So he bought himself a striped suit and a trilby from the Oxfam shop and that's how he went about. Now in some circles it transpired that it was actually Dave that went back to rescue Ted. I can categorically state that it wasn't.

Also later on in this book I will tackle rumours that went round in the business that at some point there appeared a fake Dave. There have become 'Fake Dave' spotter anoraks. Those who say they have proof that today's Dave isn't the real Dave. And those that say they know where the real Dave is. But later.

For the moment Ted is the protagonist. So what happened about Ted? Did we keep him on? What do you think? Of course we did! I always think everybody is allowed one mistake. But not two. So Ted was given another chance. In the weeks that followed Ted did his job okay. One or two suspicions of a slug or two on the side but his job was being done. Now bear in mind Ted's job was chief roadie and soundman. It was his job to make sure all gear was set up ready to go and his job to balance the sound out front. And yes, he was doing it OK. Until one night. In a theatre down south somewhere. Ted had been acting a bit strange when we arrived at the gig but we waved it aside as being 'Well, that's Ted.' As long as he does his job. We finished the gig and went down well. But five minutes later Ted was in the dressing room.

'Twenty people walked out tonight. Why? Because you were too fucking loud they said. And do you know what? I agreed with them. They were right!' Now do I hear this right? Ted does the sound out front! The sound out front is utterly and completely in his hands.

'Ted. What was too loud?'

'Micky's hi-hat.'

'Eh? That's impossible. It's not even miked up!'

'Well it fucking well was, and it was squeaking and that's why those people walked out.'

Something ain't making sense. Not sure what yet. Then I looked closer into Ted's eyes and I saw it wasn't water that lubricated his eyeballs. It was vodka.

'Ted. A squeaking hi-hat, un-miked, in a thousand-plus seated theatre, cannot be deemed to be so loud that it sent punters running.'

'It wasn't only that. It was the rest of the sound!'

'But you control that Ted!'

'You boys are fucking exasperating! You won't listen will you? You were too fucking loud but you won't have it will you?'

It was Ted's second mistake. Oh well. So long Ted!

Stanley Mills, our publisher in New York, has become a good friend. His dad ran the most famous American music publishers of the last century, Mills Music.

In 1998 Stanley put us in touch with Steve Popovich of Cleveland International Records.

'Steve will love your stuff!' said Stanley. And he was right. We got our first proper American release on Cleveland International Records and 'Flying' was the one that the Americans picked up on.

Then came the year 2000. As the new century began, so began a new era for Chas & Dave.

Chapter 29

Millennium and the USA

In the year 2000 we went over to America to do some gigs. Steve Popovich brought us over. 'Flying' was selling well on Cleveland Records' on-line service, which meant that orders came in from all over America. Our first gig was the Town Hall in Milwaukee. It held about a thousand people. They had come to see us from all parts of America. New York, Phoenix, Nashville. All Americans digging what we were doing. We did a record signing next day in quite a big record shop in Milwaukee. We were big in Milwaukee. The local radio stations loved us and played our stuff all the time. The manager of the shop said he absolutely loved it when the record rep came round, as they do, to check on record sales.

The biggest selling artist of the month, above Michael Jackson, Queen, Sting, Rolling Stones or whoever that month, was Chas & Dave. He said it will always be a highlight in his life. That moment when the rep said, 'Okay, who's this month's biggest seller?'

'Chas & Dave.'

'Who?'

'Chas & Dave. Have you not heard of them?'

'Can't say I have but they sure seem to have heard of 'em around here!'

Top radio play on the local Milwaukee Radio stations had put us top sellers in the local main record shop. Like we've always said. Play our music to the *people*, wherever they're from, and they will like it and want to buy it. Proof was here in Milwaukee, which also provides the answer to anybody wishing to know what the Americans think of our music. Never been any question as far as I was concerned. Pure Rock 'n' Roll that came from Jerry Lee in the first place, mixed with our own London earthiness, a perfect cocktail for the Americans.

The next gig was in Cleveland, Ohio. A Heritage Festival of Ethnic Music. It was there that we met the legendary Jack Clement. He flew in with his wife Ayleene especially to see us. He was the main engineer and producer alongside Sam Phillips at Sun records, Memphis in the '50s. He discovered Jerry Lee Lewis and recorded the famous 'Million Dollar Quartet' tapes with Elvis, Johnny Cash, Jerry Lee and Carl Perkins. He did the liner notes on our first American release which I am pleased and proud to reproduce here. It was actually a letter he wrote to Steve Popovich in 1999.

Dear Steve,

I feel the urge to thank you in writing for introducing me to the wonderful world of Chas & Dave. I don't just like the record, I love it. It lifts me up and takes me backward and forward in time and space and makes me feel good and even optimistic about music of the future. It is a class act for all times. They say it all with great rhythm and whimsy, interlaced with variety, tenderness, swingability, rockability and loveability. Ayleene loves it too and we never leave home without it.

In my opinion, everybody in the world should have at least one CD of *The World of Chas & Dave*. I have six or seven copies of it by now. I suspect a good way to tell how much I love a record is how many copies of I have of it.

The World of Chas & Dave is a program I can trust. All I have to do is play it and it always entertains me and never tries to fake me out. It's all-American enough for me. I think that time will prove that it is also futuristic, certainly well in to the twenty-first century. I believe that when music is good in the first place, it will always be good.

As for going backwards in time and space, I can only imagine how much fun Chas & Dave would have been to have around when I worked in the Sun Records studio in Memphis back in the rockin' fifties. I think all of us, including Jerry Lee Lewis, would be better for it and I'm pretty sure that Sam and Elvis would have been entranced by them. Johnny Cash will have a personal copy of it soon. I'll take care of that. In the meantime, I could use three or four more copies to share with some of my other music loving friends and neighbors.

The point is, Steve, the record really touches me, perks me up and makes me feel good about things in general and sort of like Jack Nicholson said in the movie *As Good as it Gets*, 'It makes me want to be a better (music) man.'

I'm a Chas & Dave fan. I love everything they do. What else can I say?

Thanks again for sharing them with me.

Your friend, Jack Clement

When someone you've admired since being a teenager comes out with things like this about you, well there ain't no buzz like it. There ain't nothing greater in this world for someone you grow up admiring to reciprocate in such a way. Jack engineered and produced 'Whole lotta Shakin' Goin' On' and my favourite (and Terry's) Jerry Lee record, 'Mean Woman Blues'. A fine example of a talented singer and piano player giving his best owing a lot to a talented producer who knew how to get the best from him. A good producer has to know how to relax an artist but at the same time be in command. Careful control and thought is called upon at all times. You've got to know how far to go to get the best out of your artist.

Jack said he cued him on the 'growl and laugh' that is so effective on the record. Any other producer wouldn't have captured the feeling that Jack did. Because of Jack's laid back but positive style, he was perfect for Jerry Lee. Sam Phillips may have produced the A-side, 'Great Balls of Fire', I'm not sure, but it wasn't such a good performance as the B-side. It was a more wooden, regimented Jerry Lee, whereas 'Mean Woman Blues' wasn't. Jerry Lee was at his best when he was out to out do Elvis at his own game. Elvis had recorded 'Mean Woman Blues' first, but Jerry Lee told me, 'He turned white when he heard my version!'

In 2000 I got an allotment. Joan got it for me. Growing my own vegetables was something I hadn't done for a while and I was feeling the need to get back into it. I did at home when the kids were growing up but had drifted out of it. I was missing it. It mixes well with this music business. My Grandad had an allotment and it's in the blood. It is the perfect pastime for anybody. You're in the open air. It's gentle exercise if you do it right. Watch an old person do it and copy their fashion.

Especially digging. They have a slow, methodic rhythmic style. Every so often resting briefly, hand on fork, before continuing. It frees your brain to think of wonderful things. Song ideas if you want. And you've got the bonus of organic spinach, beans, peas or whatever to take home.

I've had my allotment now for nine years. I'm really enjoying doing this book and just a few days ago I thought, 'I must write another one.' I write this book between one and three in the morning when all are in bed. I love it. But what shall I do when it's finished? Watch a video? Watch telly? Not likely. So what?

Something will come naturally like it does. And it did. I was looking at a gardening magazine a couple of days ago and thought, 'They ain't actually done that. They've got facts from somewhere else!' The pictures of veg weren't all that either. Well dodgy specimens by my standards. Me and Joan were relaxing round the old log stove (perfect setting). 'Look at this beetroot!' I said.

'You could show them a thing or two!' she said.

That's it! My next book! *Chas's Allotment.*

In 2001 Bob England got a call from a record company who wanted to bung us dough to do a 50th Anniversary album for Queen Elizabeth. An album full of the hits of the day. The beginning of the '50s. Fuck that! Didn't fancy it at all, but Bob got humpy.

'So how come you went for the wartime album and the Jamboree albums then? They're just a bunch of old songs ain't they?'

'Yes, but they meant something to us. They were songs we grew up with. Songs our families sang at parties. Fifties songs were pretty much crap until Rock 'n' Roll came along. One or two were OK but not enough to make an album of!'

Especially as Bob's idea was '50 songs from the '50s'. Fuck me! As I said to Bob at the time, I'd sooner do three months inside! But Bob being Bob couldn't see that it couldn't just be treated as a job. Clock in. Do your day's work. Clock out. Bob couldn't see why a substantial amount of dough was not enough incentive to make any record. Bob had heard of artistic incentive but didn't believe there was any such thing.

Now I liked Bob but sometimes he was just a fucking nuisance. All his decisions on what he thought the right thing to do was easy for him. It was simply based on who offered the most money. His 'dough' attitude often had its advantages in that he never interfered as to artistic content once the deal was done. He didn't care what the artistic content was. But I did. Dave didn't want to do it either. Dave would sooner be at home driving horses. Bob suggested a meeting. No point, I said but on his insistence I agreed so as to clear it up once and for all. I knew what was going to happen though. I would stand firm and then he'd be on the phone to Dave. Par for the course.

A similar thing had only just happened about a year before, when BMP, the ad agency who did the Courage adverts, wanted us to do a spot at the Albert Hall performing some of their famous ads live. Great. We'll do 'Gertcha' and 'Rabbit' and 'The Sideboard Song'. But Bob said no. They only want one Chas & Dave song and then they would like you to do a medley of their other successes. Like for instance one of them was a crap '70s Elvis song. 'Suspicious Minds' or something like that. Bollocks!

'But they won't pay the money if we don't!'

'Well then, we don't! We're not learning crap songs we don't like!' Then in the band car next day Dave says, 'I don't think it would hurt to do what they want on that Albert Hall gig you know. It's only a one off.'

Here we go. Dear Dave's been got at. Well we did the Albert

Hall. But we did just Chas & Dave songs. A person I think a lot of was there, doing the compering. Mark Lamarr. He came over to me and gave me a compliment on my piano playing. To think, I could have been doing, 'Suspicious Minds.' Dave harmonising. Then instead of a compliment on my piano playing he could have come over and said, 'I see you like Elvis. But what made you pick one of the crappiest songs he's ever sung?' Good job I keep my head while all around lose theirs.

But here we go again. Not far into the new millennium and another crap management idea. Singalonga Liz. But no thanks. A stop will I put to it. So we had a meeting about it in a big hotel over a big dinner. I said to Bob there's no point, but he insisted. OK. I'll come for the ride. I'll have a nice steak.

He brought someone else down with him who he'd just gone into partnership with. Between them they both went into crap ideas meant to persuade. Also slinging in that there's a big income tax bill on its way that will need paying. Pathetic persuasion. I weren't buying or budging. Fuck the money. I said to Bob, 'All these years we've been with you we've earnt well but fought all the way against corny promotion. There are people out there at last that are saying, "These boys are good! These boys can play!" I ain't going to let go of that. There'll always be wankers out there with no soul. Nothing we can do about that. Fuck 'em if they don't get what we're about. But it's not getting on the shows we *should* be on that's fucking annoying. Jools Holland is a friend and has got a respected show on TV. We're on the verge of doing his show but on the back of a 'Singalonga Liz' album he ain't gonna want us on it and nor would I.'

So Bob did what he usually did. Dave was my mate. He'd get to him like he'd done other times before. He knew he could get Dave to talk to me and it was his last chance of getting that percentage in the bank. His approach this time was a 'chance' distant meeting in the car park. Me and Dave had arrived in separate cars. Bob spotted Dave across the car park. Dave told me this later. Bob shouted across to Dave, 'So are you going to do this album or what?'

Dave said he didn't answer but just raised his arms and shrugged. I told Dave it didn't matter. I wasn't going to do the album, full stop, and Bob knew it, so that was that.

And so normal service was resumed and into the year 2002 away we went, merrily gigging along. Then one sunny autumn afternoon the phone rings. It's Bob.

'Charlie! Great news!' said Bob. Oh no. Now what? Singalonga 'who the fuck'?

'Okay. What?' I say.

'Allison Howe, producer of the Jools Holland show rang. They want you on this New Year's Eve's "Hootenanny!"'

'I would say it's okay for a "Yes" on this one.' I said. No big dinner deciders in big hotels needed! Good! The steak was rotten.

Chapter 30

Hootenanny!

The New Year Hootenanny was absolutely first class for us. Everybody who was interviewed on the show mentioned, without prompting of any kind, how good they thought we were. Vic Reeves and Nancy, John Sessions, Hugh Laurie, Ben Elton, Ronnie Ancona, Joe Brand, all spoke favourably of us. It heralded the beginning of our new resurgence.

Ironically, just at the birth of the new beginning, came the death of Bob England. January 2003. He had had stomach cancer and it finally got him. Bob did get to see us on the Hootenanny though. And he smiled. Proud.

Around the middle of the year Pete Doherty and Carl Barat of The Libertines began telling the public about how Chas & Dave were a big inspiration to them when they were young. All this makes those who wouldn't normally, sit up and take notice, although like Danny Baker said to me a couple of weeks back, 'They think they've suddenly discovered you. We knew all along!' He's right of course. But it does help. We've always had a mixed audience, but now, more and more young people began to appear at our shows.

In October of that year Dave decided he didn't want to be involved in songwriting anymore. Dave has other interests. He has horses and loves driving them. He is a master painter of gipsy wagons. He completely rebuilt and painted his own gipsy wagon from scratch. It was a work of art. He wanted to spend more time on these pursuits and so he should. He has a real talent for this and there is nobody to touch him.

Dave's decision in not wanting to be involved in writing anymore, to be honest, really spurred me on. I knew it was actually a relief for Dave not to have that pressure and now I could write freely without feeling guilty that I should be conferring with Dave all the time along the way.

In December 2003 we got a call from The Libertines management. They wanted us to support them at the Forum in London. We done the gig and went down an absolute storm. Pete came on and joined us for the encore. We supported them again in 2004 at the Brixton Academy. Another first class gig. Things were getting better all the time. Respect was creeping in at last.

By now I had got myself into a writing routine and was thoroughly enjoying it. Rise at midday, eat a bowl of roughage (egg and bacon later), pour a cup of tea and sit myself at the piano. Or pick up my guitar. Then I would write.

I can tell you now that I'm in the 2004 stage of this book that in 1999 I had to pack up drinking. I didn't want to tell you then when I was at that stage of the book because you would have kept thinking about it as you read on. I waited 'til I got over it. Which is about now I suppose. (In this stage of the book, 2004.) It was fuckin' hard though. I ain't gonna dwell on it but it's the hardest thing I've ever done. But it can be done. It's all down to habits. They can't be changed and feel right overnight but give 'em time and they can. You can't just cut out your habit. You have got to think of something else to do instead. Which I did. I'll tell you what I did in a minute. My habit was going down the pub. It began to happen very often. I can remember when I first started going down the pub at five o'clock and thinking, 'Why didn't I think of this before? What a good idea!' And then going down the pub regularly at dinnertimes and thinking the same thing. I was having a great time. Mixing with and having a laugh with 'Avitrite' and Coombsey and the crowd. Coombsey was our funny little mate. He was a lazy little git. He had a job helping the head gardener in the hotel next door to the pub. One day I've turned up at the pub and Coombsey's in there. It was snowing outside.

'What you doing in here?' I said, 'You s'posed to be at work next door!'

'They want me to go out clearing snow!' says Coombsey.

'That's alright! What's wrong with that?' I said.

'I ain't fuckin' goin' out clearin' snow this weather!' He said. He had a way of making you think that you sort of knew what he meant and nearly agreed with him. I had some wild fun boozy times in that pub. The Sow and Pigs in Cold Christmas (lovely name) near Ware, Hertfordshire. We used to conduct most interviews from there in the old days. We did an extensive interview for a Scottish newspaper there one afternoon. They reported it spot on. Like the Scottish do. Not interested in the fashion of the day. They got Chas & Dave in one, from day one. Good music. Talent. Fun. While the English newspapers in general reported 'drunken knees-up'.

That day the Scottish paper came forth with a writeup that said, 'Interesting interview with Chas & Dave in their favourite pub. Full of their mates who looked like they'd turned up for the casting of a movie, that was to be a cross between a Carry On film and *Deliverance*.'

I knew I was overdoing it booze-wise but I was having a good time. I was never the dozy incoherent drunk. I would stay as bright as a polished button, but my liver was getting well fed up with all this extra work. 'Ain't that cunt up there got no respect? I'm only one liver. He expects me to do the work of ten livers. Well the crap's gonna just have to build up then ain't it? 'Cos I can't cope with all that brandy. Why don't he put more lemonade with it? I love lemonade. Poxy brandy. Fucks my filters up.'

So what was it I did? I joined a health club and instead of going down the pub I went swimming. Sounds boring don't it? But I had to do it. Anyway I'd well used up my rations. I'd drunk enough for about three normal lifetimes.

But it's 2004 and all that's in the past. My writing was going well and I wrote my first rag-time piece for piano. I called it, 'Little Toe Rag.' Then I had to learn to play it! I'd written things in it outside of boogie woogie and Rock 'n' Roll that I'd never played before. It was so good for me. I conjured a motto, 'When in Doubt, Play the Piano!' It's what I did on those days when not positive what to do. Finish this? Start that? Not sure? Play the piano! So I'd make myself a cup of tea and do just that. Still do.

We got our first release in Japan in 2004. It did well. The Japanese company went on to release two more albums.

That year I began to do a few gigs with my Rock 'n' Roll Trio. Just pure 'Back to my Roots' Rock 'n' Roll. Me on piano, Mick on drums and Nicky Simper on bass. Darren Juniper took over on bass later on. (The son of Brian Juniper.) I got asked to play at the Eddie Cochran Memorial Festival in the spring.

Little Richard was topping the bill on the Saturday. I was to do my show on the Sunday and had the Saturday off so me and

Joan went a day early to see Little Richard. Little Richard is the King of Rock 'n' Roll. At his best there was no one better. My favourite Rock 'n' Roll sax player of all time was Lee Allen. My favourite Rock 'n' Roll drummer (apart from Mick) is Earl Palmer. They were both in the New Orleans session band that played on most Little Richard recordings. Well at least the best ones. A friend of mine and Dave's is Diz Watson, a piano player and singer. New Orleans style. An alright bloke. Him and his band, Diz and the Doormen, supported us on tour in the '80s. Diz is a sort of unassuming quietish chap and a nice person but there is something I will never ever forgive him for. He casually gave me a tape sometime in the '90s.

'Have a listen to this Chas. See what you think. Pete, our sax player was doing a couple of gigs with Fats Domino when he was over (I know. I saw him) and the band had a couple of days off so I got a couple of 'em in the studio and made this record. Lee Allen's on it.'

'What! *You made a record with Lee Allen and you didn't tell me*!?'

'Do you like him then?'

'Like him! I sing all his solos note for note and even sing harmonies that ain't there but could have been. Dizzy! I will never ever forgive you for this!'

'But Chas, I didn't realise...'

'No excuse. You should have known through instinct. "This man has got to be Chas's favourite sax player. I'll give him a call".'

'Chas, I'm sorry!'

'And so you should be.'

Some things you'll always have the hump about. Dave sawing up the classic bass amp I gave him and now this. Dizzy sneaking Lee Allen in the studio and not telling me. And then the pathetic excuse, 'Chas, I didn't realise...' Well, when I invite Fats Domino round to Sunday dinner, I ain't gonna tell him.

I got sidetracked there. Little Richard. The king of Rock 'n' Roll. Me and Joan went to see him on the Saturday before my performance on the Sunday.

There were some magic moments. And yes, not so magic half hours. But what do you expect? The man's in his seventies for Christ's sake. He had a great piano sound though. A grand piano digitally amplified and the soundman knew his stuff. Not always the case. In fact quite often not the case. There are quite a few wankers out there going under the name of 'soundmen'. But this man had it. What's more I knew him. He'd worked with us before.

'Can I use this piano for tomorrow's gig?' I asked him.

'Well, it was only hired in for Little Richard. But let me see what I can do.'

He done well and I took advantage of the magic moments that Little Richard left for me in that piano. It turned out to be a magic half hour. My old pal, Geoff Barker compered and it was a very enjoyable gig. I did it again the year after.

In the summer we did our first ever punk gig. The Wasted Festival, Morcambe. It was absolutely wonderful. If I had to choose, I'd put Glastonbury 2005 as our best ever gig and The Wasted Punk Festival 2004 as our second best ever gig.

There was more Rock 'n' Roll in store for me before 2004 was out. I went to Nashville in November to produce an album for Mike Berry and the Crickets. It was recorded at Jerry Allison's studio just outside of Nashville. Me and Jerry have known each other for years. Jerry (or 'J.I.' as he likes to be known – 'There were too many Jerrys around', he says, 'So I became "J.I."') and I spent some time together in LA when me and Dave went over to do Albert's album in the '70s. J.I. lived in LA then. But we had never really played together much. Apart from one or two songs on a couple of Paul McCartney's Buddy Holly nights. After the Mike Berry sessions were finished J.I. said to me, 'We've gotta record again together Chas. Your piano playing makes me play better.' I was well up for it and the seed was sown.

Jerry Allison wrote songs with Buddy Holly like, 'That'll be the Day', 'Think it over' and 'I'm Gonna Love Ya Too.' All records I went out and bought when I was young. Buddy and Jerry were heroes of mine. There ain't nothing like it when you get compliments paid to you by one of your heroes. Think about the people you most admire in the world of the 'Talented and Famous'. Now think about them giving you genuine compliments on your talent. Can you think of any buzz better?

I really enjoyed making this album. All the originals played on it. Sonny Curtis, Joe B. Mauldin and of course J.I. Allison. It had to be done quick as we only had something like six days in the studio, but Rock 'n' Roll is all the better for that. It keeps the excitement and energy up. And it comes across on record. The album is on Rollercoaster Records and is called *About Time Too!*

And so into 2005. It turned out to be the most eventful and certainly the most enjoyable year since we became successful. Right in the middle of it we did a gig that I will never forget.

The year started off with Jack Clement coming over to England in the spring with a few of the original Sun recording artists to do couple of gigs at the Royal Festival Hall. He rang me and said him and his wife Ayleene wanted to see us while in England and if possible come to see a gig and if there was a chance he could sit in, all the better.

My brain got to work and it worked out perfect. We were at the Millfield Theatre, Edmonton, my home town, while he was here. A perfect gig to get him down to and get him up. He was staying in town about 30 minutes away from the Millfield Theatre. We had a run through at his hotel a couple of days before and on the day Terry picked Jack and Ayleene up in his cab and brought them down to the gig. We had a sound check and the show went up.

I spoke a bit about Jack and we brought him on in our acoustic set to close the first half. It felt great and not really believable, sitting there picking alongside the man who had discovered Jerry Lee Lewis – who I had seen, not a few hundred yards from this theatre, in 1958. The man who changed my life. And here was the man who discovered him. Now a Chas & Dave fan! Jack went down absolutely beautifully. It was a magic night.

Chapter 31

Glastonbury
and On

Then in June 2005 came the gig of all Chas & Dave gigs. Glastonbury. I don't want to sound too self-confident but I knew we were in for a good gig. The timing was right for us to do it. Great things were being said about us. Chris Moyles was saying nice things. Christian O'Connell was saying nice things. Phill Jupitus wrote in the *Radio Times* that whoever decided to put us on deserves a big kiss on the lips!

But my expectations – and I had big ones – of how we were to go down were at least going to be multiplied by ten. Me and my wife Joan arrived about an hour or so before the gig. She nearly didn't come. Some weedy reason, I can't remember what. She loves gigs.

'You're going to miss us at Glastonbury?' I said.

'No!' she said, straightaway, 'Where was my head at? I'm not!' She was sure glad she didn't!

Me and Joan went on our own that day. We arrived about an hour and a half before showtime. I think the gig was due to start around 2.30. There were about five or six hundred sitting on the floor around the stage area. 'That's not bad,' I thought. Should be well over a thousand by the time we go on. Might even reach two thousand.'

Me and Joan went to the backstage area. About an hour before the gig, the crowd started chanting, 'Chas & Dave, Chas & Dave, Chas & Dave!' It now sounded like there was a fair few out there. The minutes ticked by. The chanting continued. It was now twenty minutes to showtime. Mick and Dave hadn't arrived. The chanting began to grow in volume and power. There were definitely more than a couple of thousand out there! I'd heard that strong sound of many voices before. At the Tottenham Hotspur football ground. There's got to be some crowd building up out there!

Ten minutes to go. Still no Mick and Dave. The crowd were giving it stick like I'd never heard before. I am going to have to go out there on my own, which I was prepared to do. Then just before my big chance of going solo, they turned up. We walked on stage to the biggest roar we've ever had in our lives. The crowd filled the tent and the whole field we were told later. Phill Jupitus said to me after, 'I looked at my watch and thought, right, I'll creep over to the Chas & Dave tent.' But he couldn't get near the field. Let alone the tent. Some thirty thousand people had trekked across to see us. We'd played to bigger crowds before, like when we supported Led Zeppelin for instance but these people had come to see *us* and *us* alone. There have been many highlights in our career and most you have already read about but I would say this was the best for me. Playing live has always been my biggest buzz and Glastonbury was the ultimate.

A month later I got a call from Steve Davis of EMI Records. He wanted to see us up at EMI with a view to putting a new

CD out. They already had one of ours on current release which Joan instigated. A year earlier Joan got in touch with them about getting the rights back to our original EMI recordings as they weren't putting them on the shelves. It turned out that they didn't know they had them! Then, 'No', we can't have the rights back.

'OK,' said Joan, 'But it would be nice if they were available on CD.'

Jon Wilson at EMI arranged between him and us an immediate release on CD the recordings we made for EMI. *Live at Abbey Road* in 1978, plus the *Rockney* album.

It did very well. So a follow-on was called for. Steve Davis had seen us at Glastonbury so we didn't have to sell the 'New Chas & Dave' to him. Me and Dave met at his office with Joan and Sue. It was a good meeting. The album was to be a mixture of old stuff and new. We were asked where we would like to record. I said we'd like to record at Abbey Road. Steve said he wanted a photo session in our suits and the album was to be TV advertised. But there was one request that I politely turned down on Dave's behalf. He wanted us to include a Coldplay song. I saw his reasoning and I quite like some of their songs, but our new revival was due to our own songs and I wanted this to continue.

Steve understood and we were soon back in the good old Abbey road studios. The engineer who did our original *Live at Abbey Road* recordings back in the '70s was still there! Pete Mew! So a good time was had by one and all.

On the second day in the studio I spotted an old covered up upright tucked away in the corner. Like some blokes cannot resist trying out different women, I can't resist trying out different pianos. I carefully removed its protective covering to reveal its cool, nut brown frame. It was a Steinway. Pure class.

Its lid was saying, 'Lift me up! I got something here you can have a lotta fun with!' I'd never played an *upright* Steinway before. As I lifted the lid I was getting excited. But what I discovered underneath, told me this piano had been around. Many white ivories were missing and many black gaps gaped up at me. But it was saying, 'Don't go by my looks! Run your fingers over me. Try me out! Don't just cover me up and walk away!' I had no intention of doing that.

I was the kind of piano player that having got this far, I had to see what she was made of. Yes she had been well used, and by the look of her, abused, but she looked solid brown and proud for all that. She weren't budging. 'Try me. I think you'll find you'll get some warmth and response in return.'

I gazed at her. Sitting there. Waiting for me to make a move. I spread my fingers and my arms. Then onto her ebony and ivories I smacked a gentle chord. Her response was pure honky tonk. Twenty-four carat and beautiful. 'Do that again!' I seemed to hear. I did! And again! And again! Pretty soon we were as one.

Then Mick came in. I stopped. I was almost embarrassed. 'That's a fuckin' good piano!' said Mick. 'You were rockin' there!' That was it. She had to be on the session. I used her on '12th Street Rag'. It turned out it was The Beatles favourite piano. They used her on 'Obla Di, Obla Da'.

Yes she had been around. But she'd been around good company. A great time was had back at Abbey Road and the album was finished in time, along with the new photos for release that Christmas. Yes, it was like the old days only better. As I said, musicians had always seen us for what we were. Eric Clapton, Jools Holland, Paul McCartney, Jerry Lee, Jack Clement and the like. Now at last, wanker TV people were not asking questions like, 'Don't you think you were really lucky you couple of knees-up blokes down the ol' pub made it famous?'

'No. It wasn't quite like that.'

TV people were beginning to ask questions like, 'You are excellent musicians. So much so that Eminem sampled Dave's bass playing, and in fact your guitar playing Chas, to give him his first worldwide hit. And Chas, didn't Jerry Lee Lewis tip you as the next piano king?' They were doing their research.

Yes. It took a while, but they were catching on. It was nice.

In November '05 me and Joan went to Nashville and stayed at J.I. and Joanie's ranch. As J.I. said, Joan and Joanie bopped giggled and shopped, while me and J.I. rocked, giggled and bopped in the studio. Me and J.I. had to play together again and here we were. Just the two of us. We used Ronnie Lynn's 'Merlot Sound' studios just outside of Nashville. Most of the tracks were recorded with me on piano and J.I. drums, but one or two we put down with guitar and drums in the same way J.I. did with Buddy Holly all those years ago. It was a great feeling. Some overdubs were done while I was there, but basically I went away with enough solid tracks to be finished back home. I planned to finish this in 2006. In the meantime some good stuff was in the book for Chas & Dave for December '05. Jim Driver, a great London promoter, who's booked us for some wild nights at the 100 Club, Oxford Street, booked our Christmas Beano at the Shepherds Bush Empire. Just before that we did a guest spot on a TV show starring the most talented and funniest female of all time; Catherine Tate. Catherine and the crowd came down to the Shepherds Bush gig. It was a wild night and it got filmed for release on DVD in 2006. So all in all I would say 2005 was a pretty good year.

In 2006 I set to work to complete the *Chas'n'J.I.* album. The gear I had at home was basically analogue stuff and not wanting to transfer the digital tracks to analogue, I decided to finish it elsewhere. We'd done some stuff at Jools Holland's studio in South London and he said if I ever wanted to use his studio, I could. Me and Dave had a pretty full gig sheet, so in between gigs I began demoing up ideas on each track to save time when I eventually got in the sudio. I'd play these demos down the phone to Terry.

'Great!' he'd say. 'I hope you're going to be able to recreate that same feel in the studio. It's a shame they ain't the masters. Why don't you think about getting a digital multitrack for yourself? These demos you're doing should be put on a top quality machine for release to the public!'

I knew what he meant. It was great of Jools to offer his studio but time was tight and I could be rattling off masters instead of demos in the same space of time at home. Also, although demos save time, it can be boring trying to recreate what you've already done. And then it can be so easy to lose the 'feel'.

So Terry checked the machines out up town (he's good at this) and I got myself a digital multitrack. Best machine I ever bought! It didn't take too long to get the hang of it and I was soon getting sounds out of it that pleased me. Best of all I wasn't under pressure to finish it. I don't need pressure to do what I love doing. I spent many odd pleasurable hours finishing that album.

We did a couple of gigs with Jerry Lee in the summer promoted by Jim Driver. The Rhythm Festival near Bedford and the Shepherds Bush Empire. I did 'Breathless' for Jerry Lee at the Rhythm Festival. He knew I was doing it for him. He told his manager so. 'Proms in the Park'(Hyde Park) was another highlight among the gigs and the year ended with the release of the DVD we did year before, *Live at Shepherds Bush*.

Chapter 32

Better all
the Time!

In January 2007 I did some recordings with Linda Gail Lewis
(Jerry Lee's sister) and her daughter Anne Marie. Her record
producer, Paul Diffin, sent the tracks over from America and I
worked on them here adding vocals and guitar. Dave added
some banjo too. I was enjoying myself immensely with my new
recording gear.

I'd been adding to it in the last few months. Mikes etc and I
now had a good set up. The *Chas'n'J.I.* album was now
finished. It was time to get it in the shops. Roger Dopson who
I'd known for years was with Sanctuary Records who were
currently putting out some early Chas & Dave stuff. I sent him
a copy. Roger liked it and it got released in May.

Great! Job done. Now it was time for the 'Chas Hodges'
album. I had already made a start on it. My plan was to write
all the songs and play all the instruments. 'All my Own Work'.
Terry spotted up town an electronic drum unit he thought I
might be interested in. It had good sampled sounds that you

could programme or play yourself. I always fancied myself as a bit of a drummer so this was for me. I was away on another pleasurable journey.

June 2007 and we were back at Glastonbury! We played the new Park Stage on the Friday afternoon. It pissed down right up until five minutes before showtime. Then the sun came out. Five minutes after we came off, thunderclouds appeared and down came the rain again! Someone up there must have wanted a clear view while we were on. It was another wild one. We were told we'd pulled the best crowd.

That evening we had another gig elsewhere on the site. It was basically a private show for all the TV people. This time, there we were, set up and ready to go, but no Mick! To be fair, Mick has always been the most punctual member of the band. Mobile phone calls revealed (what did we ever do without them?) he'd taken a wrong turn and now wasn't (he thought) on the site at all. He didn't know where he was. 'Just get here as quick as you can.' I said. 'Where?' he said. 'I dunno! Hang on, I'll find someone who does.'

Five minutes before showtime still no Mick. The poor girl who was organising it was starting to panic. 'We must go up on time, a lot of the guests have to be away and back to work straight after.'

All my family were there. And of course my son Nik. 'Don't worry!' said Joan. 'Nik can play the drums.'

The girl still looked nervous until Nik got up with me and Dave and started to play. He played superb! Nobody could have done it better. Well he has heard those songs a few times before in his life! Then the girl was so, so pleased and excited. Mick got there for the last song. We didn't dock him any money.

We did a gig in Peterborough on the Saturday and were back to Glastonbury on the Sunday for another show on the 'Lost

Vagueness' stage. So three gigs at Glastonbury that year. They wanted a fourth. A live radio gig, but it was at 10 o'clock in the morning! My day don't start 'til noon. (My bedtime is 4am.) The 'Lost Vagueness' stage was great. All ethnic folky type bands. It was like one big circus. So Glastonbury 2007 for Chas & Dave was almost a summer season!

I'm coming towards the end of the book and it's ironic that it's going to end, more or less, where my music career began.

On the subject of Joe Meek.

If you remember I made my first professional recordings with Joe Meek when I was 16. Now in this year of 2007, they are making a film about him called *The Telstar Man*. It's the story of his life in the music business up until he murders his landlady and shoots himself.

Okay. I've spoilt the surprise. I've told you the ending. But I'm not going to reveal any more of the story, you'll have to wait until the film comes out. But then you might have already seen it by the time you are reading this book. What's it like? No, don't tell me. But back to the present. (Which is actually – my present now, you understand – exactly four minutes past three in the morning on the 1st of May 2008.)

I can tell you a bit about who's in it. Ralph Little plays me as a young 'Chas' in the Outlaws. Con O'Neil plays Joe Meek. Kevin Spacey plays Joe Meek's business partner, Major Banks and my wife, Joan Hodges, plays Joe Meek's mum. Joan's done loads of work on TV. *The Bill, Fools and Horses, Roger Roger*, (Marilyn) feature TV specials, but this is her first film part. Oh, by the way, I play the part of Mr. Brolin, a complaining neighbour. Not a very big part, but a loud part!

We finished off 2007 with a sell out well lively gig at the Electric Ballroom, Camden Town. We had on the bill our old friend and me and Dave's favourite British singer, Chris Farlowe. He's booked for our next Christmas gig. Albert Lee's on it as well this time.

By the time you read this my own solo album should be out. I'm thinking of calling it 'All my Own Work' at the moment but the title may change. I've played everything on it. Electric drums, guitars, piano, vocals etc and written all the songs. 'So who plays the saxophone break on "Skinny Cats"? Didn't know you played saxophone Chas?' Yes! You assume correctly. I don't. It's the only other musician apart from me on this album.

My darling granddaughter Charlie Hodges (a 'Chas & Charlie' album?) is thirteen. She plays mainly guitar now, but also piano and sax and is writing songs. She's got it. All my kids have got it. And they've all found perfect spouses. Juliet and Chris Sutton, Nik and Mym and Kate and Paul.

Juliet, a great piano player and a top artist. Nik, great musician all round. Composes and records film and TV music. Kate, top piano player, singer and songwriter. Her husband, Paul Garner, ain't no slouch in the business either. A highly regarded TV writer.

I had a listen to most final mixes of my album last night. Strung together for the first time. I was pleased with what I heard. It'll be interesting finding out what you lot out there think of it.

There won't be another original Chas & Dave album. Time has moved on. Dave's retired from the writing and recording involvement. He's happy doing a few gigs and spending more time at home with his horses. But in no period of my life have I ever felt more creative.

I enjoy the pace that I am working at. Little and often. Use this for whatever you do in life and you won't go far wrong. Like running a successful allotment plot. I've seen neighbouring overgrown plots being took over by newcomers. Sweat their nuts off for a fortnight getting it in shape and don't turn up for a couple of months. Find all their seedlings are swamped with weeds and that's the end of that. They treat gardening like painting and decorating. Go mad for a week and you won't need to do it for another five years or so. But growing your own ain't like that. It's like writing a song. The germination is of utmost importance. The moment, however small, it springs into life it needs attention. Just being there, on the piano, or the guitar will help it along. But if you can't be there, on an instrument, just keep it ticking over in your thoughts. In fact it will invade your thoughts if you don't. And why not? You gave birth to it. It is your duty to bring it up.

Music is a marvellous thing. My Mum always said, 'Music keeps you young.' She was so right. It makes you feel so good that you wonder why it ain't illegal.

And so, Ladies and Gentlemen, we are finally up to the present year of 2008.

Already there has been an event of such magnitude that I am going to dedicate the whole of this book to that person who is at the centre of it.

Harry Albert Bob Garner.

Our first grandson. Born to my daughter Kate and her husband Paul on 13 March 2008.

Life is good! See you on the next gig!

Discography

Albums

1974 Signature (Bob Thiele's 'Flying Dutchman' label)
Oily Rags

1975 Retreat
One Fing 'n' Anuvver

1978 EMI
Rockney

1979 EMI
Don't Give a Monkeys

1979 EMI
One Fing 'n' Anuvver

1981 Rockney
Musn't Grumble

1981 EMI
Live at Abbey Road

1981 Warwick
Christmas Jamboree Bag

1982 Rockney
Job Lot

1983 Rockney
Christmas Jamboree Bag No.2

1984 Rockney
Well Pleased

1985 Rockney
Jamboree Bag No 3

1987 Bunce Records
Flying

1988 K-Tel
All the Best from Chas & Dave

1989 Rockney
Best of Live – The Chas & Dave Show

1995 Telstar
Street Party

1995 K-Tel
Boots, Braces and Blue Suede Shoes

1998 Cleveland International (USA)
The World of Chas & Dave Vol. 1

2002 Cleveland International (USA)
The World of Chas & Dave Vol. 2

2003 Sanctuary
One Fing 'n' Anuvver (reissue)

2005 EMI
The Very Best Of Chas & Dave

2005 Demon
Musn't Grumble / Joblot (double album reissue)

2005 EMI
Greatest Hits

2006 Demon
From Tottenham to Tennessee

2007 Sanctuary
Country Pies, Black Claws & Oily Rags, the early years of Chas & Dave

2007 Sanctuary
Chas and J.I. Before We Grow Too Old

Rare albums featuring Chas and Dave

1983 Enterprises REC460
Make Like Rock 'N' Roll
14 tracks by various artists release Chas & Dave on two tracks, 'That's Alright Mama' / 'Big Blonde Baby'

1985 Autobiography ASK794
Buddy by Mike Berry with Chas & Dave
A-ten track cassette of Buddy Holly: 'Peggy Sue' / 'Fools Paradise' / 'That'll Be The Day' / 'For Me & For You' / 'Tribute To Buddy Holly' / 'Rave On' / 'I'm Gonna Love You Too' / 'Think It Over' / 'Baby I Don't Care' / 'I'm In Love Again'

1986 Telstar STAR223
Chas & Dave's Christmas Carol Album
Side one 'God Rest Ye Merry Gentlemen' / 'Unto Us A Child Is Born' / 'While Shepherds Watched Their Flocks' / 'Long Long Ago' / 'Good Kind Wenceslas Last Looked Out' / 'Coventry Carol' / 'Wassail Song' / 'O Little Town Of Bethlehem' / 'Hark The Herald Angels Sing' / 'Good Christian Men Rejoice' / 'Silent Night'. Side two 'O Come All Ye Faithful' / 'See Amid The Winter Snow' / 'Yes Jesus Loves Me' / 'It Came Upon A Midnight Clear' / 'The Rocking Carol' / 'In the Bleak Midwinter' / 'The First Noel' / 'Once In Royal David City' / 'Away In A Manger' / 'We Three Kings'

Singles

1975   Retreat Records RTS262
'Old Dog and Me' / 'Scruffy Old Cow'
Retreat Records RTS267
'I am A Rocker' / 'Lazy Cow'
Retreat Records RTS269
'Old Time Song' / 'Dry Party'

1977   EMI EMI2874
Strummin" / 'I'm In Trouble'
EMI EMI2902
'Massage Parlour' / 'Pay Up and Look Big'

1979   EMI EMI2947
'Gertcha' / 'The Banging In Your Head'
Rockney EMI2986
'The Sideboard Song' / 'Sunday'
Rockney EMI5002
'What A Miserable Saturday Night' / 'It's Only the B Side'
Rockney PSR439
'Send Me Some Lovin" / 'Breathless' / 'Sunshine of Your
Smile' / 'I Get The Blues When It Rains'
('All the Best Rabbit' / 'Gertcha' / 'Nothing More
Important' / 'I'm In Trouble – Courage Beer Promotion
EP)
Rockney9
'Rabbit' / 'I'm In Trouble'

1981   Rockney10
'Poor Old Mr Woogie' / 'Uneasy Feeling'
Rockney KOR112
'Turn That Noise Down' / 'Flying'
Rockney KOR12
'Stars Over 45' / 'Harem'

1982 Rockney KOR14
'Ain't No Pleasin' You' / 'Give It Some Stick Mick'
Rockney KOR15
'Margate' / 'Give It Gavotte'
Rockney KORX15
'Margate' / 'Give It Gavotte' (picture disc)

Rockney KOR16
'I Wish I Could Write A Love Song' / 'That's What I
Like'
Rockney 12KOR17
'London Girls' / 'Eine Kleine Kneesupmusik' / 'Word
From Anne'
1983 Rockney KOR19
'Beer Barrel Banjos' / 'Beer Belly Banjos'
Rockney KOR21
'My Melancholy Baby' / 'Knees Up Medley'
Rockney 12KOR21
'My Melancholy Baby' / 'Auld Lang Syne' / 'Knees Up
Medley'
1984 Rockney KOR22
'There In Your Eyes' / 'One of Them Days'
Rockney KOR23
'I Wonder In Whose Arms' / 'I Miss Ya Girl'
Rockney KORD24
'Harry Was a Champion' / 'Ain't No Pleasin' You'
1985 Rockney KOR26
'You're Just In Love' / 'That's What I Like'
BBC RESL176
'In Sickness & In Health' / 'Encore Medley'
Rockney KOR28
'Halley's Comet' / 'Brother-In-Law'

1986

Rockney POT1
'Snooker Loopy' / 'Wallop (Snookered)'

Other singles involving Chas and Dave

1981   Shelf 1

Tottenham Hotspur FA Cup Final Squad 'Ossie's Dream' / 'Glory Glory Tottenham Hotspur'
Other Spurs recordings were: 'Tottenham, Tottenham', 'Hot Shot Tottenham' and 'The Arsenal (We're Off to Wembley 'cos We Beat the Arsenal)

Other singles involving Chas Hodges

1983   CBS Records A3929

'Rockers We Are the Boys' / 'Great Balls Of Fire' / 'Keep a Knockin'' / 'Johnny Be Goode' / 'Roll Over Beethoven' / 'Way Down Yonder In New Orleans' / 'Chantilly Lace' / 'We Are The Boys' / 'It'll Be Me' / 'Something Else' / 'Dance With The Guitar Man' / 'Bird Dog' / 'The Girl Can't Help It' / 'We Are The Boys' / 'Rockin' On The Stage'

Copyright Notices

Song lyrics on pages 176 and 177 from 'The Love In'
Writer: SHEB WOOLEY (TM)
Publisher: CHANNEL MUSIC CO-ASCAP a division of
DOTSON-WOOLEY ENTERTERTAINMENT GROUP
INTL, LLC.
*Courtesy of Linda S. Dotson-Wooley- Nashville, Tennessee
(c) (TM) World rights secured